OUT OF DARKNESS

A Testament of Love, Endurance, and Survival

MICHÈLE ISRAEL

Michèle Israel

outskirts
press

Dedicated
To my brother, Joe Roy,
for his courage, his strength, and his persistence.

Our childhood was not an easy one.
We were eight children in a crowded home,
two of whom were born deaf.
Each of us required attention,
love and encouragement,
acceptance and nurturing,
while our parents had struggles of their own,
running a small business to clothe and feed us.

While Joe's struggles and mine were very different,
it was in spite of those struggles that made us who we are.
My purpose for this novel—my hope—my wish,
is to illustrate how proud of him I am;
not just of that little boy we all knew as Joey,
but of the fine man he is today.

ACKNOWLEDGEMENTS

Writing is rarely a solitary effort. There are others who play a role, either throughout the process or in the final touches of bringing the story to a close where it is at last worth sharing.

One of the best pieces of advice I was given, after my very first feeble attempt in writing my first novel, *Lessons of the Heart*, was to take writing courses and to start with short stories, before tackling a major project of a novel. This advice came from my aunt Fernande, a French and English high school teacher for many years, who not only believed in me, but has a gift of seeing the best in people; embellishing their strengths and offering the kind of wisdom we all aspire to.

To give credit where credit is due, big thanks go to the Institute of Children's Literature, where I began taking my writing more seriously. From there, I moved on to Writer's Digest workshops, where I had the pleasure of being mentored by Mark Spencer, an award-winning author, who has taught literature and creative-writing courses at the university level for thirty years, and whom I later chose as my editor. His straight-talk and honesty was exactly what I needed.

One of the best experiences of taking Writer's Digest workshops was the ability to share my writing with others in the workshop, to seek their opinions and comments. Ahmad, Helen, Pamela, Cheryl, Mo, and Susan were especially helpful, and willing to share parts of their stories as well as critiquing parts of mine. But more than anyone, a special thanks goes to Ahmad A. Sbaiti, who kept in contact well beyond the end of the workshop, and who was interested enough to read and reread my manuscript, giving me tips and advice along the way. I so much enjoyed returning the favor to his *See You in Paradise*, and look forward to seeing it in print one day.

To my brother Dennis, for sharing pieces of our past, the parts I was not there for. Any question or concern that I had, you were right there, just a phone call or email away. Thank you.

To Jim Spurlock, thank you for taking the time, as a mere favor, to read my manuscript. Your thorough English-major corrections and observations along the way preceded my expectations.

To my dear friend, Paul, who has been there for me in countless ways, who has listened to me talk endlessly about this book from the very start, your friendship and never-ending support and encouragement is a one-of-a-kind true blessing.

To Jeremy, my pride and joy—you make a mother proud, and never cease to amaze me.

To Angie, your steadiness and loyalty bring us all comfort, and set the tone for the family.

To Marissa and Elijah, who share their mother's love for reading and their father's fearlessness to reach beyond their limits;

I have no doubt you will bring greatness to the world.

Last, but not least, my gratitude goes to all my friends and family, near and far, who have supported my writing, who believed in me and cared enough to read my first novel, *Lessons of the Heart*, despite your reading habits, or lack of. Your friendship and love mean everything to me, and my writing would not be nearly as pleasurable if not for all of you.

AUTHOR'S NOTE

This story is creative nonfiction. Approximately ninety percent is based on memory, conversations, letters, and public documents. The remaining ten percent is speculation, inference, and imagination.

CHAPTER 1

December 8, 2012

He calmly pinched off the safety and took aim, when the shadow of the moving object, fifty or more yards away, stilled. With a steady finger on the trigger, he waited; the .30-30 lever-action Winchester's stock resting comfortably against his shoulder. Patience. It was something he'd learned over time. It was not a trait one is born with, like a birthmark, or in his case, being deaf, but rather a learned behavior of tolerance that hunters adopt. Nearly four hours had passed, sitting perched on his tree-stand, until finally, he was betting his luck was about to change.

A few of his buddies had already bagged their annual deer, it was now his time. His stomach growled reminding him he'd not eaten since that morning. He could have packed himself a sandwich before leaving home, but at the time, it was the furthest thing from his mind. Between odd jobs and home repairs, tinkering with his classic GTO, a work in progress, and the sporadic bouts of rain in this eastern region of North Carolina, there were few chances for him to hunt. It was not until he was mid-way through his shower that morning, hot water pulsating against his scalp, that the idea came to mind. Not just the idea to go hunting, but to try out his father's land.

The weather, not too cold, and dry for a change, was his perfect opportunity. The sun was now going down, nighttime would be settling in within the hour. Just a few more minutes he would soon be on his way, with the hope of his catch in the bed of his pick-up.

Silently, he began to count down. Ten – Nine – Eight – Seven. A flicker of movement brushed through the forest. His aim followed, when suddenly the shadow split, with a slight gap in between. Whatever it was, there were two of them. It was hard to make out through the briery patches of the wooded area, a tree hunched over with beards of Spanish moss draping its bone-colored branches. A buck would be a sweet payoff, but he could not quite make out the shape from its movement, much less the size. His nose tickled, but he ignored the impulse to scratch it. To move even in the slightest manner was a risk only an amateur would take. This was the closest he'd come to spotting what could be a doe or a buck, one that would make for plenty of dinners that winter, and he was not about to blow it. His gut told him he was seconds away from the kill and resumed his countdown. Six – Five – Four. Sensing a warning, Joe held his breath when the shadows joined together again. It was moments such as these that validated the very reason he preferred to hunt alone—how his being deaf, at times gave him the advantage to sense his surroundings with sharper instincts than others.

The most common way to hunt in these parts was to use deer hunting dogs, with a radio transmitter around the dog's neck. When groups of hunters arrived, they would send their dogs off into the woods, while they sat in their trucks on the roadway or by the field and waited for the deer to be chased out for them to shoot. Joe, however, preferred deer-stand hunting from up in a tree. Sitting alone quietly was something he often did; it was a way of life. Dealing with noises and sounds was something he could not quite identify with. Distractions and interruptions that interfered with one's concentration, however, was another thing. But even in the hearing world, something such as footsteps, the bark of a dog or slamming of a door could set off the calmest of people.

"Get him out of here!" Joey's mother flailed her arms. "I just finished mopping." Her face twisted with disapproval when she saw Tonto, their German shorthaired pointer, leap through the kitchen doorway. His toenails clacked against the linoleum floor leaving muddy paw prints as he pranced about. Joey's father was right behind him, dressed in his hunting gear, complete with orange vest and cap, his cased rifle in one hand and the two dead pheasant in the other.

"What?" his father muttered, and then rubbed Tonto's head. "He did good today. Come here, boy. Good dog." Tonto paraded about like the proud hunter that he was, leaving even more smudges on the floor. There was a different smell about him, an outdoor bird dog smell of swamp water and muck.

"Dominic!" his mother called. "Take Tonto out back, please."

Joey would have gladly taken him out, but Tonto was still a little too much for him to lead on a leash. He was five, nearly six-years-old, strong for his age, but no match for the sixty-pound dog. He remembered from the previous year when Tonto was smaller but tough enough to have his way when Dominic took him for a walk. Only eight at the time, and to keep Tonto from pulling at his arm and running off, Dominic thought it a good idea to wrap the end of the dog's chain around his waist to give his hand a rest. The good idea turned bad when the neighbor's cat appeared. Tonto hauled off after it, dragging Dominic along the coarse pavement, down the street, and into a neighbor's yard. His pants and sleeves were torn at his bloodied knees and elbows, and the pull from the link chain around his waist scraped up his belly, sides and back. When the story was first told, Susanna burst out laughing, but Dominic didn't find it funny at all. Joey figured that it must have hurt pretty badly. There were a dozen or more scrapes that scabbed over and bled between bandages, with puss oozing out, causing Dominic to cringe and at times cry when his mother tended to them. The damage took weeks to heal.

Dominic entered the kitchen, grabbed hold of Tonto's collar, and led him out the door. *Poor dog,* Joey wanted to say. He didn't understand why Tonto could not stay in the house with them, especially at night, where it was warmer. He'd been a good dog, hadn't he? Running through swampland to return with the pheasant his father shot down was a job worth rewarding. It would seem he could join them for a bit of family time, and maybe even a taste of his catch, not that Joey had any say in the matter. He was, after all, just a child in a family of eight children. There were times he tried to speak his mind and share his thoughts. But why bother, when nobody listened?

Joe's finger itched to pull the trigger. The minutes he held steady seemed endless, but now his adrenaline soared when the shadows moved again. This was it, he thought, his waiting was about to pay off. Three . . . Two . . .

It was in that final moment, when the shadows, a pair of bald eagles, flew off into the distance. Joe gasped at the sight.

It was rare to see one, but to see two of these beauties in these parts was almost unheard of. He lowered the barrel of his rifle, consumed with relief he'd not been hasty to shoot. He would never be able to live it down, let alone forgive himself for such an error.

Disappointment crept in nonetheless as he resolved it was time to wrap it up for the day. He could not ignore the twinge of frustration that he was certain, perhaps wishful thinking, that a whitetail was within his reach. He could almost smell, even taste, the venison. The mere thought of it made him hungry, but also nostalgic about the first time he helped his mother prepare a pheasant for dinner. She wore her cooking apron, motioned for him to pull up a chair to the sink where she was about to clean it. Joey removed his hearing aids before doing so. He did not understand the point of having to wear the stupid things in the first place; they did his ears no good, anyhow. All that he knew was that he and Petro, who was a year younger, attended a private school for the deaf, unlike his other siblings.

"Dad—shoot—bird," his mother said, pronouncing each word slowly and while looking at him, so that he could read her lips. She leaned over the sink, aimed toward the window, and pulled the trigger of her imaginary rifle. "Cook—for—supper." She pinched her fingers near her mouth, making chomping motions, and then rubbed her belly, smiling.

But Joey already knew all that. He remembered it from the last time his father brought home pheasant. Because he was younger then, he was not asked to watch or help his mother prepare the meal. With the dead pheasant in the sink, she plucked its feathers one by one by anchoring the skin down with one hand, a quick snap of the wrist with the other. Joey got the hang of it.

"Only—one—feather—at a time," she told him, holding up a finger. "Pull—fast, okay?"

Joey nodded, followed her lead, first with the drumsticks and then up around the neck area. It was a long and messy chore, but his mother did not seem to mind. By the time they reached the breast area, Joey wanted to show her that he was strong enough to pull more than one feather at a time. It was tiring work for a boy his age, and he was already getting hungry. He took hold of three feathers then, yanked hard, when the skin tore open and the bird began to bleed.

Frowning, his mother waved for him to stop. "Only—one—feather, remember, just one," she reminded him gently.

He was sorry now and covered his mouth, regretting he'd not followed his mother's instructions. But then he thought of something, tapped her on the arm to get her attention, and then held up a finger for her to wait. Quickly, he scooted off into the next room, returning with a needle and thread.

"No." His mother laughed, shaking her head. "It's okay," she assured him.

"Wah?" His palms turned upward, it seemed like a good idea. Joey climbed back onto the chair and pointed to the scar on the inside of his mother's thumb where she cut herself on a broken glass while washing the dishes sometime ago. After a trip to the emergency room, she returned with a dozen stitches and a bandaged hand.

"Oh . . . you remember when I cut my hand?"

Joey nodded. How could he forget? All that blood was scary to see. The only thing strange to him was that his mother didn't seem to feel the sting of the gash, she didn't even cry.

But the case with the dead bird was different. He realized that sewing it up was not necessary since they were about to cook and eat it later. The thread might get caught in their teeth, he hadn't thought about that.

When the bird was finally plucked naked and nubby, Joey felt goose bumps prickling his arms; he knew what was coming next. His mother laid the pheasant on a cutting board, its limp head rolled off to the side, with an eye that seemed to be staring directly at him. One swift swing of the blade, the head rolled off into the sink. Joey winced, covered his neck with both hands. His mother held the bird by the feet, rinsed it off under the running faucet for what seemed like a long time, until she laid it down on the cutting board again. Another swing of the blade, she brushed the gnarly feet off the board, and then one final slice to the tail end. She proceeded to gut the pheasant, removing its innards and setting them aside. Joey was engaged with the procedure. It was something his mother did many times before, and he remembered the first time the meal tasted much better than he thought it would. When she was finished, she rewashed the headless bird a final time, inside and out, and then placed it in a pot of boiling water with a lid on top. There was nothing more to do now, but wait.

Joey stood transfixed, staring at the remains in the sink. The wet, furry head with its beak and eyes wide open, the hundreds of feathers, different lengths and sizes, were now in a soppy mess. He reached for one of the webbed feet, feeling the texture between his fingers, and wondered why there were only three long toes, and a shorter claw-like edging to the side. When his mother turned back toward the stove, Joey slipped the foot in his pants pocket, deciding it was worth hanging on to. It was something he might find a use for later.

The recollection was more than forty years ago. Joe still remembered the day, so vividly, of helping his mother; always so patient, so kind, and much more understanding than his father. She took the time to explain things in a way that made sense. His father's role, it seemed to him then, was to go to work at their beauty salon and then return later in the day, in time for dinner. A few times a year, he would hunt with Tonto, and then his mother would clean, cook, and serve the meal. But his mother also worked long hours at the salon—she did everything, all but go hunting. That was men's work.

By the time supper was over, Micheline, the oldest of them all, began to clear the table to wash the dishes. His mother was busy storing the remaining food into containers when everyone else pretty much scattered about, off in different directions.

"Susanna!" his mother called out. "Come dry the dishes, please."

"Mommm. . ." Susanna shot back from the living room doorway, "*Little Rascals* is on."

"Come and help first, it won't kill you."

"But, Mom . . . why do I always have to—" Before she could finish what she was about to say, their father entered the kitchen from his bedroom, having heard the exchange.

"Get your ass in here now! Listen to your mother before I knock some sense into you."

That was all it took. When it came to their father, Joey noticed, Susanna was not nearly as brave at speaking her mind as she was with their mother. With pouty lips, her eyes lowered, she grabbed a clean dish towel and did what she was told.

Stefano was still strapped in his highchair, his hands and face smeared with gravy and rice. He slapped his palms against the tray, drumming away, chanting a happy babble. It was what Joey suspected, at least. He could not hear him of course, but Stefano's toothless grin indicated he enjoyed his dinner. He reached for his empty plastic cup, held it out to his brother. Joey knew what he wanted, poured him some milk from the refrigerator. Stefano clapped happily, raised the cup to his lips, beginning to drink, his eyes never leaving Joey's, who mimicked his little brother, pretending to drink from his invisible cup.

Stefano cackled hysterically. Joey took pleasure in the easy manner in which he could amuse and entertain his baby brother, until Stefano sneezed, causing milk and snot to run out of his nose and all over the place. This time it was Joey's turn to laugh.

Micheline saw the mess and rushed to clean it. She then scooped the baby out of his highchair to whisk him off for bath time. That was Joey's cue that it was time to move on to more important matters, his favorite tasks.

"Maaa...." He waved to his mother. "Daaawg," he muttered, rubbing his belly.

"Yes . . . go feed Tonto." She pointed to the pantry where the fifty-pound bag of food was kept.

Joey filled the metal bowl, paused a moment before removing a single pellet and then tasting it.

"Don't eat that!" his mother chided. "You're not a dog."

"Woof," Joey said, and then giggled, remembering *Buster*

in his Animal Friend's book. He watched his mother rake the scrap remains she had gathered from the dinner plates, onto the dry dog food. Content with his chore, he took the bowl outside, walking carefully so not to trip and fall like he'd done once before.

In the backyard, Tonto's excitement started to build when he saw Joey approach, up until he set the bowl down before him. Joey watched him dive in, satisfied to just sit on a log stump and wait for him to finish, or at least come up for air.

When the bowl was half empty, Tonto paused to look up. Joey observed him, saying nothing at all. Tonto slurped sloppy sips from his water dish, and then approached Joey to offer his left paw. Joey shook it, rubbed the top of his head, the shade of a tootsie roll. Tonto licked Joey's face, making him giggle, and then worked his snout down to his pants pocket. He sat, and barked this time. Joey reached in his right pocket, pulled out the pheasant's foot, and grinned. But Tonto was neither fooled, nor interested. He pranced around, sitting once more, though impatiently, before nudging the edge of Joey's other pocket and then offering his paw a second time.

Joey retrieved the extra piece of meat he saved from his plate, a bigger chunk than all the scraps put together, and held it out to him. In one swift lick, Tonto devoured the treat, sniffing around for more. Joey giggled, shook his head. He hugged Tonto's neck, and then curiously, lifted one of his long floppy ears, to check inside. Peering into what looked like a dark tunnel, a maze of tiny bones and deep crevices that were so much more interesting than humans ears, he went on to lift Tonto's other ear. Holding them both out wide, like wings of a plane, he tilted right and then left, pretending to soar higher and then lower, while humming what he perceived to be the sound of a roaring engine. He learned his alphabet at school, but also practiced the sounds of each letter, and in forming words especially, when his mother read him picture books and placed his fingers on the side of her throat when she pronounced them.

When Tonto tired of the game, he shook his head free. Joey laughed, and Tonto barked in amusement. He jumped up then, resting his front paws on Joey's shoulders. The two danced about, forming a bit of a circle, until the weight became too much and Joey set him back down again.

As he was about to leave, Joey pointed to the food bowl, urging Tonto to go on and finish his supper, like a good dog. Tonto sat, his head cocked to one side as if he knew what was coming. That once he returned to his food, Joey would head back to the house. Tonto remained still, refusing to eat. Joey reached for a dry pellet from the food bowl, offered it to Tonto between two pinched fingers. Tonto's eyes danced from Joey's to the pellet and back again. When he made no move to take it, Joey slipped it in his pocket, causing Tonto to bark. Joey cackled, amused. He pulled out the single pellet again, brushed off the lint, offered it once more to Tonto, who gobbled it up this time. Joey patted his side and rubbed his fur.

"Good dawg," he said, hugging his neck before scooting back toward the house.

Joe shook his head, pushing the memory, so long ago, from his mind. What sent him back there, he no longer remembered, but noticed how the sun drifted lower and lower beneath the edge of the forest. After hours of sitting, waiting, with nothing more than his random thoughts to keep him company, he had not seen a single deer.

Although peak time for the rut in Martin County had long passed, Joe nailed several bucks during off-peak season in years past. Bucks were known to be extremely cautious, letting their guard down as the peak of the rut approached and their thoughts turned away from food and safety to round-the-clock sex. Joe and other hunters knew they needed to get in the woods whenever possible during the time when bucks' behavior was the most affected. Yet, unlike others he knew, Joe was not so much a follower of the crowd, but one who preferred doing things in his own way and time, and who prided himself on defying the odds.

Nighttime was closing in. Without a watch, he guessed it to be four-thirty or so, and then reached into his vest pocket to retrieve his cell phone. He pressed the unlock button, when the screen came to life, reading 4:34 p.m. Just a few minutes off, he grinned. This, too, was just another little pastime he took pleasure in. When his stomach growled, he didn't need another reminder to get going. He was twenty-five minutes from home, would pick up a pizza along the way, a large supreme with the works. Growing hungrier with just the thought of it, he would have them add jalapeños. Delia didn't care for hot and spicy, it sometimes upset her stomach. But she would be working late, as usual. By the time she dragged herself home she would have already eaten, or be too wiped out for food, begging for sleep to make her feel whole again.

His idea to go hunting was a spur-of-the-moment decision, and Delia had already left for work by then. Not that it mattered, he thought, slipping his phone back in his pocket. She would never have known he'd gone hunting, not until he told her, anyway. He sure would have liked to surprise her, though. Their freezer was nearly empty of meat, and money was tight. It would soon be time to pay their insurance premiums for their vehicles and, soon thereafter, their property taxes.

Ever since Delia bought and managed the Tipsy Teapot, she worked as many as twelve to fifteen hours a day, and at times seven-days-a-week. It was a dream of hers, to run her very own shop someday, to be her own boss. Joe figured it was a lot to take on, but he was not about to stand in her way. She was highly intelligent, he'd give her that, and when she set her mind to do something, there was pretty much no stopping her. What she didn't know, she told him, she would learn. It was as simple as that. Her original plan was to launch a coffee shop. But when another coffee house opened in the storefront next to the one she planned to rent, Delia switched her concept to focus on tea and a few healthy desserts and sandwiches. Eight years later, the place was barely making ends meet, but Delia didn't seem to mind the long hours, or be discouraged by the meager wages it gave them. It was her home away from home. Literally, she did everything there but sleep and shower. Joe wanted her to be happy, and she never kept him from doing what he wanted, so he tried not to complain. But her being gone all the time, it sure got old.

Joe gathered his things. Adjusting himself on his tree-stand from twenty-feet up, he slipped the end of the rope through his gun case and lowered it to the ground. It was an act he performed dozens of times before that he could go through the motions with his eyes closed. His hunter's knife, first-aid kit, gloves and canteen were all set to the side, away from his movement. With his rifle now safely to the ground, the case leaned up against the trunk of his tree, he undid his safety harness, reached for his equipment on the adjacent tree to begin his descent, when something shifted beneath him. The movement was slight, yet enough to alert his good senses that something was wrong. In that moment of pause, mere seconds, his stand collapsed, falling freely, and his body along with it. His arms flailed wildly for something, anything, to grab onto. The hairs in his nose and of his flesh stiffened, the roof of his mouth went dry as flashes of trees, shadows, and sky whipped through his mind's eye, with no time to brace himself before crashing to the ground.

CHAPTER 2

Bones snapped, breaking through the skin of his right shin. The pain shot all the way up to his head. He could not move, could barely breathe, when he coughed and spewed out fits of scalding bile. Surrounded by muddy swamp, the water from the wet leaves seeped through his clothing. On his back now, his eyes took hold of the place from where he'd fallen. His safety gear, every item he had, including his canteen and first-aid kit were right where he set them, perched on a tree limb. His fall, apparently, did not disturb the gear in the least. He tried to lift his head, now heavy, when dizziness thrust him back again.

With a hammering in his chest, he closed his eyes to think, be still, and to steady his heart rate. After taking several slow, deep breaths, he opened his eyes again. Minutes passed before he was able to lift his head up and steady himself on his elbows. Twisted awkwardly, he cringed at the sight of his mangled leg, the shinbone tip protruding from the tear of his camouflage pants. Blood seeped through his outerwear, causing a paste-like substance to form against his skin. The damage was far worse than he would have imagined. He'd known others who fell from trees, roofs, or scaffolding. The unlucky ones wound up with a broken arm or fractured ankle that most often a six-week cast would mend. His fall, however, where the bone snapped and severed the skin, was indescribable agony.

He grunted to try and force the leg straight, but it was no use—
he gave into a swirling pit of darkness.

The swamp was full of white oaks, shagbark hickory, red ma-
ples, and blackgum trees, the largest of them as tall as a hundred and thirty feet, and a hundred inches in circumference.
There were dogwoods much smaller, briar patches, stumps
and fallen logs. It was a month, maybe two, since the fall's
foliage covered the ground and the rains that followed gave it
a soggy, uneven, somewhat padded terrain.

As the evening lingered, all but for a hooting owl, though
unseen, was the only sound in the vicinity. For Joe, though,
whether asleep or awake, there was no concept of sound, no
hearing at all.

He opened his eyes, slowly at first, blinking once, seeing
nothing more than shadowed trees and a hue of darkness. He
was half lying on his left side, with his left leg curled up below the mangled one. There were muddy, limp leaves, damp
and smelly with a faint odor of sewage. He remembered trying
to straighten his right leg, the image of the break fused into
his brain. If only he'd just imagined it, a bad dream, he'd had
those before. But this? This was like a knife digging, twisting
into his flesh, chipping through cartilage and bone, a kind of
pain that caused his heart to sink deeper and deeper at his reality. On the one hand, he thought, he could have broken his
back or his neck, and died instantly. Dead at forty-seven—and
no telling when his body would be found. On the other hand,
the damage he sustained, his location and time of day, his lack
of necessities, did anything but make him feel as if he 'dodged
the bullet'. He was alive all right, but for how long? Blood

seeped from his wound, the bone exposed to the elements.

It was darker now. The thought of moving at all, to cause the busted up bones to shift terrified him, and yet to do nothing terrified him more. Through gritted teeth, he attempted to ease himself over onto his back. His body was shaky and he was uncertain he should be moving at all. But the leg needed to be dealt with. As he rolled from his left side to his back, a fiery pain shot up from his lower right limb, urging him to stop. His head rested then, against the soaked up leaves until his labored breathing subsided.

For several moments, he stared at the sky and could not move, did not want to move. He lay there, perfectly still, sensing an incredible calmness, but there was something else, too. It was as though he was not quite alone, as though someone was watching over him.

God.

Jehovah.

Until now, he had not thought much about it, not in a long while, anyway.

"It's called Armageddon," his father told his mother. "The end of the world is coming in 1975."

"Is that what Sal told you?" his mother asked. Salvatore Barone was his father's brother, a baptized Jehovah's Witness, along with his wife, Rose.

"Yeah," his father replied, "and they'll be a *great crowd* of survivors. We need to study *The Truth*."

Later that evening, Joey's mother asked his father something at the dinner table, though he could not grasp what exactly, other than it was to do with the little blue book his father brought home, titled *The Truth.*

"All it took to convince me was that one-hour cassette. I'm telling you, the end is coming."

His mother listened, not having much to say, either for or against. At least not where Joey could tell. He knew nothing of what the talk was all about, not until a few weeks later, at the start of the new school year, when they began to attend meetings at the Kingdom Hall—two hours on Sundays, two more on Thursday evenings, a Friday night study of the *Watchtower*, and the occasional Tuesday night gathering at someone's home, all to read more text. With no sign language interpreter, it made understanding what the speaker was saying no different than his attempt at reading one of his *Grandmaman's* letters to his mother, written in French. Though he tried to make out some of the words, aside from *Bonjour,* the rest was all jibber.

At the Kingdom Hall, Joey focused on the speaker's lips and then his body adjustments, one hand on the pulpit, the other to straighten his tie. He noted the color and style of his watchband, whether silver tone or gold; the shade and length of his mustache, compared to the color of his hair; whether his teeth were straight or crooked, or in Brother Calhoun's case, the gap between his two front teeth. His favorite person to observe, however, was Brother Domakas. There was something about his smile that intrigued Joey and the people around him. The way his mouth moved and his jaw angled in a peculiar manner displayed a larger portion of his gums that kept Joey from looking away. It was not until later that his mother explained to him that Brother Domakas wore ill-fitting dentures. It also explained the reason his teeth did a little jiggle when he spoke, and when he laughed, the edges could be seen against his pinkish gums.

Of everyone in the congregation, Brother Domakas was definitely the oldest man that Joey knew, but also one of the friendliest, too. He greeted everyone he came in contact with, whether he knew them or not, with a jovial smile that was infectious. And then one day, Brother Domakas stopped wearing his dentures altogether. When he laughed, Joey was reminded of his baby brother Stefano, before he grew teeth. Cringing at the thought, he wondered if Brother Domakas ate baby food out of a jar. There was no way he could chew meat, bear down on an apple, or eat corn-on-the-cob, not without teeth. And with his ill-fitting dentures that might fall out if he tried, he might be better off eating Jell-O, chocolate pudding, and ice cream, which did not seem so bad to him.

Aside from his idle thoughts that kept his mind wondering all sorts of things, Joey spent most of his time absentmindedly looking at the pictures in the *Watchtower* magazine. Until he could learn to read well enough, the pictures were all he had. When he tired of those, he would scan the room and survey the members, see who was paying attention and who was not. It was easy enough to figure out. All it took was a quick gaze around without being too obvious about it. The secret was to let your eyes do the roaming without much movement to the head. Anyone old enough to understand knew the rules. No talking. Sit still. Face forward. No blowing bubbles with your gum or tapping the chair in front of you with your foot. Pay attention. Be quiet. Joey knew the rules well.

Paying attention, for him at least, was the tricky part. He would thumb through the Bible, the New World Translation of the Holy Scriptures, stop at a section, and then cut his eyes to catch Heather passing Emily a folded-up note, who quickly hid it in the palm of her hand. Most of the adults kept their attention forward. Brother Jackson's son, Jimmy, swung his feet to and fro until he propped them against the seat in front of him, breaking a rule, to check out the shine on his noticeably new shoes. Joey looked down at his own pair. The edges were scarred and scuffed, with the sole of his right one slightly detached. He was due a new pair, for sure, he would later tell his mother. But not so much like the ones Jimmy wore, he would rather have a new pair of sneakers. Jimmy's younger brother kept fidgeting in his seat, until finally; he grabbed hold of his private area, and his mother quickly led him by the hand toward the back of the room.

It was not until they got back home, after a full week of ongoing meetings, that Joey asked his mother why they needed to go to the Kingdom Hall so often.

Before she could answer, his father asked, "What'd he say?"

"He wants to know why we go to the Kingdom Hall."

Joey did his best to read his father's lips. "Tell him . . . world . . . coming . . . end!" His father said something else, but Joey didn't know what. He often missed much of what was being said, as no one spoke in sign, other than Petro and their teachers at school.

His mother looked down, tapped her fingers against the table to help her find the right words, and then stopped to scratch the side of her neck.

"What are you waiting for?" his father snapped. "Tell him what I said."

She faced Joey, making her best attempt to spell the words in sign.

"The w-o-d-l-f . . . c-o-m . . ." She stopped, reached for a pencil on the table and wrote: "The end of the world is coming soon. We need to be ready, be part of the great crowd."

Joey drew a circle around the words 'great crowd'. "Wah mean?"

"What'd he say?" his father muttered.

His mother turned the paper towards him, where his eyes narrowed. She wrote a new sentence: "Everyone who believes *The Truth,* believes in Jehovah, will be in the great crowd."

Joey held up a finger, reached for the pencil and wrote: "Will crowd go to hevin?"

His mother shook her head, began to write.

"What's he asking?" His father stretched his neck to read the writing.

"No." His mother wrote: "Only 144,000 people will go to heaven."

Joey's head jerked a cockeyed grin. His mother kept writing, while his father exhaled a deep sigh, glancing at the clock on the wall. "Are we gonna eat, or what?"

His mother went on to explain. "The great crowd will live on a paradise earth."

Joey pointed to the words 'paradise earth'. "Wah?"

"It means there will be no more violence. No more sickness. No more disease," she wrote.

Joey nodded. He liked the sound of that and wondered if maybe he would no longer be deaf on this paradise earth, but when he asked, his mother shrugged, she didn't know. That was the end of his lesson and explanation. His mother got up to fix them all some lunch. This new information gave Joey something more to think about.

In late October, all of a sudden, there were no Halloween pumpkins to carve, no costumes or trick-or-treating. In December, there was no Christmas tree or presents that year. And the worst part of it, there was no cake or blowing out the candles for his birthday and no Easter egg hunts or hidden chocolate candy the following spring. Each time he asked why, he was given the same answer.

"Jehovah's Witnesses do not believe in these traditions," his mother told him. "They are *pagan* activities," she concluded on a scratch piece of paper.

"Wah pagan mean?"

"What's he want now?" His father asked, having just arrived home from work.

His mother repeated the question, while they all sat around the table for dinner. "He wants to know what 'pagan' means."

"It means worldly," his father said, pulling out the chair at the head of the table, loosening up his tie, before taking his seat.

"He won't understand that, what's another word?"

"Aren't we all worldly?" Susanna asked in the matter-of-a-fact logic of a child.

Jena piped in: "If we live in the world that makes us worldly. If you don't I guess you're unworldly."

"That doesn't even make sense," Dominic interjected.

"Well, you're a pagan," Susanna quipped, "so what do you care?"

"I'm getting baptized, and besides, you don't even know the meaning of the word."

"Shut up, I do too!"

"What's it mean, then?"

"That's for me to know," Susanna smirked, "and for you to find out."

The back and forth banter, mixed with laughter, was halted the moment a fist landed firmly on the table. Everyone froze.

"You think this is a joke?" His father spat, making eye contact with each and every one of them. With his cold, hard stare, no one said a word. "Huh? You think this is funny?"

Confused, Joey wondered what happened. All he did was

ask a simple question. Did his father not want him to understand what was going on?

"Eat your dinner," his father told them.

Joey looked to his mother, about to ask why his father was mad, when she raised her finger to her lips to quickly shush him. He understood then that he'd asked enough questions for now.

At the age of ten, Joey took matters into his own hands and looked up the word *pagan* in the dictionary. The definition read: *Heathen. A follower of a polytheistic religion. One who has little or no religion, which delights in sensual pleasures or material goods.* He reread the definition a second and third time, trying to make sense of the big words as best as he could. Next, he looked up the word *heathen. An uncivilized person who does not recognize God of the Bible.* This only baffled him further, because as Catholics, they believed in God and the Bible. He then looked up the word *poly-the-is-tic. Belief in or worship of more than one God.* To sum it all up—pagan, heathen, and polytheistic had little or no religion, or the belief of more than one God.

Joey slammed the dictionary shut. His head hurt. He was no closer to understanding any of it. It was all a bunch of twisted words and fancy talk that did not make sense to him. All he knew was that life was better before the *pagan* and *heathen* talk, and all the many rules and restrictions.

Eventually, he came to understand one thing, and that was to stop asking questions. They only seemed to make his mother nervous and annoy his father. When his mother raised her finger to her lips, in order to change the subject, he did as he was told. It did not matter whether he was able to follow along or that he understood what was being taught. As a child, he had no say in the matter, and whether he liked it or not, it was the new way of their lives. There were no open discussions that he was privy to, no clear explanations, or sharing of views. And still, the Kingdom Hall became the focus of their lives.

But Joey was not the only one unhappy with the situation. Micheline too, voiced her own opinion.

"Mom, you always said I could date when I was sixteen."

"Yes, but that was before."

"And now, I'm supposed to wait until I'm ready to marry? That makes no sense at all. How will I know if I want to marry someone if I don't date first?"

"You can go out in a group, get to know one another that way."

"But there aren't even any guys my age at the Kingdom Hall. And it's not just that. Being a teenager is a time to go to school dances and parties, have fun with my friends, and experience going to the movies with a guy, without a chaperone. It's not about wanting to get married."

The two of them ignored Joey's presence, unaware he was following their discussion, at least enough to understand Micheline's frustration.

"Now, Dad expects me to give up my 'worldly' friends. And he won't even let me try out for the basketball team."

"I know it's hard, but it's for your own good. Your worldly friends might get you in trouble. You're better off with those from the congregation."

"And being part of the basketball team . . .?"

"Will take time away from your school studies."

Micheline rolled her eyes, and the conversation ended. She went along with the rules, seeing that there was no other choice, though she clearly was not happy about it.

Several months later, in the spring, Micheline rekindled

a friendship with Frankie, an eighteen-year-old boy she was paired up with as a bridesmaid, at their aunt Lisa's wedding several years past. Their friendship was more in the way of letters and phone calls.

"Mom . . . Frankie wants to take me to the movies. Can I go, please?"

"Your father will want Frankie to come over for a Bible study first. Invite him over for dinner."

The following weekend, after sitting through an hour lesson of *The Truth*, Frankie and Micheline were permitted time for their date to the movies.

"What did you go see?" their mother later asked, after Frankie left to go home.

"*Blazing Saddles*." Micheline smirked. "A bunch of men sitting around a campfire, farting and telling jokes. It was embarrassing, but Frankie laughed like it was the funniest movie he'd ever seen."

CHAPTER 3

Ignoring the growling in his stomach, Joe was still now, and for the moment the pain lessened. He wanted to keep it that way. The world above him was a clear view of stars and galaxies. Having once read, while waiting in a doctor's office, about the ten brightest stars that could be seen from Earth, their names mostly weird and unusual, *Little Dumbbell* and *Bridge to Heaven* suddenly came to mind. The one that caught his attention and stuck with him was the *Dog Star,* known as *Sirius*. Strange, that he would have retained that information, and even stranger still, that until now, he had not tried to locate them. The Dog Star was said to be the brightest one in the sky. Of all the millions of them looking down on him, he could see it now. It seemed logical, a fitting name, when he, too, believed that dogs, more than any other animal, made the brightest pets.

Joe knew that he ought to be moving, that he should figure out a way to get help. But the steady Dog Star was shining down on him like a beacon from a lighthouse at sea. The glow of its brightness captivated him like a magnet pulling on metal, taking him back to another place and time.

The first lighthouse Joey ever saw was the one in *Grand-maman's* backyard, at the edge of her property near the village of Verchères.

It was June of 1971. School was out when they loaded up the Suburban and headed north, to begin their two-month summer vacation. It took six hours before reaching the customs border, where they were asked about their citizenship, their length of stay and reason for entry, and then two more hours to Verchères, an off-island suburb of Montreal, located on the south bank of the St. Lawrence River. It was there where *Grandmaman* lived, in the same house that his mother and her twelve siblings were born and raised. The house, however, was not the focal point of Joey's excitement, but the river that flowed behind it. He'd only seen pictures, most of them in black and white, with the many ships and cargos that traveled it. His parents, he was later told, purchased a portion of an island, with a summer cottage. It was a place they would all be seeing for the first time, and something that his mother pressed upon, when his father moved them to the city, to have a safer place where the children could run and play during the time that school was out. Doing so in the town his mother grew up in, made it all the more appealing.

This was Joey's first ever vacation away from home. He could not wait to see the place, and would finally get to meet his other aunts and uncles and the seventeen cousins he only heard stories about. In a way, they would all have something in common, he thought, a language barrier that would put him on an even keel. Aside from Micheline, who had already learned to speak French, there was the foreign language barrier. He and the rest of his siblings, and he suspected his cousins too, would have to rely on hand gestures to converse with one another. This was something he was already accustomed to.

When they arrived, finally, it was all that Joey could do to keep from bursting out of the car and run to shore, but *Grandmaman* was soon outside, at the edge of her balcony. She was gray-headed, wore glasses and a peach-colored cotton dress that hung loose around her hips, with square pockets she could easily dip her hands into. She flashed an excited smile, an excited wave, and made her way down the steps of the gallery to greet them.

It took several minutes for the hugs to go around. *Grandmaman* spoke to their mother in French and the rest of them in broken English.

"Long trip, eh?"

His father nodded. "Not too bad."

"Look at you," she gave Joey's shoulder a squeeze, "you are big boy. How much old are you?"

Joey smiled, held up seven fingers.

"You are bigger than Jena. Soon you be bigger than Susanna, eh? You almost there."

Joey beamed, held himself a little taller, encouraged by the compliment. It was then he noticed the lighthouse at the edge of her property, beside the river. The concrete tower and cribwork pier that surrounded the wooden lantern above it was painted white and the lantern roof, red. It served to indicate the axis of the ship channel. Joey looked up, and pointed.

"Yes. That is one of Verchères lighthouse. It's big one. It helps boats on the river see at night," *Grandmaman* explained.

Joey nodded, smiled, while eying the river, both upstream and down, though he saw no ships. He then followed the others to the house, noting the outside was box-shaped, covered in cement siding sprinkled with pinkish gravel. Inside, there was a large square-shaped kitchen, three small bedrooms, and a tiny entry way with an itty-bitty chair-like couch that no one was allowed to sit on.

"This sofa not for sitting, okay? It has a sick leg, glue not work good. No sitting, just looking. Okay?"

Everyone got the message.

"We eat supper soon, okay? Then you sleep tonight. Rest. Tomorrow, you have big day."

Joey looked to his mother to better understand.

"Tomorrow," she motioned, "we go to the island."

He understood, though he hid his disappointment of having to wait yet another day to cross the river.

From the edge of the inlet behind *Grandmaman's* house, he later noticed he could practically see the place that awaited them. It was a straight shot over, but a good enough distance away, the house behind a set of trees was nothing more than a shadow. He would have to wait, be patient, his mother would say, until they were ready.

So wait was what he did. He could barely sleep that night, the anticipation of it all. The eight of them were all sharing one bedroom, with a mattress on the floor for the smaller ones. His parents were in the front bedroom and *Grandmaman* was in her own. It was more fun than Joey imagined it would be, all cooped up in the same room, sort of like a camping trip, only indoors.

Come morning, after breakfast was over, and his parents had gone shopping for groceries, the time had finally arrived.

"Bonjour! Es-tu prêt? Regardez les petits, ils ont vraiment grandi." Uncle Leo and *Tante* Marie-Jeanne stopped by, and then commented on how much the children had grown. They brought their motorboat to lend them a hand in crossing them over with all their stock and luggage. It took two motorboats and a canoe to get them to the other side.

Joey's eyes grew bigger and bigger the closer they got to

the opposing riverbank. "Look," he pointed to Petro, and then signed. "H-o-u-s-e. B-a-r-n."

Petro grinned, shading the sun from his eyes, but he was more focused on the size of the ship that was headed downstream.

Upon reaching the other side, everyone got out of the boats, and the oldest ones helped to pull them up on shore.

"Everybody, grab a box or bag to take to the house," his mother ordered.

All of them hauled items up, with a better view now, a first tour of the place. The home, high on the embankment, was once painted a pale yellow, but had long ago faded to the color of dishwater, matching the yard that surrounded it. The wood was rotted in areas and the shutters drooped on rusty hinges. There were broken slats and holes in areas of the ramshackle porch that ran the width of the house and along the side entry way, with columns to support the corners of the metal roof. Weeds sprouted through the holes of the porch, and the paint was chipped in long strips everywhere. Poison ivy crept along in wild bunches, overgrown bushes staggered, the grass was knee-high, and the apple trees out front kept the sun away.

"Wow!" his mother said. "We have a lot of work to do."

Inside the kitchen, was a table and chairs, a long bench to sit on, a black potbelly stove, and yellowed linoleum flooring. From the ceiling hung long strips of sticky fly paper.

"Wah for?" Joey asked, pointing to the fly paper.

"When the flies come in the house," his mother explained, "they get stuck, and then die. See," she showed him, "no screens on the windows. Lots and lots of flies come inside."

Joey pointed to the metal-handled fly swatter that hung on a nail beside a wall calendar.

"Yes, we can kill the flies that way, but it takes too long."

His mother then proceeded to tell the older ones that when she was a child, she earned a penny for every hundred flies she swatted and killed. Micheline later told Joey this.

"Fooling. No true."

"No fooling," Micheline assured him. "They were very poor."

Joey thought about it, and then pointed to the fly paper, agreeing it was a better idea. There was no electricity and no running water, only what came out of the hand-operated well pump. Without lights, they rose with the light of day and went to bed when everything got dark. Whatever food they needed was carried over from the mainland, and nothing that could spoil was brought over. They chopped wood for the old Franklin stove where they cooked their meals and toasted their bread.

On that first day, after a tour of the upstairs loft, where the girls, Micheline, Susanna and Jena would share, and the dusty old attic beside it, all seemed content enough to be back downstairs again.

Joey signed to Petro, "Maybe g-h-o-s-t-s live here."

"Where?" Petro wanted to know.

Joey pointed upstairs. "I think maybe a-t-t-i-c," he said, shrugging, trying to keep a straight face.

Petro thought it over for two seconds. "Me," he pointed to himself, "sleep downstairs."

Joey giggled. He liked messing with his siblings, but he did believe the place held a haunted vibe to it, which intrigued him all the more. Not that he believed in ghosts. Not that he didn't.

It was during that first summer, in a group effort that the house was fully painted and repaired. Every other weekend, his father would drive up for a visit and to check on their progress. Micheline was often left in charge whenever his mother needed to run errands on the mainland. Each day, after the work was done, there was always time to play.

One of his favorite hide-a-ways was in the barn, where Joey climbed the bales of hay to the top, to peer out the loft window for the perfect view. Dominic was out a ways, fishing from their canoe, baiting the hook before throwing the line in. Alanzo and Stefano were making mud pies down by the river. Jena was swinging from a tire swing. Petro was riding his bike up and down the lane from where the tractor pulling the hay wagon left a path. And Micheline was inching her way on the metal roof of their home from where she climbed out of her loft window, to reach the best apples from the tree beside it.

Joey spotted the black and white ship headed upstream. After a beat, he pulled the slingshot from his pocket, the one he'd made with a Y-shaped piece of branch he found and a thick rubber band he'd located at *Grandmaman's* house. The ship had a peculiar look about it, long, black and lean along the bottom, low to the water, with a smokestack near the back. *Pirates*, he thought. *You not come on our land. I destroy you!* He pulled the band hard before releasing it, pretending to have hit his target. *Pfshh!* He barely made a sound of what might be an explosion, and then applauded with bravado.

His time in the barn always came with something new to discover. It was there that he found a pair of stray kittens, orange and black in color, apparently abandoned by their mother. Another day, it was a bird's nest hidden between a bale of hay and the barn wall, with blue-spotted eggs yet to hatch. Never having seen anything like them before, he wanted to hold them, and considered whether to take just the eggs or the entire nest, to hide under his bed, and keep watch for when the eggs hatched. But when he reached for the nest, the mother bird burst out of nowhere, her wings flapping madly, her beak squawking in a panic. Joey got the message that the eggs were not to be touched.

It was during their second summer, though, when two of the farmers that tended their land brought them over a pony.

"Bonjour, Madam," Monsieur Lacoste greeted their mother.

"Bonjour. Qu'est que tu a la?" (What do you have there?)

Monsieur Lacoste stroked the pony's mane, and said the pony was theirs for the summer, if they wanted him, but he would need to have the bit on before anyone could ride him.

"Oh my goodness," she exclaimed, "he's leaving the pony with us!" Excitement and interest brewed. Everyone gathered around to get a closer look, but soon stepped back when it became apparent the fitting of the bit was no easy task.

Monsieur Lacoste held onto the colt's head gear with one hand, the bit in the other, while Gaétan held the reins and saddle horn in attempt to keep him still. Pony seemed to fight them every which way, two steps forward and four steps back. For several minutes, the farmers were shuffled around the courtyard, their feet dribbling along the dusty ground, nearly tripping over themselves, struggling not to let go and to stay on their feet.

Joey and others could not help but chuckle at the sight of them. For a moment, he thought he was watching an episode of *The Three Stooges*, only this time with Moe, Larry, and Pony. Even his mother, who tried unsuccessfully to hide it, wore a pained expression, her lips pressed together tight, but her shoulders shook at her failed attempt not to laugh. It was easy to see, though, that the farmers were not at all amused, maybe even embarrassed, Joey thought. Despite the comical scene it caused, Monsieur Lacoste and Gaétan refused to give up. They hung on to Pony like their life depended on it, getting shambled about, pretending to ignore the sniggers of their viewers, until finally their efforts won over, and the bit was secured in place.

Everyone cheered. "Who wants a ride?" his mother asked.

Joey raised his hand, took a step forward. The only ponies he'd ever ridden were the coin-operated ones outside the grocery stores, or the wood-carved ones on the carousel at the Chester Carnival.

Monsieur Lacoste boosted Joey onto the saddle, and then led him around the courtyard in a wide circle. Joey held on to the sturdy saddle horn, feeling taller and older, as his body swayed slightly, like a real cowboy's did. He would have liked to trot a little, but the ride was soon over for the others to have a turn.

The moment Joey was helped down, Pony backed away. Monsieur Lacoste pulled him closer, but Pony refused to advance, looked him straight in the eye in a mocking manner, before jerking his head up.

"I'm next," Susanna shouted. "It's my turn."

There was an exchange between Monsieur Lacoste and his mother. It seemed to Joey that Pony was getting even, having been forced to wear the bit, and was acting out now.

"Mom, it's my turn," Susanna insisted. "Can I go already?" The others, who were interested in a ride, stood by and waited.

Pony jerked back again, doing everything he could not to comply. He raised his head high, yanked it down low again trying to free himself and then shimmied back in the other direction.

Monsieur Lacoste scowled, said something more to his mother, where she agreed, and turned to the others.

"Okay, the pony is tired now. Everyone, go play."

"Hey!" Susanna bellyached. "How come I don't get a turn?"

"He's tired, I said. Go find something else to do."

"How can he be tired after just one person?"

"Susanna . . ." His mother looked agitated now.

"That's not fair! Joey gets to do everything. Little brat."

Joey knew his sister was angry, and he knew why. But he was older now and decided he was better off ignoring her when she got this way. Besides, he had better things to do, like planning ways to make friends with the colt. And once he did, he would teach him to do tricks.

By the end of the first week, the others all but lost interest in Pony, for his constant attempts at trying to nip at them. Not Joey. He walked him each day and knew that if anyone was able to teach Pony, it was him. He patted him down in the barn, with all sorts of thoughts running through his head.

Good Pony. He rubbed the bridge of his nose, the two of them eye to eye. Joey removed the hairbrush from his back pocket and began to brush Pony's mane. He enjoyed his time alone, with Pony calm and complacent, taking pleasure in his rubdown, until the mood suddenly changed when Susanna walked in.

"What are you doing?" she asked.

Joey made no reply, as she could clearly see what he was doing, and he didn't want to get into a tangle with her and upset Pony.

"Hey!" Susanna squealed, her eyes big as moon pies. "That's my brush. You stole my brush!"

"Nooo!" Joey said, pulling his arm away when she lunged at him. Pony jerked his head high, showing a good portion of his teeth, and then positioned himself between Joey and Susanna, making a move towards her.

Susanna stepped back quickly before Pony was able to nip

her, stumbling, and nearly tripping over her feet.

Joey smiled, but more to himself, so not to agitate her. "Gooo!" he told her. He didn't need her interfering with his time alone with Pony, or to be involved in what he planned to do.

"Give me my brush!"

"Nooo!" There were several brushes in the house, he thought, all of the same color, that came from his parents' salon. He'd found this one, with a broken handle, lying on the bench near the kitchen table, when the idea came to mind to brush down Pony.

Susanna turned to leave, with her hands planted on her hips and her jaw squared. Joey knew just where she was headed, too. His mother, however, had better things to do and would tell her to go find herself another brush.

Moments later, Petro joined him in the barn. "What matter S-usanna?" He signed.

Joey filled him in. "Same. Complain . . . complain . . . complain . . . all the time. You want help me walk Pony?"

Petro agreed. The three of them walked out onto the courtyard along the edge of the embankment a good ways down, when they came upon a fallen tree. It was a few feet off the ground, wedged up between two other trees.

Joey waved his hand to get Petro's attention. "We teach P-ony jump over tree." It seemed like a really neat trick, he thought, and that Pony was ready for the challenge.

Petro nodded, liking the idea. Holding onto the reins with one hand, Joey climbed over the tree trunk to show Pony how it was done. With a flick of the strap, Pony leapt over with ease. The boys laughed, pleased at how easy it was. To make sure though, Joey wanted to give it one more try. This time, he walked Pony farther out, and then flipped the reins over its head before releasing it to show his trust in Pony. With his hand he motioned for him to "Stay!" He then signed to Petro, "We run—hop over tree—show P-ony how. Okay?"

Petro agreed. He liked this idea all the more.

"Stay!" Joey motioned to Pony again. He and Petro, the two of them, ran toward the tree, hopped on over, and then waited for Pony to do the same.

With his chestnut colored head to the ground, his tail swishing as he nibbled the grass, Pony ignored the two.

Joey clapped his hands again and again, with Petro joining in, the two of them waving and shouting for Pony to come on.

Tossing his head up, his long mane flapping in the breeze, Pony did a two-step frolic. His attention back on point, he galloped the distance before leaping through the air, clearing the tree log altogether.

Amazed, Joey never thought it would be that easy. He could not wait to show his mother and the others. He knew that he could teach Pony, just knew it.

Then Petro came up with a new idea. "You—me—P-ony—ride same time—jump tree."

A bit skeptical, Joey liked the idea. But would Pony go for it? He led Pony back alongside the fallen tree for his brother to get on first. Joey, barefoot and giddy, positioned himself behind Petro, the two of them fitting snugly on the saddle, their hands secured to the horn. With a slight tug of the reins, Joey steered Pony far enough away, giving them plenty enough distance to manage a trot before making the jump. Once they were lined up, a hundred paces or so away, Joey dug his heels into the colt's side, the way Little Joe did on *Bonanza*. Pony started off with a light trot, the three of them bouncing along. Joey felt proud of his efforts, really proud, that he refused to give up when everyone else had—all but Petro, that is. His bonding time finally paid off, and his mother and the others would all be in for a real treat. But just when he expected to brace himself for the leap, Pony slowed to a near stop, lowered his head close to the ground, and buckled his front legs to make his way under the fallen tree.

Pulling hard on the reins, Joey bellowed, "Woooah!"

Ignoring the order, Pony forged on until his two riders toppled off, legs and arms splattered, one on top of the other.

Joey hollered, "Nooo! Nooo!" The two of them now on the ground, tangled as one, with Petro on top, trying to get off of him.

Pony trotted off a short distance, and then stopped to look back at the pair. With a thrust of his head, he circled himself about, his jaw slacked open, exposed teeth and gums in a mocking manner.

Joey saw Pony laughing at them. Laughing! He didn't know that horses were capable of such a thing. He got himself up, balled fists and all, stomped over to get hold of the reins to lead Pony back to the barn. "Bad Pony! Bad!"

Petro, at first, just stood there, bewildered. The plan had been simple, so perfect, and yet played out so miserably wrong. He, too, had seen the way Pony ran off, just far enough to be out of their grasp, but near enough to turn and scoff at them. He had watched Joey bolt, his body stiff with disbelief, as he stormed off to get hold of Pony. The fields of hay yet to be baled swayed slightly beneath a clear blue sky. Petro swatted at a horsefly flittering around his face, as he hurried to catch up to his brother. He waved to get Joey's attention, to stop him, to talk things out, maybe try something different, but Joey pushed past him, looking straight ahead, and in no mood to hear any more of his bright ideas.

CHAPTER 4

If there ever was a time that Joe wanted to believe, to have faith in a creator of mankind, a loving God of mercy, this was it. But believing in God was not the problem. The sky above him was proof enough of that. He gazed up at it now, captured by its beauty. Through the starkness of the trees were billions of tiny lights. Without a God, how could one explain their existence? If only he could somehow rearrange the stars to spell out a signal for help, like an Etch-A-Sketch. He needed to get home to Delia, but how? Relying on God alone was not the answer. There were many who attended church and prayed regularly, who lived a clean, wholesome life and bad things still happened to them. People often ask themselves, *why me? What have I done to deserve this?* Was it a test of faith, a plan in the making, or simply a case of odds and rotten luck? Searching for answers that aren't there was a waste of time and effort. If there was one thing that Joe was sure of, for him to stand a chance at getting out of the woods alive, was entirely up to him.

He had rested long enough now, his mind suddenly clearer. And then, it hit him. His cell phone was in his vest pocket and not with the other items still up in the tree. Why did he not think of it sooner? Delia could have already been on her way, bringing help with her: a flashlight, some bottled water, an ambulance. Most important was the ambulance. Delia by herself would never be able to get him out of the woods. At two hundred fifteen pounds, last time he checked, he was too heavy even to drag on a tarp. He would have her call nine-one-one. Joe reached in his pocket, now empty.

The cell?

Panicked, he jerked his head up. The cutting edge pain jolted him like a lightning bolt. His leg throbbed with such brutality; he didn't know how long he would be able to endure it before he blacked out again—or worse. He was three weeks shy of his forty-eighth birthday, a middle-aged man, by American standards. It was a reality he was often reminded of when thumbing through picture albums, even those from ten years prior. His prematurely thinning hair and receding hairline did not come from his father's side of the family, who now, in his mid-seventies, still had a full head of hair.

Joe was not vain about his looks, and refused to become one of those wannabes who, by way of a comb-over, fooled themselves into believing they were still in their twenties. Did they not know they were the brunt of women's jokes? That the slightest breeze would cause a man's comb-over to wave like a child's flag? It was either sparse hair flailing in the air, revealing a bald spot, or so much gel or hairspray that he wound up looking even more ridiculous. The flag still waved, only more stiffly. Instead, Joe shaved his head bald. It was easier to care for, and Delia liked it even better. She massaged his scalp with the tips of her fingers, relaxing him in a way that only her touch could. What he lacked in hair follicles, she told him, he made up for with the rest of his body. His biceps, thighs, and chest were still as solid as when he played sports in high school. He never smoked, and the only drug he took was a Tylenol for the occasional headache. His years of labor—swinging a hammer, an ax, hanging sheetrock, or tuning up a car's engine kept him fit and out of the doctor's office.

Joe shivered from the wet clothing against his skin, as the swampy marsh began to close in on him. He couldn't just lie there and do nothing, time was wasting and the night's temperature would soon drop. He was out in the country, a remote wooded area, on his parents' land that ranged in the vicinity of fifty acres or more. The problem was that he didn't tell anyone of his whereabouts. To make matters worse, he never hunted here before. It was not a place that anyone would think to search for him. He'd chosen the location this time on a hunch he might get lucky, away from other hunters and the dogs that accompanied them.

Some dumb luck.

He gritted his teeth now, willing himself to sit up, to check his surroundings. The pain was sharp and unrelenting, but his spirits lifted at the touch of his cell phone that was lodged between the wet soiled leaves he was lying on. With his thumb, he swiped the dirty water from its face, drying it against his upper sleeve. He pressed the power button, and waited. The usual image failed to blink on the screen. Again, he pressed the button, harder this time.

Come on . . .

Had he charged it the night before? He couldn't remember. The phone was wet, obviously, maybe even damaged. He popped open the back to try reseating the battery. His fingers, cold and shaky, lost their grip on it and the battery slipped into the murky waters. Frantic now, he reached through the muck, searching, relying on the feel of his fingers that were close to being numb. He cursed his clumsiness and rotten luck, pitched the useless phone away, watched it slam against a tree and shatter.

His leg ached. It was a kind of ache he'd never before

experienced, and he needed to do something to make it stop. Something other than destroy what might have been his only means of connecting to the outside world of his area of confinement. He would need to be strong now, and rely on his intuition and gut instinct to get him through this. His heart pounded, his head spun, and yet he knew what he needed to do. The thought of it sickened him, terrified him, but there was no other way than to position the twisted leg straight. Only then would he stand a fighting chance to crawl his way out and back to his truck.

He steadied his breathing and tried to think positive.

Flip the script, his English teacher, Mrs. D, used to say.

Things could always be worse.

Joe thought about that. Had it been colder, rainy, or with snow on the ground, he wouldn't stand a chance; not for long anyway. In summertime, the mosquitoes would torture him alive. And without water he would dehydrate that much quicker. It was nearly Christmas, and yet the evening temperatures remained in the low forties. There was always a worse scenario.

But at the moment, it did little to relieve the pain or lift his spirits. Having read survival magazines for most of his adult life, he always figured he would be prepared to deal with whatever. What he did not count on was that his gear would be unreachable and his mobility constrained, with an injury too serious to do much of anything about it.

The slightest movement of his leg from the knee down triggered a sunburst of pain. Bleary-eyed, his gaze stopped at his rifle case against the tree, right where he lowered it from his perched position. It held three bullets only. He could drag himself to the gun, fire off a shot or two for a signal. But who would hear them? Even if someone from the lot across the road were to hear the shots, it was nothing unusual in these parts, and it was, after all, hunting season. He was better off saving those bullets, for his own protection through the night. Judging from the water around him, he knew he would never make it through the swamp in his condition. For any chance at all, he needed to fix his leg first.

He swallowed hard before reaching behind his right thigh, lifted it upward, allowed the heel of his limp foot to slide along the ground gently. He grunted through the motion that sizzled every nerve ending, sending shivers up his spine to the edges of his earlobes. Joe stopped to catch his breath, to swallow the bile that formed in his throat. With his leg now bent, he pressed himself up to a seated position and proceeded to un-lace his right boot. The breakage along the shin had begun to swell, and the puncture wound oozed blood. His leg shook and wobbled and then flopped off to the side. There was no telling how much damage he suffered, fragments of bone and ligaments possibly crushed beyond repair. If infection set in, he knew what could happen. Gangrene. The mere thought of an amputation made him cringe. No way would he let that happen.

He made the decision then to straighten his leg. At first, he could not bring himself to touch it; the idea made him light-headed and nauseous. But when he thought about the pictures he'd seen on the Internet, when a random ad popped up on his screen—toes and limbs turned crusty black as if dug out of a campfire pit, charred down to a nub of coal. It was one of the most sickening images he'd ever seen. Gangrene was such an ugly word. And yet, there were folks diagnosed with diabe-tes who refused to watch their diet and exercise, increasing the risk of Gangrene, who chose to take their chances. Like a game of Russian roulette, cross your fingers and hope not to die, a reckless and foolish gamble he was not about to take, few as other options available to him were.

Before he could change his mind, Joe gave a swift shove with the use of both hands and twisted the leg straight. "Aughhhh!" He moaned an anguished cry, felt the bones pop and shift, before collapsing from sheer exhaustion.

In a state of haziness, slipping in and out of consciousness, his thoughts went to Dingo, Prince, and Jester, his loyal companions, alone at home. They were not accustomed to being penned up in the house for this long of a stretch. If only they were with him now, he thought, they would get him out of this mess.

Dingo and Prince, a lab/shepherd mix hand-selected from the pound, gravitated towards him the moment he set eyes on the pair. They were found abandoned in a rotting shack, turned in by some locals, the pound keeper told them. They appeared to be of the same litter, were devastatingly underweight and infested with fleas and ticks. One started off with a limp, though no broken bones were found, and the other was skittish when trying to be held. They were cleaned up, examined, and given their shots.

When they took the pair home, Joe named one Dingo, for his sandy-to-reddish brown coloring, his long muzzle and flatter skull, all traits of a Canis lupus dingo Australian dog. Prince, on the other hand, was simply named for his dark coloring, the way his ears perked up when he heard a strange sound, and his unwavering devotion to his new owners. It was not until a few years later, after moving to North Carolina, that he found a stray curled up on their front stoop.

The mixed breed lifted his head slowly, with pleading eyes, making no attempt to move at all. Joe squatted down, offered the edge of his knuckle to show there was nothing to fear. The stray was spade black in color, hopelessness in his pale gray eyes with pupils as dark as the fur on his back. He sniffed Joe first, licked his hand second, and then rested his head against his front paws. It was then that Joe saw the specks of blood.

Was he hit by a car?

He stroked his velvety head, gently worked his way down the length of his neck and back, when the stray flinched from the touch just above his right hind leg. There didn't seem to be a break, but he was definitely hurting.

After fetching a bowl from the house, Joe filled it with cool water, set it down near the dog's nose. Without getting up, the injured stray tilted his head to slurp some of the water.

Joe had been on his way out, headed to town to purchase materials for a ramp he was building for Ms. Viola, an elderly woman who lived alone. Already late, he wondered what to do about the stray. If Delia were home, she could call the animal shelter to come get him, but there was no telling what time she'd be back, and he suspected the dog may be lost or a runaway and the owner might come looking for him. Joe sat on the edge of the porch, rubbed the stray's head again, whose pleading eyes looked up at him, the two of them quiet.

Where you come from, boy?

You live around here?

They treat you good?

Joe took his cap off, scratched his head, and fixed it back on again, when the stray inched in closer to rest his head on Joe's lap.

You no make this easy on me.

I have two dogs already.

Two dogs who eat a lot.

We need find where you live. Owner look for you.

After a bit more stroking, Joe managed to break himself free, long enough to locate some bright neon construction paper in the house. With a black marker, he printed in large block letters: LOST DOG FOUND on Leggett Mill Rd (Black). Beneath it, he added their phone number.

On his way to town, Joe posted the sign at the Stop-and-Go on the corner of Prison Camp Road. It was the nearest place where farmers and locals mingled, a constant traffic of people on a daily basis. If the owner of the dog was anywhere in the vicinity, it was the best place to get the word out.

Nearly two weeks later, Joe realized he was getting more and more attached to the stray, and had already thought of a name for him.

"Did anyone call about the dog?" he asked Delia, hoping that no one had.

"No. No one. We'll give it another week. I know someone who can maybe take him."

"Who?"

"S-h-e-l-i-a. She's been talking about getting a dog, or a cat, since her h-a-m-s-t-e-r died."

"A dog . . . or a cat? You serious?" Joe made a face. If she wasn't partial to one over the other, she wouldn't be a good fit for *Jester*. Jester needed love and attention, someone who would understand him, play with him, and care for him. Not some woman wanting to replace a dead rodent. He was guessing that Shauna or Stella, or whatever her name was, wouldn't know the first thing about caring for a dog. He shook his head, and honestly did not understand people, sometimes.

"What's on your mind?"

Joe shrugged. He looked down from his chair and then to

where Jester was lying by his feet. His head perked up as if he knew he was the subject of conversation. *You want stay here, boy?* Jester scooted close enough to be patted on the head.

"You want to keep him, don't you?" Delia, at times, could read him so well. He couldn't deny wanting the dog, or that Jester belonged with them. Because of her sheepish grin, and that look in her eye, Joe knew she was okay with it.

Thinking of them pained him now. When he needed them most, there was no way they could get to him. He trained them well, through sign; the three of them were amazingly loyal and not just good guard dogs. There were no worries about break-ins or stolen property. If so much as a raccoon took a stroll in their yard, their nose and ears perked up like radar antennas. It was especially good when Joe was home alone, if someone came knocking at the door, the three of them would alert him of a visitor. They were quick learners, too, much quicker than humans, Joe thought, and could smell trouble when it presented itself.

Pulling his elbows back, Joe forced himself up again. He rubbed the pins and needles from his legs, and then leaned back again. There was a pair of trees beside him, with roots wrapped around a decaying log. The water, full of black leaves, smelled dank, musty. He quickened his thoughts and movements toward forming a splint, and then doubled over with dry heaves. Joe rested his temple against his forearm, closed his eyes with the idea it would help him think, and consoled himself with the notion that he'd been in tough spots before.

"I told you, I am not going to school today! I'm sick. Leave me alone." Chloe sassed him before slamming her bedroom door shut, and then locked it.

Joe pounded on the door to get her to open it. "Chloe!" He jiggled the handle, had a mind to bust it open, but thought better of it. It was one of the many same arguments she'd had with her mother. He didn't like being the one to push the issue; she was Delia's daughter, after all. Despite the possibility she was on her period, having menstrual cramps, she was caught twice skipping out, once the house was hers. And while Joe did not believe she was really sick, he was not about to stand guard outside her door. He had more important things to do, like going to work. If Chloe missed too many days and failed any of her subjects, that would be her problem, and not his. Of course, with having to attend summer school, they would be responsible for getting her to and from the school, since the busses didn't run in the summer. It was not just the students who paid, but the parents as well.

Joe ran downstairs, saw the time, and shoved the storm door with the heel of his palm. When his hand hit the glass, it shattered instantly, cutting the main artery of his right bicep. Blood spurted in a high, wide arch. He located a dishtowel from the kitchen counter, tore it in half, and made himself a tourniquet. He kept his arm elevated above his head, forgetting about the broken glass at his feet. His shirt was sopping wet with blood. He was about to head outside when the room around him began to spin, and a heavy buzzing sensation in his head slowed him down, when he buckled to his knees so not to lose consciousness. There was no way of getting Chloe's attention. It was a sure bet she drowned him out with the music from her headphones. She thought herself clever, smarter even, given his hearing disability, Delia once told him. But that was where her daughter underestimated him. Not just as an adult who knew better, but as a person who had lived in a silent world all his life who has had to rely on his gut instincts. It was the little things he noticed, a simple white lie, a guilty glance that passed from one to the other or avoiding to make eye contact. The fact that Chloe was going to get away with missing another day of school was something Delia would have to deal with later. With his arm lifted over his head, he made his best attempt to steady himself back onto his feet, when another wave of dizziness engulfed him.

Joe never quite believed in miracles before, not until Delia showed up, having returned to retrieve something forgotten. He was still conscious then, long enough for her to help him to the car. All that he remembered after that was waking up in the ER.

"That was a close call," Delia signed, tears in her eyes. "We almost lost you."

CHAPTER 5

Joe aimed his thoughts toward making himself a splint, something that would support his leg as much as possible, before he could even attempt to crawl his way out. He inched himself up again, when a sharp pain shot up his leg straight to his groin. Clutching himself, he allowed it time to ease, and then carefully shifted his weight on to his right hip. In doing so, his right leg stretched out a bit, enough to feel the bones move, this time with a bit of relief. The bones, he wanted to believe, were positioned straighter now.

He reached for some long, sturdy branches roughly two feet in length, the busted tree-stand for the harness strapping around it and the camouflage cloth beneath it. With the items, he fashioned a makeshift splint using his boot lace, the strap and cloth, and his belt to secure the branches that extended to his thigh area. He tightened it, just enough to keep the limb straight for the time being. He didn't know how far he would get, but felt certain he was in better shape now.

To preserve his upper-body strength, and to keep his head down low to avoid getting dizzy, he lay back down, just long enough to take a deep breath and brace himself for what would come next. He then carefully rolled over onto his belly. With his elbows, he inched his way toward his rifle, a half dozen yards or more from within his reach. Sweat dripped from his forehead with every movement until finally he latched on to the strap of the case and slipped it over his shoulder. It was a small victory, a start. He was now ready to get moving in the opposite direction, toward the edge of the woods. Darkness made clear recognition impossible, but he remembered trekking an approximate hundred yards or so when he found the tree he would climb. By foot, at nighttime, would be tricky enough, with the fallen trees and brier patches, but a belly crawl with a bum leg through soggy terrain and no water to stay hydrated was enough to discourage most people. Joe, however, would be the first to let it be known he did not fall into the category of *most people.*

He pushed off from the inside of his left thigh and foot, his elbows digging through the mush, and imagined the life of an inchworm, and then a caterpillar. It was a topic that Delia once posed to him.

"If you were to come back as an animal in your next life, what would you be?"

Joe had never considered such a thought. Why would he, when it seemed so unrealistic? But, for the sake of playing along, he told Delia, honestly, "I don't know. What about you?" Delia's response, a *caterpillar,* was instantaneous and could not have surprised him more. Of all the many choices available, an insect would likely be on the very bottom of his list. When he asked her why, she proudly gave him all the reasons.

"C-a-t-e-r-p-i-l-l-a-r-s have as many as four thousand muscles in their body compared to a human's six hundred twenty-nine. Crazy, isn't it?" Joe raised an incredulous eyebrow, but before he could respond, Delia went on. "They have twelve eyes, six tiny eyelets on each side of the head. They produce s-i-l-k and have six legs with several more sets of fake legs to help them hold onto p-l-a-n-t surfaces and be able to climb."

Joe had no idea she was so interested in the life of a caterpillar, but often found her reading one thing or another, her nose always deep in a magazine or book.

"You want be c-a-t-e-r-p-i-l-l-a-r because have twelve eyes and legs?"

Delia grinned before going on. "That's only part of it. What made me decide is that c-aterpillars have only one job, to eat. Can you believe they increase their body m-a-s-s by as much as one thousand times?"

"So . . . wait. You want eat and eat so you grow one thousand times bigger? Did you forget one time you ask me if I think you g-a-i-n weight, I tell you yes, and you mad and not speak to me for one week?"

"That's why it would be c-o-o-l to be a c-aterpillar. It would be my job to g-a-i-n weight, and I wouldn't have any hang-ups about it." She laughed at what she was saying, and then got serious again. "But that's not even the best part."

"Okay, tell me."

"One day, after I was big and fat, I would stop eating, h-a-n-g upside down from a branch and s-p-i-n myself into a c-o-c-o-o-n, before t-r-a-n-s-f-o-r-m-i-n-g into a beautiful butterfly."

The ability to transform into a butterfly now would come in handy, Joe thought, but a caterpillar still would not be his choice, were he given one. Breathing heavily, he fought not to think about his unreachable canteen, or a drink of cool water. He hadn't even filled it full before leaving home, figuring he would only be gone a few hours. Not that it mattered now. Thinking back over his years of planning, taking precautions, reading safety tips, especially when hunting from a deer-stand, keeping a first-aid kit on hand, and not cutting corners when it came to the hunter's guide book; all of it was totally useless now. There were no tips on what to do if your stand broke, if your equipment was out of reach, or your cell phone died.

Joe had not been counting his forward movements, but with each onward stroke, however small, he knew he was making progress, and refused to stop, even long enough to see how much ground he'd covered for fear it would diminish his hopes. His breathing grew heavier with each awkward shove, when suddenly, he felt himself sinking.

The water hole, a foot deep, was covered with matted leaves. The wetness against his lips provided a bit of relief, until a maggot started up his nose. Joe swiped it off, his right hand landing with a splash. The gritty taste of foul water, the smell of rotted wood and fungus caused him to spit and cough. His clothing was now saturated throughout his mid-section. He shivered, dragging himself back out onto marshy terrain. His strength was quickly wearing thin. Like a shard thread on the verge of breaking, he drifted wearily.

Delia will be home now, maybe . . .

A crushing sense of regret overtook him. He could have left her a note, but why would he when he planned to be home long before she would. Out of sheer habit, they were so used to doing their own thing. Both of them independent, there was no need to report their every move. Each allowed the other a certain amount of freedom. It was about trust. With Delia's schedule, telling her of his intentions that day, or any day, wouldn't much matter. By the time she got home from work, he was usually always there waiting for her, having already fed the dogs and eaten himself.

There was one time, though . . . when he stayed out later than expected.

◇━━◆━━◇

It was four in the morning after a night of poker with the guys. Joe was on a roll, having a good night for a change, the hours flew by.

Quiet now, so not to wake her, Joe eased his way into the house, slipped off his boots by the door, and then padded his way to their bedroom, careful not to step too loudly. When the lights flashed on, startling him, Delia was there, arms crossed, glaring at him.

She awake? By the looks of it, she'd been awake all night.

"Why didn't you t-e-x-t me?"

Joe watched her abrupt hand gestures. Her body went still then, but her eyes, full of fire and contempt, stayed on his face. He shrugged, didn't consider a text necessary. It was not often he saw her this way, and honestly, he didn't get why she was making such a mountain of things. She knew where he was. Why the need to text? He wasn't a child who needed an extended curfew. Besides, she should have been asleep.

"I was worried about you." Delia signed, still uptight, look-ing anything but relieved. She said some other things too, but was signing so fast that even Joe had trouble keeping up. Her eyes were red and smoldering, her hands and arms flapped about till they landed firmly on her hips. And here he thought he was about to crawl between the sheets, and get a few hours of sleep before the sun came up. He gave her a moment to settle down before saying anything at all.

"Why you not t-e-x-t me, if you worry?"

"I did. Twice!"

Joe checked his phone and saw the texts, one at 2:05 a.m., the other at 3:00 a.m. He shrugged sheepishly. Obviously, he was okay. There was no need to worry. So why did she look like she was ready to pounce on him? To put her at ease, he pulled out the wad of bills from his pocket.

"Look," he splashed out the cash and grinned proudly. "I won three hundred forty dollars!" He was certain now that all would be forgiven. That she would lighten up a bit, maybe even attempt a smile, a hug, something. Only, she did none of those things. Not a one, and not until several days later.

CHAPTER 6

The stench of swamp brought him back, like a swift kick in the gut. Joe pried open his eyes. How many times had he blacked out? Three? Four? The vibe of the nighttime air, the setting of the moon and his own intuition, all of it suggested it was between nine and ten o'clock. He lifted himself up, adjusted his splint to keep the leg from flopping about. The pain and nerve endings were a constant reminder.

The rest must have done him some good; he now felt ready to carry on again. He hitched his rifle a little higher on his shoulder, filled with grit and purpose, the fighter in him egging him on. It was something ingrained in him, since he was a boy, when he wrestled with his siblings on the living room carpet, and then later in school, on the wrestling team. Forging through the muck, he crawled like a wounded animal, determined to pick up his pace. Getting help for his injuries was his main concern, but to achieve that, he needed to block out the pain and keep his mind on the goal.

Minutes were drawn out to feel more like hours. His head ached as if he'd been balancing a bowling ball, and the ache only compounded the one in his leg. Quitting, however, was not an option. He counted his strokes, if only to occupy his mind. When he made it to twenty, he promised himself the next twenty would be easier and that much closer to dry land. At what seemed like one-fourth of the way, with his leaden leg dragging behind him, his good leg buckled, and the rest of his body went limp.

Joe collapsed, resting his head against his forearm.

This is crazy! I get nowhere.

The thirty strokes he managed felt more like three hundred, and still he could not see his truck. Was he even going in the right direction? Did he somehow get off course? It was too dark to make heads or tails of his whereabouts, and his brain was beginning to zone out. If only there were something liquid to drink, it would help to keep him going. Fighting the urge to sleep now, he wondered what would happen if he failed to wake up.

I maybe die out here. Just fall asleep and die. No one will find me. No one.

He imagined his remains getting eaten up by the wild, or worse—the crows feasting on his open wound first, while he lay helpless to do anything about it.

Why I not tell Delia? Why my phone die. Stupid-Stupid phone!

He never wanted the damn thing to begin with. Everyone insisted it was a good idea. *For emergencies,* Delia told him.

Fifty dollars a month! What good do me now?

Joe was tired, more tired than ever. But giving in to sleep was a luxury he could not afford. If he could make it to his pick-up, he would somehow figure out what to do next. He pushed off his left foot to continue on, slithered his way along the murky ground, full of outdoor odors that made him think of a farm. He pushed again and again, until the rest of his body denied him once more, and his world, as he knew it, shut down into total darkness.

Joey motioned to his mother from the backseat of their Suburban. "How long?"

She held up ten fingers. "Ten minutes."

Satisfied with her answer, he grinned. They were riding for a long time, he was anxious to get there. Aunt Bert and Uncle Freddie would be happy to see them, and surprised too, to see how much he'd grown, now that he was eight. He thought of the fresh-baked cookies that Aunt Bert would have waiting, still hot from the oven. He remembered they lived down a long country road, in upstate New York. Their youngest child, Ellen, was Micheline's age. The two of them would go off fishing down by the creek, while the rest of them stayed behind.

Little Freddie was his father's cousin, and known to everyone as *Little Freddie*, to differentiate between him and his father, Uncle Freddie. He lived in the area, on a farm, with goats and pigs and a dozen or more chickens.

Petro nudged Joey, they were sharing the backseat, and signed, "Will we see Z-e-u-s?" Zeus was Little Freddie's pet goat, who, to everyone's surprise, was permitted to roam around indoors, like a member of the family.

"No. We no see Little F-r-e-d-d-i-e." Joey already knew, he had asked his mother earlier. Everyone likely remembered their last visit, and Joey thought of it again now.

"Come on in," Little Freddie had said. One by one, they all gathered inside the old single-story home, to first tour the place, with four-legged Zeus following closely behind. Susanna and Jena were squeamish of the idea, not wanting to get too close to him. The rest of them all laughed. It seemed to Joey that Zeus was touring the home with them, as a guest, rather than an outdoor farm animal. But it wasn't just Zeus that entertained them; it was the craziest thing Joey ever saw. There were no cages or fences to keep the animals separated.

The chickens clucked around their feet, pecked at their shorts, hoping to be fed. The ducks and roosters were free to roam about in the field with the cows and the rabbits. Joey had counted six dogs and seven cats that mingled in with the goats and pigs, and an old, over-weight pony.

"Can we ride the pony?" Susanna asked.

Little Freddie cackled, making his eyes go all squinty, nearly shut. "No, I'm afraid not. He's retired, this one."

"Well, what does he do then?" Susanna wanted to know.

"He keeps us company," Little Freddie replied. "Oh, watch out there, where you're stepping."

Susanna looked down; saw that she landed smack center in some pony dung. "Ewe! Gross." Everyone laughed. Everyone that is, except for Susanna.

Joey smiled to himself, remembering the look of disgust on Susanna's face, and the smell that stayed with her throughout the day.

When they arrived at Aunt Bert and Uncle Freddie's, the scent of chocolate chip cookies wafted from the kitchen.

But it was later when the real fun started, when his father practiced his skeet-shooting with Uncle Freddie. Joey compared it to a batter's cage, what he'd seen on TV where the balls were pitched from an automated machine, and you get to practice your batting skills. In skeet-shooting, a puck-like object was shot into the air from a fixed position, his father and uncle took turns shooting at the clay targets, grinning proudly whenever they hit their mark. When their aim was good, the clays shattered into bits and pieces, landing somewhere on the open ground. Joey and his brothers collected the broken objects, savored them like a basket full of Easter eggs. He loved the game and could not wait for the day he would be old enough to try it himself.

With a long knobby branch, Joey pretended to be a hunter, aimed it high toward the sky. When the puck went soaring through the air, meant for his father or uncle to shoot at, Joey pulled the trigger of his imaginary rifle, and then watched the pieces break apart into smithereens. He laughed and he cheered as if he'd just hit the bulls-eye on a dartboard. These were his practice sessions for when he was old enough to handle a gun, and when the time came, he would show them all he could hunt as well as his father and his uncle did.

CHAPTER 7

Joe smacked his dry pasty lips, lifted his head, only to be pulled back down again. Dizziness swept over him and scalding bile gushed from his throat. He barely managed to choke it down before spewing it out. If only for a swallow of water, something cool to drink, it would keep him going. Having gone without food was not the problem. Water starvation not only depleted his strength and energy, it had a way of messing with his mind and his senses. But regardless how much he wished it, there was no water, other than the muddy swamp water that was filled with bugs and dirt, and no telling what parasites. The smell alone was enough to deter him, even if his lips thought otherwise. He needed to stop dwelling on what he didn't have, and focus instead on getting on with it.

He lifted his head, slower this time, to regain his bearings, blinked hard, and then gazed at the light up ahead.

A light!

It was coming from a trailer beyond the edge of the woods, across the roadway of someone else's property. Whose trailer, he didn't know; he was not all that familiar with the area, not enough to know the people. Little did it matter. The trailer was well out of his reach to crawl to. Getting to his truck was half the distance, and out of view to even alert a nearby neighbor of his whereabouts. At this projected hour, it may have been someone who just returned from a bar or nightclub, or maybe even from working the late shift. He thought once more of shooting off his gun, as a plea for help. But then who in their right mind would venture out into the woods so late at night? Even if someone were to call out, "Who's there?" he wouldn't hear them. The light, he decided, would serve another purpose. One that would guide him through the night. He could only hope that it remained on for a good while, to help lead him towards the bed of his pick-up. Each time he lost consciousness and slept the time lapse could be minutes or hours, but beyond the darkness and through the trees, his focal point became the light.

Forging onward, he dragged his achy useless leg like a ball and chain, the pain always with him, always there. Every now and then, he touched it to assess the swelling. Each agonizing stretch, he managed a few inches further.

Keep your eye on the prize. The words flashed through his mind like a bright neon sign, until his head grew foggy again.

Focus! Don't let him catch you off-guard.

Concentrate . . . Focus . . . Keep your eye on the prize. The words bounced around in his head like a pinball machine. Words that finally resonated to what his coach drilled into him, time and time again. He'd learned it all in high school, on the wrestling team.

Never take your eyes off your opponent! You have to want it enough to stay focused.

Was it Coach . . . or from a scene in one of his all-time favorite movies? Yes, that was it. Joe wondered now if this was how Rocky Balboa felt, getting his face and body pummeled in the fight of his life against world heavy-weight champion Apollo Creed. Rocky was just a working-class Italian-American small-town club fighter, an unknown. The odds were stacked up against him. With a will of steel, the discipline to match it, and a coach that cared enough not to let him give up, his shot of a lifetime changed his life when he went the distance. It earned him respect. Not only from those betting against him, but a deep down to the core self-respect in knowing that he gave everything he had, and then some. Not just as a fighter from the slums of Philadelphia, a nobody who grew up on the streets, but one whose name became known overnight.

It was not just about his ability to box, Mickey told him. A big part of it, more than calculating each move or knowing your opponent's weaknesses, was believing in yourself. Joe memorized the story, watched it countless times, reading the subtitles carefully. From the shy Adrian, who became Rocky's wife and number one fan, cheering from the stands to Mickey, the coach who took him under his wing, who taught him everything there was to know about the sport. He remembered too, the sight of the crowd cheering in their arrogant banter, banking on his opponent's victory of a knock-out, and the oath he'd made to himself when Rocky focused not on the crowd, but everything that Mickey taught him, both big and small.

There were portions of Rocky's life that Joe could identify with in a big way. The memory served to feed his mind like a drug. That no matter where you came from or what disadvantages you may have growing up, anything was possible.

Joe's father repeated his own hardship story so many times that Joe lost count.

"My old man would throw away his paycheck each week drinking and gambling, often leaving my mother with no money to feed us. I was the unlucky one," his father said, "the oldest. I was just a kid, about ten or so, delivered newspapers door-to-door, shined shoes in town for tips. Didn't pay much, but it was something."

"So what happened, Dad?" Micheline once asked.

"What happened was . . . I wasn't working to put money in my pocket. I gave it all to my mother, so she could put food on the table, and feed the seven of us kids."

Those who were still sitting around the dinner table remained quiet and listened, knowing how the story went.

"Then one time near Christmas," he continued, "I made five dollars in tips. Five dollars! So I asked my mother if I could keep the tips this time, just this once. And you know what she told me?" His father's face tightened and his eyes went hard.

Those who remembered knew the answer, yet no one said a word.

"She said, 'No-No, Leroy, give it here. I need that money.' I was ten-years-old, and I was the one putting food on the table. Not my old man. Me!"

Everyone just stared. No matter the many times he recited these happenings, the bitter disappointment was unmistakable, just as raw as the first time he told it.

"While my old man's out playing cards, smokin' and drinkin', his ten-year-old kid was feeding his family."

Micheline spoke up then. "Grandma must have really appreciated you, Dad."

"She didn't appreciate nothin'. Never got a thank you. Never got nothin'."

When no one said anything further, and Micheline lowered

her eyes, his father shared a new piece of the story.

"When I was eighteen . . . and I enlisted with the Navy, my checks were deposited into my bank account back home, for when I got out."

"The Navy?" Micheline questioned. "I didn't know you were in the military."

"Yeah." His response was more in the way of a solemn nod than a verbal one.

"How come you never mentioned it?"

"I wasn't in for very long," he said, lowering his eyes before he continued, his voice lowered, too. "Didn't even make it through basic training when the doctor told me I had tuberculosis."

"What's that?" Dominic asked.

"It's a disease that affects the lungs and your breathing. I was sent to the military hospital there for about a year."

"A whole year?"

"Yeah . . . Doctor asked me who my undertaker was."

Dominic paused, glanced to his mother, to Micheline, and then back again before asking, "You mean . . . he thought you were gonna die?"

His father gave a somber nod. "While I was in the hospital, a few months later, right before Christmastime, my mother said she needed a new coat, so . . . I gave her access to my account, told her she could buy herself one for Christmas."

"That was nice," Micheline said. "So what happened, then, after you got better?"

"About nine months later, they sent me home with an honorable medical discharge. During that whole time, my monthly paychecks were being deposited. I figured I'd have a good amount saved by then, make a fresh start, move out on my own. But when I got back, the money was gone."

"What do you mean, it was gone?" Dominic stared incredulously.

"They spent it all."

"Who spent it all?"

"My parents."

CHAPTER 8

It was a part of his father's past that Joe got wind of as a child, but it was not until later in life, after the story was retold over and over again, that the bits and pieces began to make sense, and why his father harbored ill feelings against his parents, even long after they died.

Although Joe's circumstances were different than those of his father's, he could identify with the pressures put upon him. He could identify, too, with Rocky, his feelings of inadequacy and of not quite measuring up to others' expectations.

There were times when he wondered if his father was disappointed, embarrassed even, at having sons that were deaf. Did he blame himself? Blame his mother? He couldn't communicate with them like he could the others. Whenever they were alone with their father, any attempt at conversation would often fall flat. "Where's your mother?" he would ask. When Joe shrugged that he didn't know, his father would sit at the table, glance up at the clock, with him and Petro making small talk about school that day. His father, looking ill at ease, watched them for a moment, before reaching for the newspaper to avert his attention to. Joey tapped the table to get his father's attention, began to sign about the fight the previous night. The blank look on his father's face told him he wasn't following. On a piece of paper, Joey printed out: Spinks – Ali. His father shrugged, either disinterested or without a clue about the fight that everyone was talking about, and then turned back to what he was reading. When he flipped the page over, there it was, at the top of the Sports section, the caption above their photos read: *Leon Spinks beats Muhammad Ali in 15 rounds for Heavyweight Championship boxing title.* His father pointed to the area, nodded as if he got it now, but then turned his attention away again.

Joe's mind wandered from one thing to the next, as he crept along, the light as his focus, things he hadn't thought about in ages. Like why his family never took the time to attend a class together to learn sign, or to have an interpreter come to the house to teach them while they all still lived at home? A child's mind, Delia once told him, adapted quicker when learning a second language. And it must be true, he thought, Micheline was an example of that, having spent the summer with her Canadian cousins at the age of ten. With practically no English spoken during that time, she returned home speaking French fluently. She'd gotten so accustomed, in fact, so comfortable with their way of speaking that for the first day or two she struggled to remember her own language. Joe found this to be quite funny when he was first told. And from that point on, Micheline was able to easily converse with her Canadian relatives.

But sign language, he thought, more than French, was a family necessity that would have benefited them all and stayed with them for the rest of their lives. As adults, they would have retained that connection. By the time each of them got to be of age and left home, a few of them out-of-state to make their own way, returning home only for the occasional short visit, made learning a new language less of a necessity for them. Aside from Petro, it was his two youngest brothers, Alanzo and Stefano, that were the most exposed to sign from an early age. With the two still at home, the others grown and gone, it provided Joe an outlet for constant interaction.

However small his movements were, Joe turned inches into feet, and feet into yards, with short periods of rest along the way. The light of the trailer lured and enticed like bait on a hook. So he carried on, blocked out the distance he knew was still far up ahead.

Keep your eye on the prize, the voice in his head urged him on.

He stopped again, this time to dry the sweat from his brow. Cold one minute, clammy the next.

Get off your ass, and get to work!

A black mangy-looking dog leapt from the shadows with pointed fangs, an angry snarl.

Joe shook his head to clear his thoughts, the tips of his fingers pressed firmly against his temples to make it stop. He waited a beat, and then opened his eyes again.

The light appeared closer, so close he could almost touch it. *Is someone coming? Someone there?* The next moment, the light seemed to drift farther and farther away. Joe began to question whether there was even a light on at all. With each stroke, he moved onward, until the light dimmed, and then vanished altogether. He blinked over and over to bring it back, when his head hit something, a barrier blocking his path.

Susanna slugged Joey in the chest first, and the head next when he retaliated and swung back. The fight started after she caught Joey playing with Gilligan, her pet hamster. He didn't know why everyone else was allowed to hold him, scratch his ears and tickle his nose, but he was made to wait for someone older to be around before doing so? He was seven-years-old, not a baby, and he knew how to handle a tiny hamster. Besides, it was Susanna's own fault for snatching Gilligan out of his grasp that she was bitten. She was the one to hit him first, when all he did was to stand up for himself. He was not about to be her sissy-punching bag. What's good for the goose is good for Susanna. She was two years older, and yet she lied and blamed him for everything. Did she think he didn't know what she was up to? The times she would pinch him and then point to one of his younger brothers. Usually, it was Petro she accused, assuming he would not be able to defend himself. She might think she was smarter than he was, but Joey always knew what she was up to.

Like the time when he colored a page in his *Incredible Hulk* book and his mother praised his work, Susanna tore part of the page, claimed it was an accident, and then faked an apology. The moment his mother turned her back, Susanna stuck her tongue out at him, and walked away grinning, as if she got away with something. The reason why she did those things he couldn't figure out.

Several days after the incident Joey started noticing that someone was coming into his room and messing up the blankets on his bed, after he made it, only his and not Petro's. He thought of Susanna first, but to be sure, he would hide in his closet, leaving the door cracked open enough to see. He did this a few different times before catching her in the act.

Joey stepped out of the closet to show himself, when Susanna's face went all scared-like.

"I can't find Gilligan," she stammered, fixing his covers again.

Did she really think he was that dumb to fall for that one, that Gilligan might crawl up into his bed for a nap? To prove she was lying, Joey ran past her and upstairs to her bedroom, with her hot on his heels. It was just as he thought, Gilligan was right there, in his cage.

"Lie!" Joey told her, taking a stance.

"So?" Susanna shrugged indifferently, gave a snarly grin. Caught at her own game, she could hardly defend herself, and didn't even try to. That was when Joey decided he would have to teach her a lesson.

He waited a few days until the timing was right and then hid her school bag in the living room coat closet. The following morning, she was forced to go to class without her homework. Her teacher sent a note home about the missing homework, and his mother was not happy.

"Mom, I told you I searched the whole house," Susanna argued. "Someone stole my backpack. You need to buy me a new one."

"No one stole your backpack. Now, go look for it, and don't stop until you find it."

Joey picked up on the word *backpack*, and knew, of course, where it was. He simply wanted to give Susanna a taste of her own meanness.

He hid the bag behind the assortment of winter boots, hoping she would get the message, and stop her lying and being hateful towards him. His sister was not very good at finding things, though—she didn't even bother to check the closet. Joey planned to slip the bag back in her room later on, when no one was watching, shoving it deep under her bed, to make it seem like it was there all along. He felt proud of himself for the smart hiding place. But his mother unexpectedly spoiled the plan when she decided to vacuum the carpet. It so happened that the coat closet was where she stored the vacuum cleaner. About that time, Susanna came running downstairs, her lopsided pigtails flapping against her shoulders. Her face was all twisted as if she'd just seen a Tarantula the size of a dinosaur. Not that she could tell one from a Daddy Long Leg. Girls her age exaggerated the tiniest of things, as if a baby spider had the power to gobble them up in one swipe. In Susanna's case, Joey wished it so, and smiled at the thought, when she was being mean to him.

Joey snickered at the sight of her, but not so much to risk drawing attention to himself. Instead, he pretended to play dumb, since that was what she always called him anyway. Dumb. Stupid. Well, he would show her who of them the dumb and stupid one was. For sure, not him.

A moment later, Joey put on his *surprise* face, raised eyebrows and dropped jaw, when he figured out what all the fuss was about. Gilligan was not in his cage. Susanna cried like such a sissy, mumbling something Joey could not make out. This did not seem to faze their mother, with more important matters to tend to, like jerking on the vacuum cleaner that seemed to be hung up on something inside. Frustrated, she stuck her head in to locate the problem. It was all that Joey could do to keep from bursting out laughing, when after a hard jolt, the missing schoolbag surfaced.

Susanna's tears stopped instantly. Her first reaction was surprise. Her second, relief. She retrieved the bag, openmouthed, her eyes the size of gumballs. While examining her books, she pulled out her completed homework.

"See, I told you, Mom." About that time, Gilligan shot out from the bag, darted across the carpet to hide beneath the couch. It was that very second, Joey noted, that *Godzilla* herself turned on him.

"It was you!" She pointed her bony little finger in his face.

He wanted to ask her how it felt to have someone do mean

things, to be accused and blamed unfairly. But because he was deaf, he could not speak or express himself the way others could. When he tried, no one seemed to understand him. He knew that his sister was not his friend, but what he didn't know was why she hated him. She blamed him for everything, always. So, it served her right for the way she treated him. He was not afraid of her, even though she was nine and a little older than him, she certainly didn't act it. He would show her that, even though he was deaf, he was not stupid or dumb.

With a straight face, the look of innocence, Joey shook his head denying anything to do with her missing bag or with Gilligan. To be truthful, he did want to say they were even now, and he would like for them to start over with a clean slate, but he didn't know how. It didn't matter, though, because Susanna socked him in the chest with one fist, grabbed hold of his hair with the other. The two of them went at it, rolling on the carpet, arms and legs thrashing about, until their mother pulled them apart, sending them off to separate corners for time-out. It was a good thing too, because Joey was about to let her have it. He was hurting and his pride was bruised, but he cried no tears. Crying was for sissies. It was what his father said, and what his sister did best—she cry-babied to get attention. What she needed was to be punished for all her meanness against him. He might be younger and a bit smaller, but everyone knew that boys were stronger than girls. Besides, with enough time, he would grow taller than his sister. A lot taller, he was sure of it.

When his mother looked away to begin vacuuming, Susanna smirked, then stuck her tongue out at him, her eyes like the devil's. Joey imagined her with sharp, curved horns sprouting from her head, all twisted and ugly, wearing a black cape and holding a pitchfork. She thought she was getting away with something, but that was only her first mistake. Joey lunged toward her to show she did not scare him. Their fists went flying this way and that, a shirt collar was torn, a sleeve overstretched. Before long, they were at it again, rolling on the floor when their mother parked the vacuum cleaner and pulled them apart once more, this time shouting.

"Stop it! Stop it right now, I said!" She then sent them off to their rooms, but Susanna, being Susanna, started up the steps, and then refused to go further.

"It wasn't my fault!" Susanna yelled. "Joey should be punished and sent to his room, little brat, not me!"

If their father was home, Joey knew she would already be upstairs and would never dare to talk to their mother this way. But he wasn't home, and Susanna knew it. With pinched lips and arms crossed, she stood there on the first landing, her hip cocked, in her defiant way.

Joey was headed toward his room when he stopped to see what would happen next. His mother, who was usually the patient one, was in no mood to be pushed.

"Susanna, I want you to shut your mouth, and go up to your room, now!"

Instead of doing as she was told, Susanna did the unthinkable, and said, "Make me!"

Joey saw that his mother's face turned several shades of red. She reached for the nearest object, a child's shoe, and flung it toward Susanna, where it caught her square on the mouth. He didn't know if his mother planned it that way, but if it was, her aim was perfect, and it managed to get Susanna's attention alright.

"Ouch! Mom . . ." Susanna hollered, clutching her mouth and then examined her fingers. She was about to yell something else, when his mother started towards her, but Susanna bolted finally, and ran up the steps.

The moment she was gone, Joey headed to his room, his childish pride refusing to give either of them the satisfaction that he cared one way or the other. He did feel a little better, though, that Susanna got clobbered. If he wasn't so surprised at the time, he might have smiled, but it served her right for talking back. Maybe it will teach her to keep her mouth shut next time.

Joey examined his scratches and carpet burns, swiped the specks of blood from his arms with the edge of his shirt that was now torn, his favorite one now ruined. He would never understand why his sister was the way she was, so mean and hateful towards him. Even when he had tried to be funny she attacked him for no reason.

"That little brat stole my money!" Susanna bellowed, pointing a finger in his face.

Joey had no idea what she was talking about. His only clue was the mention of money.

"Calm down," his mother told her. "What's the matter?"

"I put my tooth under my pillow last night, and he stole my money. Little thief! I know it was him, Mom, I know it!"

Joey knew that Susanna had lost a tooth, but not what all the fuss was about. He saw, then, the surprise look on his mother's face, as he waited to learn more.

"How do you know it was him, have you asked him?"

"I don't have to ask him, Mom; I already know."

"Well, maybe you're mistaken. Did you ever think of that? Stop accusing him, already. Maybe the tooth fairy forgot. She's probably busy with all the other kids in the world that lost a tooth. You're not the only one, you know. Was it still under your pillow?"

"Yes, but she doesn't always remember to take the tooth."

"I think she must have forgotten."

"No Mom. Why do you always take his side? You think he's such a saint. But he's not. He stole my money, and I have the proof."

"You do . . . what proof is that?"

Susanna plopped the evidence on the table, a dried up pheasant's foot. "He left this under my pillow."

Joey snatched it up, giggled, without saying a word.

"See . . . I told you, Mom. Do you believe me now? He stole my money, and I want it back."

"Wah?" Joey shook his head, confused. "Noooo moneee."

"Liar!" Susanna lunged at him, but his mother blocked her with her arm. "He has my quarter, Mom, and I want it back."

"There's nothing to give back, Susanna. The tooth fairy didn't come last night, alright! She didn't come."

"How do you know?"

She gave Susanna a piercing look, taking in a deep sigh, as if contemplating a response. "I just know. And if you don't drop it right now, I'll make sure that she doesn't come back. Do you hear me? Now, apologize to your brother for accusing him."

Susanna looked incredulous. "I will not! He shouldn't have been in my room, anyway. I want him to stay out!"

CHAPTER 9

The obstacle blocking Joe's path was the trunk of a fallen oak. No longer could he see the light that guided him. With his left hand, he felt along the knobby bark to estimate its size, and then let out a groan.

There was no way he could climb over it. With barely enough strength to snake his way along the ground, a two-foot climb might as well be twenty. He gave a wary scan to his left and one to the right, to figure his best route. Through the hazy darkness and his mangled thoughts, it was impossible to remember which way the tree had fallen or even be certain that when he first entered the woods he climbed over it. He was turned around, his directional compass off-kilter. *Was this tree here before?*

He shifted onto his side to ease the soreness in his limbs and regain a second wind. Through the sparseness of the trees above him, the nighttime stars were the only thing keeping him steady. But more than anything, he wanted to sleep. With his eyelids getting heavier, as if a weight was pulling them down, what could it hurt to rest awhile? He needed to pre-serve his strength in order to keep going. And if he slept hard enough, maybe this would all prove to be some outrageous, hyped-up nightmare. If only he could be so lucky. But deep down, he knew. He knew there was no way his reality was anything other than what it was. That he was stuck out here, and would stay stuck unless he could somehow keep going and make it to his truck. If only things did not keep getting in the way. His thoughts were conflicted, his senses tearing him from one extreme to the other when his eyelids fluttered. Out of nowhere, as if someone poked him with a stick, he blinked his eyes wide open, and froze. It was then that he saw it, saw the shooting star soar above him from west to east. He moved not a muscle, barely breathing, until it fully disappeared.

His gut told him to follow its direction, that the little voice inside would steer him to make the right decision. He dug his elbows through the muck with newfound energy. To move too quickly made him cringe, so to not risk another setback, he kept his movements slow and low to the ground, as he crept alongside the tree trunk with one hope in mind, that once he reached its end, the light from the trailer would still be there.

Delia would be worried sick by now . . . or angry. He rarely stayed out this late; not without a quick text when his occasional poker game ran late. He learned that lesson, and wondered if she called anyone in search of his whereabouts. She was not the kind to hunt him down, but more the type to stay at home and stew about it. She didn't have a phone number for Alex, the neighbor he planned to help move that day, and it certainly would not be like her to go knocking at his door, even if she were to notice his truck in the driveway. Not that any of it mattered, though. Alex had no more knowledge of his whereabouts than Delia did.

For the first time, Joe realized the ground was getting drier. This seemed to encourage him, he must be getting closer. Not wanting to stop, not yet, he puffed rapid breaths between his cheeks, another push off his left foot when he came up against a briar patch. He stopped to assess the width and could not see where it ended. There were likely several patches lumped together. Joe was not about to backtrack and make yet another detour, so he plowed his head through, grabbed hold of whatever branches were in his way, and snapped them; digging through the matted leaves while the briars jabbed at his head, poked and sliced at his hands and fingers. When he reached the other side, the majority of his body clearing the area, his right knee hit something sharp in the worst possible way. Pain, so intense, the pressure was as if his leg was caught in a vise. He felt the blood from his wound oozing freely when he stopped and curled up into a fetal position. It was then that he saw the problem, the cause of the pressure wrapped around his leg, its head rose above its tightly coiled tail, a forked tongue protruded, the snake hissed.

There was no time to examine whether the snake was poisonous or not, Joe needed to alleviate the pressure, and fast. He snatched at its throat when the pit viper struck back. Its tongue seared into his hand between his thumb and the knuckle of his forefinger. The agitated snake vibrated its tail rapidly, emitting a strong musk. Joe slammed it hard against the tree trunk until it relaxed its hold on him. Again and again, he smashed its head until it snapped off, its jaw wide open from the shock. It lay there, two to three feet in length. He could not make out its coloring, but suspected a copperhead, its venom relatively mild and rarely fatal. The way his luck had gone that day, he was not about to take the chance. He slung the decapitated snake as far as he could throw, and then wiped away the crusted mud from his hand, where he sucked hard against the bitten area, now sensitive to touch. He spat out what appeared to be nothing, sucked a second time, spitting again and again, his heart drumming a singsong of dread. The only thing he remembered reading on snake bites was to keep the victim calm, restrict movement, and get to a hospital.

If only he could. He would not have thought that the pain in his leg could get any worse, but it did. Why was he so oxygen-deprived that his hands and feet were now tingling? His stomach was reeling, but there were only dry heaves that left him buckled over, blinded and disoriented.

Zapped of all energy, he rested his head against the bicep of his arm. A grayish-white fogginess swooshed around in his brain, in the shape of a funnel, reminding him of an approaching tornado. Everything spun around and around like the time he mixed alcohol at a party. He didn't have all that much to drink, not really, when he started with Crown Royal and Coke, but then someone passed him a shot of Tequila. It was the first time he tried it, and the last time too. The mixture of both alcohols was punishment enough that he swore he would never repeat that mistake. When he drank at all, beer was more to his liking, preferably out of a bottle than on tap or from a can. With his palms pressed firmly against his temples, he tried to make the swooshing inside his head stop, but instead, it took him down a winding, unpaved road at the speed of a Tour de France racer.

Joey pedaled as fast as he could. He was in a race to get home before his father, in time for dinner, so not to have to explain his reason for being late. He was twelve, and still, they treated him like a child. He spent part of the afternoon near the high school several miles away, practicing his donuts and ramp jumps in the community parking lot. When his friend Wesley told him what time it was Joey hauled his butt on out of there.

He raced from Bartley Road to 4 Bridges, up the steep hill, before crossing over Route 206 onto Hillside, and then followed it back around to town. When the road turned to gravel, he didn't let up, took a turn too sharp, the bottom of his jeans caught in the link chain. The pull nearly knocked him off his bike, but he was able to come to a stop before crashing into the side of a parked Volkswagen Beetle. He tried to work it loose, but the denim was coarse and torn, mangled between the chain-ring and the crank set. If only he had a pocketknife on him, he would cut himself free. With a half-mile still yet to go, he needed to think of something. To keep from drawing attention to him, he hobbled over to a wooded area with a path that would lead him to the auto repair shop behind their home. There was no way he could ride the way his pants were caught, and no way could he walk either. He tried again to tear it loose without causing too much damage that he would later have to explain, but the darn thing would not give. Just when he thought he was doomed for yet another lecture from his father, he spotted a cigarette lighter on the ground. His plan was to burn just enough of the fabric to free his leg, but once the flame took hold, the denim, caked with oil, caused it to intensify. His attempt at blowing it out was like adding fuel, and caused it to spread. He tugged and he tugged, feeling the heat and then a scorching burn, when he stripped off his shirt that was covered in sweat, balled it up and jabbed at the flames over and over until the fabric broke free. Rolling his body through the dirt, he kicked and clawed at the ground to be sure the fire was out.

No one saw him; at least, he was grateful for that. Finally, he sat up and ever so gently peeled back the blackened tattered edge of his pants, careful not to make contact with his skin. The inside of his ankle and calf turned a shiny, deep red with blisters beginning to form, the hairs on his leg now singed. The pain and the pressure made it too unbearable to touch, and then nausea hit him. Joey heaved before chucking up some vomit, allowed the swirling in his belly to settle. He needed to get home. It looked really bad, but first he rolled up his pant leg high enough to keep the fabric from touching the burnt area. His mouth was dry and pasty. He stood up, used the handlebars to keep him steady, and walked an old man's walk, while grunting through the pain.

By the time he stepped into the kitchen, shivering and feverish, his family was all gathered around the dinner table.

"Oh my God!" His mother cried out. "What happened?"

Joey had already played it out in his mind. "My pants . . . stuck . . . c-h-a-i-n," he began to explain with the use of his hands to get across how tight it was, when a wave of light-headedness hit him and he grabbed the edge of the counter to keep from falling.

His mother was at his side in an instant, with a chair for him to sit. Joey leaned forward, cradled his head in his hands to allow the queasiness in his stomach to pass. It felt as though his leg was still on fire, but he knew they were all watching him, waiting for an explanation. Moments passed, and without looking up, his mother handed him a glass of water. With a shaky hand, he drank it down. He was then able to finish telling them, that the friction between the bike chain and his jeans was the cause of the burn.

". . . s-p-a-r-k-s," he spelled out in sign, adding a flutter to his fingers, and then choked out the word "fire." He pointed to show them, the skin was now a brighter shade of purplish-red that was moist with the largest blisters oozing liquid. Surrounded, were splotches of a whitish waxy color.

It was not until later, after the doctor's examination, that he gave them the news. "Your son sustained second and third-degree burns," the doctor told them. "We'll need to do several skin grafts to repair the damage."

CHAPTER 10

The memory of it all came rushing back to him now. The same leg that got burned at the age of twelve was now in even worse shape. He never told anyone what really happened, there was no reason to. It was part of being a child, he supposed, withholding certain information to conceal one's foolishness, or in his father's viewpoint, one's stupidity. Truth be known, Joe would have to admit he got himself into some real predicaments. Since as far back as he could remember he had a burning desire to prove himself. To prove that he was good enough, strong enough, smart enough, to do whatever the task called for. He grew thirsty again, just thinking about it.

During their third summer on the island when Joey was nine, he convinced his mother he was old enough to chop wood. Technically, he was a few days past the half-year mark and closer to his tenth birthday, he pointed out, the selling point that finally won her over. A steady supply of wood was needed for the potbelly stove they cooked on, as well as their evening campfires.

"You—have—to—wear—shoes," Dominic told him, prepared to give him his first lesson. "Go put your shoes on."

Joey was used to walking barefoot. Whether walking along the shore or playing at the river's edge, he got wet every day, but he went along with his brother's request, and was ready now.

"Tie your laces," Dominic motioned, "so you don't trip and fall."

Blowing air between his lips, shoulders slumped, Joey sighed before complying. Dominic placed an upright log on the flattened stump, centered it, and then motioned for Joey to watch.

"Keep—your—feet—apart," Dominic told him, and then demonstrated how to grip the handle. "Hold—ax—tight—with—both—hands." Dominic swung the ax hard, splitting the log in two.

Joey nodded. He got it. He'd watched him do it often enough, it was nothing new to him. Joey placed the next log upright, set his feet apart just so, swung the ax up and then back down again, halfway slicing the log when it stopped, the blade caught in the middle.

Dominic took over, lifted the caught log, before slamming it down to finish it off. Joey nodded. He just needed to give it a bit more strength. His second try, the log split just right.

"Good," Dominic told him.

Joey split two more logs when the one after that caught again. He lifted the ax, hammered it down, but couldn't work it loose.

"Let me have it," Dominic said.

"Nooo," Joey nudged him away. He lifted and slammed. Lifted and slammed again.

"Let me do it, Joey. You're just wearing yourself out."

Joey let go of the handle, his lips pinched tight, eyes narrowed and arms crossed firmly in front of his chest.

Dominic sliced the log with ease. "Not easy," he told him.

Joey made a face. "I nooo . . ." He waved a wild gesture before stomping off. A few paces out, he halted, yanked off his shoes and sent them flying towards the porch before heading for the water's edge.

He made his way downstream to give him time to cool off and think about what just happened. Dominic tried to show him the right way. So what that he was older, did he have to make him feel like such a child? Joey had proven that he could swing the ax and chop wood, didn't he? He would have been able to get the blade out, had it not been for his know-it-all brother to be in such a hurry to take over.

Joey strolled along the shore, leaving footprints in the sand. Where he found chunks of clay, he set them aside, to later carve into boats, and then harden under the sun. A ship liner, mostly flat in size, carrying cargo, was headed upstream. He never saw such big boats back home in the States. It was one thing to see them, but to watch the river pull away from shore, like a vacuum, he could walk out farther and farther, until the waves came rushing back. It was the best time to find crabs and flopping minnows, but he needed to be quick about it so not to let the waves knock him down. Along the river's edge, Joey wandered through random empty beer cans and soda bottles, flip flops and odd pieces of clothing that washed up on shore. There was drift wood, a crab net, a broken fishing rod, and a smelly dead fish. This one looked to be a small-mouth bass and was covered with horse flies. With a stick, Joey shooed them away. The bass's shiny eye seemed to be staring right at him. He poked it with his stick, gently at first. The stink was bad, even worse than when he shoveled Tonto's poop, so he dug a hole in the sand using his hands. With a broken shell, he dug the hole deeper, and then scooped the dead bass in before covering it up. He snapped a small twig in half, a couple inches in length, placed them just so to form a cross over the mound.

Satisfied with his efforts, he continued on his way, stopping only when he spotted stones flat enough to throw and watch them skip along the surface of the water. A yacht raced by, near enough, he could see the couple aboard waving at him. It was no one that he knew, but he threw up a hand just the same. It was how folks were out here. They pretended to know you even when they didn't, just to be friendly. He liked that. The sharp looking cruiser, with its front end in the air made their own boat look puny and dingy in comparison. He wondered what it would feel like to ride in a boat that size, and to fly along the river like a rocket.

His stomach growled. It must to be lunchtime, he thought, so he turned to head back home when something long and white, floating in the water, caught his attention. He reached down to examine it, realizing it was a super-size deflated balloon, with an extra-large opening. There were no obvious holes or tears, so he shook it free of water and blew in it. It was thicker somehow and would not take in air, so instead, he filled it with water, knotted the end, and then pitched it out into the river. The balloon landed a good distance away; he watched it float, slowly, with the current.

He wished now that he'd not gone quite so far. His mother would be setting out the peanut butter and jelly sandwiches, they were his favorite. He hoped she would save him one, and not run out of bread, or leave him with the crusty ends. By the time he reached the buried smallmouth, he noticed the waves of the yacht washed away the cross. There were no other pieces of twigs nearby, so he used his finger to draw one in its place.

Another ship liner worked its way downstream, with a

much smaller tugboat not too far behind it. He was hot and could use a swim to cool off, but he wanted to eat first and then change into his swim trunks, so he set off running to get there quicker.

It was not until he finally reached the beach area facing their home that he noticed something not quite right. The shore looked emptier than usual. At first, he felt sure that everyone was inside having lunch. Where else would they be? Except, the canoe was gone, and so was the motorboat. They would not have floated off with the waves, not while anchored down, tied to a stake. He shaded his eyes, looked across the river as far as his eyesight would take him, upstream and down, with no sign of them anywhere. He ran up to the house to see who might have stayed behind, expecting to find Micheline or Dominic, but found the kitchen empty. Upstairs he ran, and then back down again, in each room no one was there. More confused than ever, he ran back to shore.

Where everyone go?

The only place he could think of was *Grandmaman's* house. But why didn't they wait for him to get back? He was always being told he wasn't old enough for all sorts of things, to ski, to chop wood, or steer the motor boat; how could they just leave him behind, like he was suddenly old enough?

He considered what to do, and then hiked over to the *caption rouge,* the shed where they kept the generator. Towards the back was an orange and black wooden rowboat, a spare they never used. There were two oars lodged into metal holders, a plastic sand bucket on the floor board, and a spotted toad perched on top of it. Ignoring the toad, Joey pulled at the boat, but it was lodged in too tight against the planks of the wall. He scooted behind it, squatted down, and with his back against the rear of the boat, his feet pressed firmly against the wall of the *caption rouge*, he bared down, using the weight of his body and pushed hard until it broke free. He dragged it out onto the grassy area, not sure why they never used the boat, it looked fine to him. It was heavier than the canoe was, but not so much that he couldn't manage it on his own. He thought of an idea then, ran to the house and returned with two empty soda bottles, the ones worth two cents when returned to the store. He positioned them on their sides beneath the boat, one toward the front, the other centered in the middle. Like a conveyer belt, he rolled the boat over the bottles to gain a few yards, and then repositioned the one in back to the front, to keep it going. When he reached the river's edge a good ten minutes later, the armpits of his shirt were wet and his knee was scraped and bleeding. He ignored the little bit of blood for he was geared up like a Trojan warrior, ready to make his way to the other side.

With one foot in the boat, he pushed off with the other, hopped in, and sat himself on the center bench, his back and the front end of the boat aimed toward the mainland. He dug the oars in, two at a time, the way he'd seen others do, and watched their area of the island drift further and further away. He was far enough out now, well over his head, when he realized he didn't bring himself a lifejacket or floater of any kind. Not that he needed one, he was a good swimmer, but his mother always made him wear one when they crossed the river. "Just to be safe," she would say. During windy days especially, the waves were rough enough to jerk the boat around. At the passing of ships, he watched his mother explain to the others not to take the waves head-on, but at an angle. It was never explained to him directly, but he caught on just the same.

He still could not believe they just left him. His mother must have forgotten to count heads, it was what she did whenever they traveled and stopped to use the restroom. Not that it was full-proof.

The previous year, after leaving the Gas-Mart headed for the interstate, his mother cried out: "Oh no! Someone's missing!" She proceeded to count the heads in the car for the second time. "Oh my God, it's Stefano." His father turned the car around, went back to collect their four-year-old brother, who was out front, bawling his eyes, beside the store owner. But Joey was much older than Stefano. He was not about to get all weepy-eyed and would show them he was capable of crossing the river on his own. The island grew more distant with each stroke; he could barely make out their home for the sun in his eyes. Without any breeze, the air got blistering hot. His arms began to tire when he was reminded that he missed lunch and he was thirsty now, too. He could have made himself a sandwich, had he thought about it . . . or brought him a thermos of something to drink . . . and a hat to shield the brightness of the sun. He was far enough out now that when he looked over his shoulder toward the mainland he could almost see the speck of what might be their motorboat and canoe at the inlet. The images wavered as though he were looking at them under water, the fluidity making him light-headed. He was sure of what he was seeing, though, it was just as he thought. He dug the oars deeper into the river, eager to get there, but his feet were covered now and the bucket was sloshing about. The boat was taking in water, but where?

He stopped his rowing, grabbed the bucket to quickly empty the water out. He couldn't tell where it was coming in from, but it couldn't be a very big opening, he'd gone quite a distance. Scanning the shoreline on both sides, he estimated he was about one-third of the way over, with two-thirds yet to go. He could turn around and head back, but he was not about to let a little bit of water stop him. He shoveled one cup at a time, over and over, until his feet were clear again. When he got back to rowing, he noticed something was different. Their home on the island was now farther to the left, which meant he'd drifted downstream with the current. He would need to angle the boat and aim it upstream, so not to drift even further. The muscles in his arms were achy and sore, and the sun was beating down on his head, burning the back of his neck. It was good though that the river was calmer than usual. There were times when they crossed all nine of them together, six in the motorboat, and three in the canoe. The day could be sunny, warm and bright, but the river, with enough wind, would be choppy and tricky to manage. Even for the motorboat to stay on course, but especially for those in the canoe. Most often, it was the older ones doing the rowing with Dominic in front and Micheline in back, with him stuck sitting in the middle with nothing to do.

A quick glance over his left shoulder, Joey saw the *Empress* coming directly toward him. It was the largest ship of its kind, their favorite, for the amount of waves it provided. The *Empress* was a special cruise liner that carried tourists for entertainment and sightseeing. Compared to other vessels and cargo freights, it was both a beauty and a beast of a ship. The white *Empress* howled a warning. It was one that Joey could not hear, but understood when the smokestack at the rear of the ship blew out its dark smoke. His chest hammered, so he rowed harder and faster, causing the boat to slide and zigzag. He never considered that a ship might come, not as he was crossing. He knew how to take the waves, at an angle, but the *Empress* was coming directly at him. If he didn't clear it in time, his boat would surely capsize, and he refused to think what might happen after that. He pumped the oars over and over with a fearless endeavor, until water swilled about along the floorboard, covering his feet once again. The question of whether to empty it or keep rowing hammered in his head.

The *Empress* coasted nearer and nearer, there was no stopping it, and then the smokestack buffaloed a second warning.

CHAPTER 11

There are certain instances in life that stay etched in one's memory despite how many decades go by. Reliving those moments as if he were nine again, the terror that gripped him like an exposed electric wire dancing at his feet, ready to zap him, and still he had something to prove. Something his life depended on, and he was not about to screw it up.

The *Empress* came at him, sure and steady. Joey picked up his pace when he spotted over his shoulder his mother and the others approaching in the motorboat, from the other side—their arms thrashed about in a wild, wavelike frenzy. His mother pointed toward the *Empress,* her face shadowed by her cap. Their hand signals were telling him to turn around, to go back, as if he might not make it.

Joey leaned back on his bench, stomach knotted, headache brewing, as he pushed harder on the oars. He saw the *Empress* sure as they did. He was deaf, not blind, and there was no way he was turning back. Front and center now, he was lined up directly in the ship's path, but a good enough distance away, he thought, to clear it. His chances of making it were just as good to keep going as they were to turn back. He knew that he could make it, just as sure as he knew to keep the boat angled when the waves started. He'd come too far, worked too hard, was thirsty and hungry; he was going to *Grandmaman's* house, and that was all there was to it. This time, he was in the driver's seat. It was his choice to make.

With his back to his mother, he pulled and pushed against the oars, dug them deeper into the river, steady and in sync. While the boat took in a little more water, he knew this would cause him to work that much harder. He knew all of that, and still it didn't matter because he was strong, strong enough to chop wood and pull the boat up high on shore. And he was tough, tough enough not to give up, to keep rowing even when they thought that he couldn't make it. He could almost see his mother with the invisible eyes in the back of his head, telling him to *Go back . . . Go back . . . It's too dangerous. Where's your life jacket? You have to have a life jacket, just to be safe.* And he would have brought one had he thought about it, but they were all probably in their boat, anyhow.

The *Empress* was closer now. It fired off another smoke signal, a third and probably final warning. As the ship grew nearer, the size of it overwhelmed him. It was like the picture of a boy in the magazine, the one standing next to the Empire State Building that made him look no bigger than a snail. Joey hoped that the Captain would ease up on the gas. There was no veering around him, no stopping, but maybe he could ease up on the gas. With a quick glance up, he thought he saw someone looking over the edge of the ship with a pair of binoculars. He didn't know where his mother was, and there was no time to look and check. He pressed his heels firmly against the floorboards, tackled the oars in a push-and-pull symmetrical manner and a certainty that he knew what he was doing. He ignored the burning of his muscles, the ache in his belly and the blisters on his hands. None of it mattered as much as clearing the *Empress*, which was so close now he could read the inscription on the bow—*St. Lawrence Empress Cruise Lines*. Stroke after stroke, Joey powered on, his adrenalin peaking. Sweat dripped from his forehead, his hair damp and curling, splattered to his scalp. His nostrils flared and his chest pounded when a mist of spray showered him as he cleared the hull of the *Empress*. A dozen or more strokes later, he watched the ship pass before him, making sure to aim his oars directly into the wake. His rowboat, a peanut in comparison, rocked over the waves like a child's rollercoaster. He slowed down his strokes to match the timing of the ripples, and still he did not look to see where the others were. Instead, he caught sight of the folks out on the upper-deck, dozens of them cheering him on. Some of them waved their hats, others held cameras and were taking his picture. He would have waved his own cap, if he had one. But he was safe now, so with a satisfied grin, a sigh of relief, he threw up his arm, and waved back.

As the *Empress* continued on down the river, the dangerous situation now behind him, his mother pulled up alongside his boat.

"You—scared—me—to—death! Are you crazy?"

Joey ignored her question, to shovel out water. All the while he was well aware of her reaction toward him.

"That—boat—no good. Leaks. You—could—have— drowned."

He made no move to reply or even acknowledge what his mother said. She should have been happy and relieved to see that he made it, rather than scold him like a five-year-old. He wanted to tell her that she should not have left him behind and that he proved he was capable. Had he known about the stupid boat taking in water beforehand, he would not have chanced it. His mother waved to get his attention, but Joey kept his gaze down, putting distance between his boat and theirs. She threw him a cable then, in order to drag his boat behind the motorboat, but Joey wasn't having it. He'd made it this far on his own, and was not about to be towed like some broken down heap of junk. He managed just fine by himself and would finish what he started. So he choked back a cry, caught the cable with his right hand, and tossed it back into their boat. His brothers and sisters all stared at him like he *was* crazy. But he was about to show them what crazy can do.

His mother followed alongside him, the motorboat putt-putting along. He kept at it, his back to his focal point, the oars flopping about unevenly. He was beyond tired now, really tired. It seemed that once he safely cleared the *Empress*, all of his fired up energy was drained right out of him. It would have been easy, he thought, tempting, to sit back and relax, while the motorboat did all the work pulling him to shore. But he was not about to give any of them the satisfaction of knowing just how tired he was, or that his idea to cross the river was not the brightest one. So he dug the oars in deeper again, his arms bent forward and then back again, as he fought and choked back the tears. With a glance over his shoulder, finally, he craned his neck toward the inlet, the knots and knuckles of land of where he was headed. He could feel their stares and his mother's impatience, the fight within him wearing thin, but he kept at what he was doing. A dozen or more minutes passed, he gave a second look, and then he saw her. *Grandmaman* was standing at the edge of her property, waiting for him. He could almost see her clearly now. She was wearing a striped, cotton dress that fell just below her knees with a pocketed apron tied around her waist. In one hand, she held a bright yellow beach towel, in the other, a jug of water. Joey was never so happy to see *Grandmaman;* she must have known how thirsty he would be.

There were times when he wondered what his *Grandpapa* had been like. He died when Joey was four, long before they started spending their summers on the island. All that he knew about him were the pictures in the photo albums that told their own story, and what little his mother added when he asked her.

"He was a policeman in the city," she said, "when I was a child growing up." The black and white snapshots were small, and not so clear.

Joey pointed to a colored, more recent photo. "When?"

"After my father got old, he didn't like to shave much. He was a tall man, about six-feet."

Joey noted his full head of white hair and thick, bushy eyebrows above the clearest of blue eyes that matched his own. But even more prominent was his scruffy beard jaw-line. He wondered if that was how he would look when he got old, or if his mother would look like her mother did now, when she reached her age.

"Hello!" *Grandmaman* called out. She set the jug of water down, and waved.

When his boat scraped bottom, Joey stepped out into the ankle-deep water, his legs wobbly and unsure, pulling the boat up on shore, enough so that he could tilt it over to let it drain. He avoided eye contact with his mother and the others, who were in the process of tying their boat down.

"Drink?" *Grandmaman* held the jug out to him, with the lid already off.

Joey nodded, eager to gulp it down straight from the half-gallon container. He drank and he drank as the water ran down his chin, onto his neck and chest. He could not remember ever being so thirsty, so starved for water. The cool liquid felt good against his lips and even better seeping down his throat, filling up his belly. When he finally had enough, he gave a happy grin.

"Thank you," he motioned the words. His shirt was already saturated, so he flipped it over his head, balled it up and dried off his face.

"You thirsty, eh? Come," she urged him, "come have lunch." She placed the dry towel over his shoulders, the two of them headed back towards the house, with the others following behind.

It was not until later, once he'd eaten and rested up, that he decided to forgive his mother. He noticed her crying, while speaking in private to *Grandmaman*. Of what they spoke about, he didn't know, but he guessed as much it was about him. He remembered the look on his mother's face when she reached his boat. *You—scared—me—to—death! Are you crazy?* He never meant to put his life in danger or to worry her like that. The idea of what might have happened didn't occur to him. So when she approached him later, and wrapped her arms around him in a bear hug, all of his anger melted away.

"Dominic and Micheline crossed the river by canoe," she began to explain, using hand gestures. "I thought . . . you went with them. When we got here," she pointed down, "I said, where's Joey? We looked around . . . we couldn't find you. When I saw you rowing over, in that old leaky boat and then the big ship was coming . . . I was so scared . . . I thought I was going to lose a son."

Joey motioned, frantic, that when he came back from his walk, everyone was gone. He checked the house, the yard, the barn, no one was there.

"I know. I'm sorry. We didn't know. It was my fault. I'm sorry."

He could see his mother was visibly shaken, even now, just

talking about it. She never meant to leave him.

"Please don't scare me like that again, my heart is getting old. Okay?"

Joey nodded, grinned, and then noticed *Grandmaman* asleep in her rocker. Her eyes were closed, a slight tilt of her head, she smiled. He wondered what she might be dreaming or thinking about. Something good, for sure. He liked coming over to her house. Her grilled cheese sandwiches were the best, he had finished off two of them.

Just then, Dominic jumped up and ran to the window. Another ship was spotted. Everyone fled out the door, with Joey on their heels, one right after the other in a race to shore.

CHAPTER 12

Joe awoke to more darkness, regained his senses and where-abouts, and then recalled the dream of his close call of the *Empress* on the river. It was all so odd, he thought, life repeating itself. Maybe not in the same sense, but that he would find himself in another fight for his life. It reminded him of how thirsty he was, all over again. The only difference now was that when he finally made it out of the woods, *Grandmaman* would not be there with a jug of cool water waiting for him.

He felt the sting on his hand, the one from the now dead copperhead. There did not seem to be any swelling so it must be a good sign, he thought. He was still in pain, all-over pain. His legs were cramped, tight and aching, and his back hurt when he moved a certain way. Worse was a relentless throbbing in his head that pulsated with every breath and beat of his heart. If he didn't know better, he would have thought the fall from the tree-stand landed him upside down, on his head. His mouth was cotton-dry, his lips cracked, and felt as if they were bleeding.

My name is Joe Barone.
I am alone in woods, on my father land.
All right.
Good.
I remember.
He thought about the searches on the evening news,

missing persons, movies and documentaries. It normally took twenty-four hours before a person was deemed missing, unless in the case of a small child or proof of foul play. No one in his family would ever think to look for him out here, and he seldom saw his father anymore, anyway. Keeping his distance was the best way to avoid an argument. His mother would call to check on him from time to time, encouraging him to stop by the house. The last time she did, nearly a year ago, the request came through Delia.

"Your mom called today," she told him. "Your father is having knee replacement surgery Monday morning. She asked that you stop by to say hello, maybe visit for a while." The request was a simple one, and yet it made his insides tighten up. What would he say, and what could they talk about? Would they ask questions why he hadn't been by in so long? How long had it been, anyway; he barely knew anymore. A year, maybe two, since the last altercation.

"Word's out, Joe," his cousin Vincent began, "your father's been complaining about your G-T-O that's parked in his barn over on M-a-i-n."

He want my car gone? Why he no tell me? Why he complain to everyone, and not me? When Joe heard this, he arranged to have it moved the very next day. When his father saw the tow truck and Joe arrive, he approached him on the spot.

"What's going on?" his father asked. The tow-man hitched the vehicle to the back of his truck, lifting the front wheels off the ground. Joe motioned briefly he was taking the car.

"I never said you needed to move it," his father replied. But Joe was in no mood to have a face-off, and he didn't want his old man holding it over his head that his car was taking up space and then condemn him for it to the family.

It was the last time he'd seen his father, before his mother's plea came. The thought of disappointing her weighed on him, almost as much as what he anticipated to be another uncomfortable situation he would rather avoid. In the end, though, Joe had Delia call his mother to let her know he would be there.

When he arrived, he noticed the Toyota Camry with the Tennessee plates out front and was glad to see Micheline was in town.

Micheline greeted him at the door. "Hey, Joe," she said, with a smile and a ready hug. "It's good to see you."

Joe gave a sheepish grin, hugged her back.

His mother was right behind her. "There you are, my long lost son . . . it's been a long time. Too long. You look good." She gave him a motherly squeeze. Joe leaned over the table, shook his father's hand, and then took a seat beside Micheline. He couldn't help but notice his father wearing a clean white tee-shirt, and that his hair was damp, as if he'd just taken a shower in the middle of the day.

"So, how are you doing?" Micheline asked.

"Okay. You?"

"I'm good, still working for the State, twenty-eight-years now."

"Wow! Long time," Joe motioned. "I work c-o-n-s-t-r-u-c-t-i-o-n most time, here and there," he added.

"How's Delia, she didn't want to come?"

"No. Busy. Work coffee shop."

"How's business, good?

"So-so."

The question-and-answer session went on awhile longer,

until there was a lull in the room. Everyone looked to one another for what next to say, when Micheline picked up the slack.

"Dad's having surgery in the morning. He has a bad knee. Hurts a lot. Doctor told him, after surgery, he can work in the garden."

"What garden?" Joe asked, an odd expression twisting his face.

Micheline shrugged, smirked. Everyone laughed. There was no garden, and the last thing their father would be seen doing was kneeling down and tending to one, either before or after any surgery. This seemed to lighten the mood in the room. His mother pulled out the papers to show the surgery details, handed them over to Joe. He looked them over briefly while everyone remained silent.

"Hey, Micheline," his mother began excitedly, "does he know about the new house being built? Tell him about that."

"Mom and Dad—new house—in the country—Dominic is building—did you know?"

Joe gave a half-hearted shrug; he'd heard something about it. His mother pulled out the blueprints to show him the layout of the two-story dwelling that ranged twenty-six hundred square feet, with a sunroom out back, and a two-car garage.

"The house will be ready this summer, maybe," Micheline told him.

Joe scanned over the plans. "How much p-r-o-p-e-r-t-y?" he asked her.

"A little over three acres," his father said, joining in the conversation.

It was how the visit went. There were back and forth questions and answers, with his father doing more listening than talking, though he seemed to be in good spirits, just more subdued and quiet than usual.

CHAPTER 13

For as long as Joe was idle, resting, his mind seemed to wind down and relax. He knew it would be time to get moving again, soon, but with his thoughts more lucid now, less anxious than they were; he wanted to savor the moment a bit longer. The way he remembered that last visit in his parents' kitchen, it went about as well as he could have hoped for, and still, he felt relieved to be driving back home again, relieved to have fulfilled his duty. Micheline, though she lived in Tennessee, a thirteen-hundred-mile roundtrip drive, kept in contact with the family, making regular visits. As far as Joe could tell, there were no problems between her and their father, at least not since the time she moved out on her own.

The summer of 1975, the targeted year for the world to end, and that Joey would turn eleven; it was following her high school graduation that Micheline packed her bags and left home.

"Isabelle and I are going to rent an apartment in Montreal," she told them. "Her boss where she works has a waitress job waiting for me once I turn eighteen." The news was first shared with her mother, who later informed their father.

"We don't want you to move out," his father said from the

front seat of the Suburban during the break at the *Witnesses Convention.* "If you stay, you'll pay twenty-five dollars a week room and board. But if your mind is made up that you're leaving, you don't have to wait until you're eighteen, you can leave now."

Micheline had little to say, but when a few weeks later she was gone, everything that summer seemed different. It was six months after that, though, when something really set off his father.

"You are not to write or contact her in any way!"

"Why?" Susanna asked in a defiant tone.

"Because I said so, that's why!" There was an icy coldness to his stare, as if daring her to say just one more word.

Susanna, on occasion, managed enough restraint, at least where their father was concerned, to keep from crossing that line that would get her in hot water, and this was one of those times. It was later that Joey learned this did not stop Susanna, or his mother, in fact, from writing Micheline.

"Wah for . . . father mad M-icheline?" he asked his mother, finally.

She pulled out a chair at the kitchen table, thinking how best to respond. "Micheline moved from Canada. She lives with her boyfriend now, upstate New York."

"Wah boyfriend?"

"Remember Drake? He came here one time a few years ago—drives a car with a bad m-u-f-f-l-e-r."

Joey remembered the time he squealed his tires at the Shell station when they stopped for gas, and burning rubber. His father called Drake a *big shot*, said he was *trouble*.

"I remember," he nodded. "Why father mad . . . wah for?"

"Because Micheline lives with her boyfriend. Not married."

Joey asked no more questions, but wondered when he

might see his sister again. By then, several years had passed since he and Petro attended the School for the Deaf, in Trenton, New Jersey, that offered a residential program for students who lived too far for daily commute. The program offered students the opportunity to participate in recreational activities with their peers, the same opportunity afforded to students in regular education environments. This was a welcome change for Joey and his brother, who were given the chance to temporarily break away from the confusing life in a family that did not speak in sign, and also to explore a more comprehensive life among the deaf community. They would board a bus within walking distance from their home, on a Sunday afternoon, and return the following Friday evening. To Joey's satisfaction, this narrowed down their meetings at the Kingdom Hall to Sundays only.

The years passed by, one by one, and still the world remained the same. This seemed to further upset his father. Maybe it had to do with all the time they spent preparing for the end to come: going to meetings, their door-to-door service work, preaching the end was near to anyone willing to listen, when none of it paid off.

Or maybe his father was embarrassed for trying to convince his younger brother of *The Truth*. Uncle Willie was not a religious man, not even close. But to prove a point, his father made him an offer he could not refuse.

"Come with us to the Kingdom Hall," his father said, "I'll pay you twenty-five dollars, come see for yourself."

"Twenty-five dollars?" Uncle Willie grinned, the temptation of a juicy prime-rib steak dangled before his mind's eye.

There was no arm twisting, no coaxing, no upping the ante. Uncle Willie did not need to be asked twice when offered money. His father was sure, then, that Willie would see the light after a two-hour service, when it only took him one to be convinced of *The Truth* himself.

"Willie's coming down this weekend," his father said at the dinner table. "He's coming to the Kingdom Hall with us."

"What about Carol and the kids, are they coming too?" his mother asked.

"Nah." He took a spoonful of his soup. "He's coming alone. Carol said she'd come too for twenty-five dollars," he snorted.

Joey picked up on the mention of Uncle Willie coming. But then a few of his siblings laughed. He motioned to Micheline, who was sitting across from him. "Wah funny?"

"Uncle Willie," she began, "coming here Sunday, to the Kingdom Hall."

"I knooow . . . Wah funny?" Micheline filled him in on the deal made between their father and uncle, while not agreeing to extend that deal to Aunt Carol.

Joey grinned. He got the picture.

Petro signed to his brother, "Why Dad pay Uncle Willie?"

Joey shrugged. "I think b-r-i-b-e."

Petro smirked, rubbed his thumb and forefinger together, hooked his thumb to his chest.

Joey laughed. His father was no fool; he knew that once his brother was recruited, Aunt Carol would follow.

"He'll see." His father reached for a slice of bread, buttered it heavily before folding it in half and dipping it into his bowl of tomato soup. "It only took me an hour to be convinced. One hour." He shoved the saturated portion of bread into his mouth.

On Sunday, Uncle Willie showed up in time for coffee. "Good Morning," his mother greeted, "glad you could make it."

"Oh, I wouldn't have missed it," Willie said. "I'm looking

forward to it, actually." He chuckled, as if something more was going on behind the smile.

Shortly after, they were all seated at the Kingdom Hall. Joey positioned himself so that he could watch his uncle carefully, whose eyes from the start remained focused, straight ahead, serious, giving nothing away. There was no more kidding around, not since the moment they entered the Kingdom Hall.

Joey kept his attention too on the elder at the podium, whose name was Brother G. He struggled to pick up some of his words.

"So . . . be confident . . . the end is near . . . God will bring it about . . ." Brother G would speak a few words, then look down at his notes. "In the meantime . . . keep busy . . . God's service. . ."

The first hour was Joey's least favorite. There was no written material and no pictures to follow along. Today, however, with his watch on Uncle Willie, he looked for signs as to whether he was becoming a believer or not.

When finally, everyone stood to sing along from the hymn book that was Joey's cue they were halfway through the service. The pre-recorded music vibrated in the room. Uncle Willie sang along with the others, *Praise Jehovah for His Kingdom*. It felt good to be standing up, to stretch his legs a bit. Joey hoped that the next and final hour would move along quickly.

Everyone sat when the song concluded. Brother N was at the podium now, motioning for everyone to open their *Watchtower* magazine to page six.

"*Is There Anything You Can Do To Prepare?*" Brother N read aloud the titled chapter. He looked out into the congregation, gazed around for a volunteer. "Who would like to begin reading?"

Joey's eyes went from Brother N to Uncle Willie to the hand that rose up two rows over. He stretched his neck to see it was Sister Smith. With a nod from Brother N, Joey followed along in the copy he held on his lap.

"Will you fill your freezer with hundreds of pounds of food? Hoard all the canned goods you can buy? Take lessons on a pistol range to protect yourself from criminals? Or buy guns to guard your hoarded food? Will you move to some remote, primitive spot? But think how easily all this preparation could be a complete waste. When electric current or gas is cut off, frozen food is lost. When food is really in short supply, the hoarders are in danger of losing not only it, but their lives as well. For what will stop hungry people? And guns will not stop criminals. In fact, criminals usually have the 'drop' on you when they suddenly attack. Moreover, there is a much greater danger on the horizon.

"That danger is from a higher source. It is the day of reckoning that God holds with the entire system of things—religious, political and commercial. The unsolvable crises on every hand show that the world's system has been 'weighed in the balances and found wanting,' and is soon to pass off the scene.—1 John 2:17."

"Thank you, Sister Smith. Let us turn now to the First of John, Chapter Two, Verse Seventeen."

Picking up on the exchange, Joey watched as everyone opened their Bible. He looked over at the one Dominic was holding, when a few moments later, Brother N read aloud.

"Furthermore, the world is passing away and so is its desire, but he that does the will of God remains forever."

Joey's attention span veered off. He flipped through the *Watchtower* magazine, blowing air between his lips, when he turned the page, and landed on the familiar 144,000 chosen ones.

The saving of all mankind who will obediently give response to God's commands will be accomplished during Christ's thousand year reign over earth. During the past 1900-year period God has been selecting those who will be kings and priests with Christ and who will rule during that thousand years to bring blessings to mankind. This kingly governing body will be a heavenly group and is restricted in number to 144,000 persons.—(Rev. 7:1-8)

The congregation exploded with laughter. Joey instantly sensed the change in the room, popped his head up to get a take on it. Brother N was no longer speaking, he was laughing right along with every other member, including his mother and father and Uncle Willie. What triggered the hilarity among the members, Joey did not have a clue.

It took several minutes for the members to settle down before order was resumed. As the next section of the *Watchtower* was read and everyone quieted down, Joey could see his father and uncle losing their grip to contain more laughter. Their shoulders shook with each snicker, their heads bobbed and their bodies rocked. The two of them failed miserably trying to control themselves, as many sets of eyes were now drawn to them. Uncle Willie produced a handkerchief from his pocket to swipe the sweat from his forehead and dab the corners of his eyes. It was moments such as these, with his father in such good spirits, that Joey relaxed. It even caused him to smile, as if he'd been in on the joke. A few moments passed, all seemed normal before his father and uncle started up again, chuckling like two naughty boys in the back of a classroom sharing a private joke or mischievous prank. He would have to remember, once the service was over, to ask his mother what was so funny.

Joey flipped back to the section of today's topic, attempting to find anything remotely humorous that might have caused the uproar, but found nothing. He turned his attention back to Uncle Willie, who as of yet showed no signs of boredom or restlessness. He surprisingly appeared to be paying very close attention. It was almost as if he might be quizzed later. Did he have to pass a test first, he wondered, before collecting the money? Eventually, the mood in the room returned to its normal, hum-drum atmosphere with members silently reading along, or at least pretending to. Joey caught the occasional tilt of a head, the eye contact that followed, with a nod or shrug from one younger member to another.

After a while, when the members stirred, Joey knew the service was about to conclude. He wondered if Uncle Willie would return the following Sunday. He was glad that he found part of the service to be entertaining. If his entire family were to come with him next time, he and his cousins could all hang out together afterwards, shoot hoops in the backyard or play Monopoly. His cousins after all, the five of them, were of the same age as he and Dominic and his sisters. It would be something to look forward to.

Back at the house, sitting around the kitchen table over coffee, juice and donuts, his father and uncle were at it again. The same side-splitting laughter rocked their bodies.

Joey tapped his mother's arm for an explanation. "Wah funny?"

"Brother D-o-m-a-k-s," she spelled out in sign, "said something funny at the Kingdom Hall."

Joey knew that Brother Domakas was always in good spirits and that he often participated in the question-and-answer session of the *Watchtower*, but he could not imagine what he might have said, to set off the members.

"Wah funny?" he asked again.

With the *Watchtower* in her hands, she flipped through the pages to locate the section that described a prophet and his donkey.

"Brother Domakas said the prophet sat down on his a-s-s," she concluded by writing and underlining the word *ass*, and then circling the word *donkey*, as it was referred to.

When the image sunk in, Joey jolted, bug-eyed; he covered his mouth with his hand and chuckled. This set off his father and uncle into a comical marathon. Understanding finally, Joey got the gist of what happened.

"Maaa . . ." Everyone piped down to listen to what Joey had to say. "Bro D c-u-r-s-e . . . King'm Hall." Only it was not *really* a curse word, Joey giggled, not in describing a donkey. He joined in with the others, now that he was in on the joke. When finally the laughter died down, Joey noticed something else. His father reached into his pocket, counted out the bills before handing them over to his uncle. This was bound to mean only one thing—that Uncle Willie was not won over.

"Thank you," Uncle Willie said, slipping the cash in his pocket. "I'm glad I came. The songs were nice. The members were friendly." He chuckled again.

"Come back, anytime," his mother said, refilling his cup with more coffee.

"The end is coming soon," his father warned.

"Nah—" Uncle Willie grinned in his usual way, like he was on the verge of something bigger. There never was a time that Uncle Willie did not have something humorous to share. It was the reason they loved being around him so much. "Tell you what," he said, "when 1980 gets here, we'll celebrate and have a big party."

His father, more serious now, said, "That'll never happen."

CHAPTER 14

Joe was idle for a long time, it seemed, long enough to get his wits about him. *I can stay here . . . die slowly . . . or I can push and keep going.* The choice was his. Some choice. Neither of which enticed him, not when moving risked excruciating pain, and remaining still risked his not being found, at least not until after it was too late.

The icy white moon in the deepest of blue skies was calling to him now, in a strange, mesmerizing way, that he found himself visualizing E.T. tucked inside a basket, while being bike-pedaled home. He was just a teen when the movie came out and had watched it again a few years later.

E.T. phone home.

Joe adjusted himself onto his belly then, knowing what he needed to do. He was going home. Following the same eastward direction, not quite sure how, he put all of his life into his good leg and his two strong arms, through dips and mounds he moved like a phantom creeping through the night, his lungs filling and blowing. *Saving Private Ryan* flashed through his mind—infantry soldiers crawling through the dugout pits. At least here was no fear of an enemy line. The snake had been taken care of, and if his hand still ached from the bite, he was no worse off from it.

After what seemed like the length of a football field, Joe stopped moving. He lay there, motionless, his body depleted and useless. Foggy images circulated through his head, distorted faces of his father, of Delia, Dominic, even Mickey and others with no rhyme or reason. They were all jumbled up and confusing, some of them pixilated like a cable channel with interference. He fought to regain clarity, forced himself to make sense of it all. Until finally, a man from his past, someone familiar, came toward him. He lowered himself down to his level, smiled, and nodded, his left hand on Joe's shoulder, giving an encouraging squeeze. They shared an unspoken kind of respect, a mutual admiration for the other. Even now, Joe could see his expression come into focus, so clear, so sure. He could feel the impact of his words before he ever signed them. *You can do this, Joe. You can do this.*

By the time he entered high school, Joe had grown into a handsome young man. At five feet eleven inches tall, two hundred pounds—give or take, Joe was all muscle, with broad, square shoulders, round defined biceps, and solid thick thighs. Rather than the extra-lean body of a runner, he had the kind of muscle on his bones that gave him the strength and power to do whatever activity he set his mind to. During that time Joe discovered a talent for sports. English Literature and Math equations bored him to tears, but as a sports contender, he felt alive and on top of the world. The encouragement of fellow students and coaches, the discipline it required, the thrill and competitiveness, the hard work and sweat—all of it drove him. An added bonus to his athleticism and sporty physique combined with his super dark wavy hair, his bright blue eyes and unassuming smile, made him popular with the girls.

The day Joe was called in to Coach's office he wondered

what he might have done. "C-o-a-c-h, you call for me?" Joe signed, when he entered Coach Palmer's office, a bit apprehensive.

"Have a seat, Joe." Coach was leaning up against the front edge of his desk. His walls were covered with a variety of impressive certificates, awards, trophies and plaques; the result of thirty years worth, from his high school and college days when he ran track and played baseball, to what lead to a career with the Marie H. Katzenbach School for the Deaf. As the son of a deaf mother, Coach was also able to make use of his extensive knowledge speaking through sign.

"I've got good news for you. At least I think you'll agree it's good news." Coach shifted his weight, rested his right thigh on top of the corner of his desk in a half seated position, read something from a page he was holding, and then set it back down again, to give Joe his full attention.

Joe loosened up a bit, but still with no idea what Coach was about to say.

"I've been watching you, Joe. We all have. I'm not going to beat around the bush here, we're talking O-l-y-m-p-i-c-s. What do you think about training for the upcoming World Games for the Deaf?"

Joe could not believe what he understood Coach to say: he wanted him to train for World Games; the Olympics for the Deaf? Him?

"You serious? You think I'm good enough?"

"Good enough? You've broken records in both the *j-a-v-e-l-i-n* and the *s-h-o-t-p-u-t,* not once, but twice! You have i-m-p-r-e-s-s-e-d not just me, but also the A-t-h-l-e-t-i-c Director and the R-e-g-i-o-n-a-l Director, once I gave them your s-t-a-t-s."

Joe was elated over the mere thought of what Coach was

saying. For the first time, he felt that he found his niche, something he was really good at, that would gain him recognition. It was hard work alright, with all the practice sessions, competing against others who had been training for much longer, with families to support them, even encourage them to their fullest potential, but for him, it was what he loved doing. "When do *Games* start?"

"Not until next year, summer of '81. That gives us a full year to train."

"What location?"

"We'll train here, of course. The h-o-s-t-i-n-g country will be Germany."

Joe's heart sank. There was no way his father was going to agree to his going out of the country, let alone the expenses involved.

"Is something wrong?"

"My father. I don't think he let me go. Germany too far, too expensive, and he think . . ." He searched for the right way to explain that his father was not a fan of sports, any sport of this sort.

"The school has g-r-a-n-t money that would cover most of the cost involved, such as p-l-a-n-e f-a-r-e, hotel, and food. You would have to get a p-a-s-s-p-o-r-t, of course, and your parents, if they go to watch you perform, would have to pay for their own way, but why don't I set up a meeting to speak with your parents first of next week. I'm sure that once I explain all the b-e-n-e-f-i-t-s this o-p-p-o-r-t-u-n-i-t-y will mean, your father will have a better understanding and come around to our side."

"You don't know my father, Coach. He stubborn. He has own business, and I don't think he want me go to Germany to watch *Games*."

"What kind of business?"

"Hair s-a-l-o-n."

"Is your father a hair d-r-e-s-s-e-r?"

"Yes. My mother, too. They work all the time."

"Let me set up the meeting, okay—I'm sure we can work something out."

"Thank you, Coach." Joe stood to leave. It all sounded amazing to him, but also too good to be true, he didn't want to get his hopes up.

When Joe reached for the door, Coach walked over to him, put his hand on his shoulder, and said: "I've been doing my job for a long time, Joe, and I have to say, I don't come across too many students who have the kind of t-a-l-e-n-t and drive that you do. You're a real fighter, Joe. R-e-g-a-r-d-l-e-s-s what happens here, that fighter i-n-s-t-i-n-c-t in you can take you far in life. But as far as O-l-y-m-p-i-c-s go, you d-e-s-e-r-v-e a shot, and yes, you are for sure good enough."

Joe left the office feeling as if he were walking on air. It was an honor to be deemed worthy enough to attain Olympic status. Of course, he would still need to train and qualify, but like Coach told him, he was a real fighter, and if given the opportunity, he would give it his all.

The meeting was scheduled for the following Monday night. It was all Joe could do to get through the weekend; his nerves were all over the place. When the time came, finally, after the introductions were made and everyone was seated, Joe focused on the demeanor and body language of his parents. His mother sat up straight, legs crossed at the ankle, her hands rested uneasily on her lap. His father, eager to get the meeting over with, sat impatiently. Coach got right to the point.

"Your son is a gifted athlete," he said, beaming his eyes

on the father with an occasional meeting of the eyes with the mother. "He's broken records in both the *javelin* and the *shot-put*, and I'm very pleased and proud to say that he's good enough for the Deaf Olympics." Coach signed as he spoke, for Joe's benefit alone. But it was his parents' reaction, or rather his father's, that Joe waited for. He knew the pitch that Coach intended to make. What he planned to say exactly, only Coach knew.

Carefully, Joe watched his father's expressions. He had long ago become attuned to body language and vocal cues people displayed in reading their thoughts and feelings, both good and bad, especially with people he knew. Joe caught bits and pieces of his parents' conversation the night before, when they thought he wasn't around. His father didn't want to attend the meeting in the first place, and Susanna too, continued to be his rival.

"How come Joey and Petro get to play sports in school, and we're not allowed to?"

"Because they're deaf," his mother said, "and they live at school."

"So? Because they're deaf, they get special privileges?"

"Hey!" his father interjected. "You want to swap places with them? Quit your whining and mind your own business. This conversation has nothing to do with you."

Susanna muttered something under her breath before exiting the kitchen to the living room, when her eyes met up with Joe's, who was sitting there in the shadows. Susanna's reaction, though, was the least of Joe's concerns; it was his father's reaction that mattered. He waited and watched now, to find out more, as Coach continued to make his plea.

"Sports for the deaf provide the perfect outlet for meaningful interactions with others who use sign language.

Friendships, bonds, communication and responsibility help them gain confidence. By competing in sporting events, they'll expand their social relations outside the sport by giving them self-assurance and building their self-esteem. With your permission, of course, I'd like to start training him for next summer." Coach emphasized each word carefully, making eye contact with both parents, and pausing to allow them to comment or ask questions.

Joe was able to follow every word while keeping his main focus on his father. When Coach finished his pitch, he waited for their reaction.

His father gazed downward, as if gathering his thoughts, and then shifted uncomfortably in his seat. Had he been at home, there would not have been any shifting or discomfort. He would have already fired off his answer. No explanation necessary, just a firm, non-negotiable *No*. Not even a *let me think about it, No*. It was always *No, case closed*. But his father was not at home now. He was sitting in Coach's office, in the presence of a professional, who happened to be the school's head coach, someone who saw talent and promise in his son and was willing to go to bat for him. What kind of a father would he be if he didn't at least pretend to listen and keep an open-mind?

His parents exchanged a quick questioning look as Coach and Joe waited for either of them to say something. With a deep sigh, his mother dug through her purse, before finding a Kleenex just in time to cover her mouth and catch the sneeze.

"Bless you," Coach said.

"Thank you." His mother smiled shyly, returning the wadded up tissue back into her purse.

When she looked up again, Joe thought she was about to say something more, but it was his father who beat her to it.

"Well . . . we appreciate the time you've taken to explain your position, but . . ." As the words were spoken, Coach signed and then paused, waited for his father to go on. "We've talked it over, my wife and I, and uh . . . this isn't the kind of life we want for our son."

"What kind of life is that?" Coach asked.

"A life of competitions, getting his head full of ideas. These . . . fun and game activities, telling him he's good enough for the Olympics. It's not a career path."

"With all due respect, Mr. Barone, I don't think you understand that by playing sports, it can lead—"

"Oh, I do understand. I know exactly where it can lead." The moment the words were out of his father's mouth, Joe saw the heat rising to his cheeks. "I never wanted him to play sports in the first place. But against my better judgment, I was talked into letting him wrestle his first year of high school, so that he wouldn't feel left out, and he wanted to wrestle, so I finally gave in and said okay. Few months later, what do you think happens? He dislocates his shoulder."

"Mr. Barone, as a parent myself, I totally understand your concern for not wanting your son to be injured. No parent wants that. In contact sports, however, there is always a chance of that happening. The good news here is that there is no contact with *javelin* and *shot-put*, just exercise and training to prepare for it." By the time he finished signing, Joe knew he was doomed, he could see it in his father's demeanor.

"It's not just about getting injured," his father interjected, "we don't have the time or the money to waste on this . . . Olympic stuff. Running a business to feed a family of ten is what I consider to be important." His eyes glared and his lips tightened. "I've worked hard to get where I am, and believe me, I didn't get here by playing sports."

"With all due respect, Mr. Barone, might I ask what kind of work you do?" Coach seemed to have thrown his father a curveball. The question, as well as Coach's calmness, seemed to relax his father a bit, but his guard remained up.

"We run a beauty salon, my wife and I."

Coach did not flinch, nor seem surprised. He already knew what they did for a living. He and Joe covered that earlier on, when Joe shared his reservations about the meeting in the first place. But Joe suspected that Coach was doing what Coach did best, and that was to get to know his father and try to put him at ease. He had witnessed it all before. When students, even other coaches became defensive, Coach, always exuding calmness, found a way to turn things around, of deflating their anger or resistance. He was good with people. Very good. Until now, that is—meeting his father or the likes of him, he had no idea what he was up against.

"Oh really, where?"

"Chester. *Wheels of Hair Design*."

Coach nodded as if he might know the place. "How's business these days, pretty good?"

"We do all right." His father's breathing became shallow again. The huff in his chest and shoulders relaxed.

"Do you think that would be something Joe would want to carry on, working in the family business?"

The question seemed to stump his father. His expression was almost comical, but breaking out in laughter was the last thing Joe wanted to do. It was obvious his father never even gave it a thought, not that he should. Working in his parents' salon was about as ridiculous to Joe as getting his nails painted or his legs waxed. It was the last thing he would be doing for a living, of that he was certain. The only thing he did do for the business was to help renovate the shop, paint, minor repairs, move heavy equipment, stuff like that, men's work. Not shampooing and setting women's hair like his father. No way! His mom did manicures, pedicures, facials and massages, women's work. She was good at it, too. What his father did for a living did not embarrass Joe. It was what many others did back then, in the fifties, those without a high school education. His parents did not go beyond the eighth grade, and his father was medically discharged from the Navy. With his options being few, he completed a year of cosmetology; it was where his parents first met. For his father at least, it was a start where he could eventually run his own business, be his own boss, and with his hairdresser wife by his side, he accomplished just that.

"Well . . . I don't know," his father said finally. "He's never shown any interest in the business. What does that have to do with this?" His father was getting impatient again. After a quick glance at the clock on the wall, he adjusted himself in his seat, ran his hand through his hair, and then gave out a hardy cough to clear his throat.

"Sports provide a good foundation for what he might like to do with his life," Coach added. "It opens up many opportunities. And as far as the costs involved, as Joe expressed that same concern, the school obtains grant money to cover much of the costs. This is an opportunity that rarely comes along and . . ."

Joe had to hand it to him. Coach remained unflustered, calm and composed. His father, however, would not be swayed. He could feel his resistance a mile long. His mind was made up, and had been before they ever got there.

". . . I would hope that you will at least think the matter over before making a decision."

"Let's say we did let him try out," his father challenged.

"Let's say he won first place. Would he get a cash prize?" His prideful look was all but telling, but his arrogance did not deter Coach. His father, however, did not wait for a response, because oddly enough, he already knew the answer. "No! He wouldn't earn any money, would he?"

Coach was about to say something, but his father fired off another question, and then another and another.

"Will it find him a good job somewhere, throwing a javelin? Earn him a trade where he can make a living? Will it pay for his meals or a new pair of shoes? Buy him a house or a car, or even pay his doctor bill the next time he dislocates a shoulder?" He took a breath, and continued. "I get that you want to help my son, but if you really want to help him, teach him something he'll be able to use in the real world, and stop feeding him some pipedream bullshit!"

By the time he ran out of steam, the corners of his mouth formed a white mucous. A light film of sweat covered his brow. His chest heaved in and out and his eyes grew hard and unsettling, as if he'd been provoked to react in such a way.

Coach's good intentions were sucked right out of him. He saw the roadblock, barricaded by an unreasonable mind that would not be swayed by facts and figures or pure logic. There was no use kidding himself. No use trying to convince a blind man that the sky is blue when he had no concept of color and saw everything of the same shade. When Coach paused before giving a reply, his father stood.

"If that's all," he said, a bit calmer now, "I think we've wasted enough of your time. Come on, Fran."

Coach stood too. "Please . . . I really think it would be a mistake to dismiss the idea completely. Why don't you take some time to sleep on it?"

"I could sleep on it a day, a week or a month, it won't change my mind. Like I said, this is not the kind of life we want for our son. He needs to focus on what's important, something he can do for a living. Not in training to fly off to Timbuktu thinking he's some big-shot. It's not going to happen."

Joe saw defeat in Coach's posture, a look of embarrassment. He might have said more, done more, or had other qualified staff in the meeting to back up his belief, but it seemed pointless now, and his father was up and out the door, his mother quietly following.

"Thank you," she said. "It was nice meeting you," she quickly added, and just as quickly waved for Joe to come along.

For Joe, it was not about being better or outshining the others, or even the need for bragging rights. It was not about standing out in a crowd like some hero. He didn't quite know how to explain it, except that it just felt great to be really good at something. The long strenuous workouts, the hundreds of push-ups and sit-ups, sprints and weight training were all part of the high and worth every agonizing, sweat-dripping moment. Win or lose, the opportunity for Olympic status was an honor that sports enthusiasts could only dream about. It was something that most parents and families would be proud of. It made the news and TV stations, it made history. But for Joe at least, it just made him feel good about himself, like any other teen wants to feel, with dreams and goals for a promising future, while getting over whatever hang-ups or insecurities they may have about themselves. Having been born deaf was not a crutch. It was not something he was ashamed of or deterred by. He was able to learn, to adapt, and to apply himself in all the ways it took to become a man. This was a shot being offered to him that so few others were given, a shot that could change the course of his life. But if Coach could not get his father to see that, maybe his father never would.

No World Games tryouts for Joe. He was not sure, though, what bothered him more, the fact that he would never know if he could have made it, or that his father did not seem to care either way. His coach, at least, believed in him. *You have so much talent and drive. You're a real fighter, Joe. It will take you far in life.* His teammates, too, always cheered him on, high-fiving him whenever a new record was broken.

To his friend Phillip, Joe later explained. "My father said no. He no let me try out for *World Games*."

"Because location, Germany?"

"No. Even if *Games* here, at school. He think O-lympics p-i-p-e-d-r-e-a-m bullshit."

"He say that?" Phillip gave a weird look.

"Yeah. He tell C-o-a-c-h."

"Wow. . ." A stunned Phillip lowered his eyes, and after a beat, he looked up again. "When I tell my dad C-o-a-c-h want you for O-lympics, I think he more excited than me. He think O-lympics huge h-o-n-o-r. He has much r-e-s-p-e-c-t for hard work and discipline."

"Yeah . . . hard work. Not bullshit. My father . . . he never watch sports . . . never play sports. He don't understand. He only like go fish or hunt. Only care about make money."

"What your mom say?"

"I think my mom be okay. She want me be happy. But, she no make decision. If my father say 'no', that final. No means no."

"I'm sorry, Joe. I know you disappointed. You should still feel proud. My dad, he proud of you, too. He want meet you."

"He does?"

"Yeah. He never meet anyone good enough for O-lympics before," Phillip teased, gave a playful squeeze to Joe's shoulder.

Joe shook his head, grinning. He envied Phillip, in a way. Wondered what it would feel like to have parents sitting in the stands, cheering and supporting him.

CHAPTER 15

Joe wondered if everyone, at some point, experienced a pipedream—something they envisioned themselves doing during their life, not quite knowing where it might lead. Had he made it to *Games*, how different his life might have been. He wondered, too, if his father ever thought of those things for himself. Had his parents not stolen his money, his childhood been a little easier, with less of a burden to carry, would he have been a kinder, more understanding father?

His mind traveled even further, to a time when he sought out his father's approval, knowing that work in itself, with something to show for it, just might be his ticket. Not making it to *Games* was not the end of the world, he knew that now, and still, he would always wonder.

His senior year, Joe developed a new skill: woodworking. He started off making small things: a lock box, a bookshelf, a stool. Learning the different drills, the intricate tools, the wood grains and grades of sandpaper, how best to smooth edges or round corners—every bit of it intrigued him. In his final quarter, he wanted to build something spectacular, but what? Discussing his ideas at the dinner table, his father made a startling request.

"A dresser chest?" Joe formed the words with his lips, his curious eyes narrowed questioningly.

Nodding, his father pointed to the one in his bedroom. He wanted it a foot taller, with smaller, narrow drawers at the top; no more than two inches deep, for his antique watch collection. He sketched out a diagram of what he had in mind, with a pull-out tray in the center, lined with fabric, like the one he'd seen in a magazine. Its purpose was to catch the tiny watch pieces when he took them apart to repair them. Below the pull-out tray would be an opening for his high stool-chair. To the right, he boxed-out a row of drawers maybe six or eight, but deeper than the ones on top.

Joe allowed the idea to toss around in his head. It would definitely be a big project for sure. One surpassing anything he might have come up with himself. But he was not frightened of a challenge, not at all. In fact, it motivated his purpose.

For the following ten weeks in shop class, he sawed and shaved down boards. He glued, he nailed, and he sanded like a demon on a mission. There were errors he made, measurements not exactly accurate he insisted on redoing. It was not about building something that was good enough, he wanted it perfect. There were two wider drawers across the top that required a particular precision and a great deal of patience to attain that kind of preciseness. He would not settle for something that would work, but to create a dresser of quality.

Rather than deal with the standard drawer knobs, he chose a unique style that did not require knobs at all. This would alleviate the problem of a lost or broken knob that would later go missing, like several others they had in the house. After deliberating over his options, he decided on a curved opening at the top of each drawer, making it easy to slip in ones fingers to pull the drawer out. This required additional sanding with a coarser grade of paper to smooth each opening evenly. The drawer pulls alone took him a full two weeks to complete, before he was satisfied with the end product. Had he known the time it would involve, he would have opted for the knobs, but it was done now, and it looked damned good. He earned himself an A, along with recognition in the student council newsletter. Not only was it his toughest piece by far, but one that surpassed his own expectations.

When it came time to take the dresser home, he was full of anticipation. His father would surely be surprised, maybe even impressed, but Joe could not remember a time his father was ever impressed enough to praise his work.

"You have done a fantastic job, Joe," his shop teacher, Mr. Barnett, said. "The w-o-r-k-m-a-n-s-h-i-p alone and design are exceptional, one-of-a-kind. Your father is going to be mighty p-r-o-u-d of this. Mighty p-r-o-u-d."

Glowing from the compliment, Joe thanked him. The unit weighed a hefty one hundred fifty pounds. He borrowed soft, double-layered blankets from the lab to transport it in the back of his pick-up. Petro helped him load it up, and even showed the dresser off to a couple of his friends who stopped by to see the item his brother made that was worthy of the newsletter.

"Wow! You made that?" The two friends eyed the piece, long enough to see what Petro and others had been talking about. They gave Joe a thumbs-up. "Nice work. Really nice work."

Back at home, Petro helped Joe carry the unit in through the kitchen, to his parents' bedroom. They wiped it down to free it from dust and pollen. The unit smelled of fresh pine, still free of varnish. He considered a dark mahogany stain to match the other furniture, but chose to hold off, and let his father decide on the color. If the dresser were for him, he would choose a clear stain, one with a natural finish.

To be certain that nothing jarred loose on the drive home Joe opened and closed each drawer, one at a time. Each slid out and back with a smooth fluidity, as they were meant to. He stood there with a glazed expression and wondered if he could make a living doing this kind of work. There was no telling what a unit this size would sell for, but it took him roughly forty-five hours to complete. At ten dollars an hour, a decent wage, he thought, would come to four hundred and fifty dollars for the labor alone.

Joe was still standing there when his mother walked in from behind. The touch of her warm palm against his back startled him out of his daydream.

Her mouth dropped open, eyes went to shocked moons. "You made this?"

Joe nodded, pleased with her reaction. She opened and closed the drawers, just as he had minutes earlier.

"You did a good job, this is beautiful!" She lifted her right hand, paused a moment, to sign: "H-A-D-R-W-O-D-K"

Joe chuckled at her attempt, knew what she was trying to spell, helped her out by showing her first the sign for an 'R' versus the sign for a 'D'. The other letters, she'd gotten right. She was about to try it again, when his father stepped in the doorway.

"What's for dinner?" he asked, loosening up his tie when he noticed the extra piece of furniture in the room.

For weeks, Joe sanded steadily with smooth, even strokes, all the while envisioning his father's reaction. The dresser turned out even better than he could have hoped for. Thoughts of other projects entered his mind: a rack for his father's rifle and a swing set for their backyard.

"Look what he made," his mother said. "Isn't it wonderful?"

His father stepped closer, his expression blank, giving nothing away. Without a word, he touched the grain of the wood, opened and closed a drawer, a second, and then a third. His fingers slid along the curve of the drawer pulls to feel their softness.

Joe did not realize till then that he was holding his breath, waiting for his father's approval, any reaction or comment at all.

His mother smiled and, once again spelled the word, and correctly this time, H-A-R-D-W-O-R-K.

He knew just how much work was involved, right down to how many weeks, days, and hours. After what seemed like an eternity, his father gave an approving nod. Joe watched him closely, looking for clues, if there was something more, something he was not saying.

His father viewed all four sides of the dresser, stood back to examine it, and then directed his question to his mother.

"Ask him why he didn't stain it?"

His mother attempted to repeat the question, but Joe understood what was asked. Of all the positive things his father could see and have said about his efforts, he chose to mention what he felt was missing, and nothing about the quality or aptitude of his work. With a half shrug and a forced grin, Joe signed to them both. "Later, I can stain."

"Good," his father said, and then touched the smoothness of the wood one more time, offered him a second approving nod, before turning to his mother. "So, what's for dinner?"

CHAPTER 16

The thick sulfurous odor filled his lungs, waking him out of a dead sleep. There was no denying the smell and no adult person alive that did not know the scent of skunk. As if he didn't have enough to deal with, the added irritant was something more he would have to endure. If it kept him from feeling hungry, at least, he could reap some benefit, but the fact remained that his stomach felt empty, and it now demanded food. He was wavering into the wee hours of the morning, nearly a full day since his last meal. He had gone without food for a longer period of time when he was sick with flu and fever, and no appetite, but as he thought it over and accounted for the prior day, his steady movements required nourishment. His first-aid kit was usually stored with an energy bar in cases when he skipped a meal, or needed something extra to tie him over, but there was no point in thinking about that now. Joe pinched his nose to block out the stink. He wondered if the skunk came through the area or was run over in the road. In either case, the smell could linger for miles. There were folks that believed things usually happen in threes. If that were the case, his fall would certainly be number one, the snake bite number two, and the skunk stench number three. As bad as it reeked, it was nowhere near as bad as being sprayed. His neighbor Alex's schnauzer got sprayed that prior summer. The attack caused vomiting, swelling of the eyes, temporary blindness, and Alex a hefty vet bill. To make matters worse, the smell took more than a week to get rid of, and that was after trying every remedy in the book, from bathing the dog in tomato juice, to apple cider vinegar, to hydrogen peroxide.

Joe wondered again what Delia was doing. Was she in bed asleep or sitting up worried, wide awake, working a crossword puzzle? He thought of the years they spent together, the ups and downs, the reservations he had, and then back to the time they first met. If someone told him then that the two of them would be together now, he never would have believed it.

It was TGIF, the end of his work week, when Joe entered the local bar between his job site and home. There was nothing like an ice cold Michelob, while shooting a game of pool, to take the edge off. He was not a regular customer, or much of a drinker, in fact, but he enjoyed the break in monotony. Whether he met anyone new or not, won or lost a game, or simply spent his time people-watching, the acceptance among the patrons made it easy. He could sit quietly and not be bothered or place his quarter on the table to challenge the winner.

Tonight, he felt like playing. Over time, he'd gotten quite good at the game. He watched the two biker dudes duke it out, placing odds on the tall lanky one, with the big nose. He popped the striped ball in the corner pocket, followed by two more, one right after the other. Whether it was luck or skill, Joe watched him minutes later call his final pocket. He steadied the cue stick and then plucked the ball nice and easy, watched it land in the hole.

Joe had placed his quarter on the edge of the table mid-way through the game, so he racked them up. Same rules, different players. He lost the first game, but asked for a rematch. Thirty minutes later and two wins under his belt, he decided to quit while he was ahead. Big Nose shook his hand before walking away.

Joe was about to set the cue stick down, when a tall, slender woman, wearing cowboy boots placed a quarter on the table.

"Rack 'em up!" she told him.

Joe had never seen her before, and she didn't appear to be with anyone, but just to be certain she was talking to him, he hooked a thumb towards his chest, barely a whisper. "Me?"

Cowgirl tilted her head as if trying to size him up. "Sorry..." She extended her hand. "I'm Delia."

Joe was used to folks not knowing right off that he was deaf. Not that it took long for them to figure it out, especially when speaking was involved. As long as they looked at him directly when they spoke, he might make out some of what they were saying. Then again, reading lips was an acquired habit that came with its challenges. Not all lips formed words the same or moved alike. Hers, in particular, were thin and without lipstick, like the rest of her, simple and unpretentious. He liked that. A woman coated in heavy make-up was not his thing. He much preferred the earthy natural look. None of that *Silicon Valley* Cosmo stuff. It was one thing flipping through a magazine, where the women were dolled up and air brushed, some more curvaceous than others. Whether blonde, brunette, or redhead, most of them wore fake eyelashes and hair extensions, with breast implants and collagen lips. There was nothing wrong with that, if it was what a guy was into, some of them really went nuts over it. The bigger the better. *Eyecandy* was what they called it. Joe laughed the first time he heard the expression, wondered who came up with that one.

Eye-candy. It was an interesting concept for the idolizer.

Joe was not quite sure what Cowgirl's motive was, whether she actually enjoyed the game, wanted to learn, or if she might be hitting on him. Not that it mattered. He wasn't looking for a girlfriend or even a one-night stand. There were too many diseases out there, and not worth the risk. Whether or not anything went beyond the one game, Joe would not be asking for her phone number later. Girls were too needy. After a couple of dates, they assumed ties over you, wanting to label you as *theirs.* If they caught you talking or even smiling at another woman, it became a case of twenty questions, a cold shoulder or an attitude. Either that or they complained about you never taking them anywhere special. When he tried to explain that he didn't have that kind of money, that his Pontiac GTO needed new tires and a lube job, and that was just for starters, they seemed disappointed, as if he was letting them down. They just didn't get it, and he was tired of being made to feel as if he was not measuring up to their expectations. Dating, plain and simple, got to be expensive. One day, for sure, when he was in a better financial position, but right now, a girlfriend was the last thing on his mind. He had other priorities, like getting his own place, so that he could move out of his parents' home.

Cowgirl waited for his response, and he all but forgot he'd yet to introduce himself. There was something about her smile that seemed genuine. He might just have to go easy on her this game. He shrugged shy-like, took her hand in his.

"Joe." He restrained the strength of his grip, felt her gaze as he racked the balls, separating the solids from the stripes in rhythmic order, and then rolled the cue ball to the other end of the table, nodding for her to begin.

Delia stepped forward, chalked the tip of her cue stick, as she sized up her opponent, a smirk playing across her lips. She seemed comfortable and at ease in her own skin, as if she'd done this many times before. The sleeves of her faded denim shirt were rolled up to the elbow, the fabric loose against her chest. Her wrists were small and delicate, her nails unpolished and modestly trimmed. She wore no rings or bracelet, no jewelry at all, other than a plain wristwatch with a black leather band. She set the chalk down, flipped her dark hair over her shoulder, and then positioned her stance. From the edge of the pool table, her body leaned over, her hip cocked slightly. She rested the cue stick along the inside of her left thumb, slid it to and fro, and then paused to glance his way.

Joe stood silent, allowed her the time she needed, felt the heat of her stare pierce right through him. And then, BAM! She made the break. He watched them scatter around the table when a solid and then another dropped into opposing pockets. He pulled up a stool to lean against. He'd had girls approach him in the past, ones who did not even know how to hold a cue stick, let alone line up the ball properly. Cowgirl knew her way around a pool table. She assessed her possible moves and then lined up her next shot. She was no beginner, for sure. Whatever he was thinking before, Joe would give it his best. Besides, there was no such thing as a freebee in life. A win was something you earned. It wasn't just given away.

The two went back and forth. It was a close game, although she beat him fair and square. Afterward, they ordered themselves a beer, found a vacant table, and began exchanging notes using a paper napkin.

"How you spell your name?" Joe wrote. He knew it started with a "D" was all.

"Delia." She pronounced it again more slowly after printing it out.

Joe nodded, as the waiter set down their beers on the table, and since he had not yet eaten and was on his second bottle, he ordered himself a burger. Delia thanked the waiter, said she was good. She'd already had dinner at home. Someone fed the jukebox. Music pumped against the floorboards. He felt the vibration, curious to know more about Delia. The place was getting more crowded when he spotted people dancing.

"Do you dance?" Delia asked.

"No, I like better . . . watch."

"Me too." The two of them were drawn to a middle-aged couple that looked to be in their fifties. Both of them short and plump around the middle, their bellies pressed up against one another. The man, graying at the temples wrapped his arms loosely around the woman's waist. Hers were linked around his neck. Their bodies swayed to the tune of "In the Still of the Night," with eyes locked together in a sort of trance, as if they were the only two people in the room, and no one else mattered. There were others on the dance floor, moving to a quicker beat, but not this couple. Theirs was slow and precise, serious and dreamy-like, not a word spoken between them. When the song ended, he kissed her on the tip of her nose, and then gracefully spun her around, his eyes never leaving hers. The woman smiled, gave a little curtsy, and then the two of them, arm-and-arm, walked off to their table.

Joe turned back to Delia, who was just as entranced by the movements of the couple.

"Lovebirds," Delia said.

Joe gave her a quizzical look. "Love Bird?"

"Yeah. It's a saying," she scribbled on the napkin.

"Saying?" Joe was beginning to feel a bit awkward now.

"Lovebirds . . ." she said again, and wrote, "are brightly colored parrots that 'mate' for life and spend a lot of time sitting side-by-side." Delia looked up, shrugged with a smile, and spoke clearly while mimicking each of her words in an exaggerated, dramatic way. "When two people are always . . . holding hands . . . hugging . . . kissing . . . we call them Lovebirds."

Joe laughed at the way she described it all, in such an animated fashion, like a pantomime; he understood what she was saying. The waiter reappeared, set down Joe's burger and fries, and was off with a plate of food for some other customer. Joe added ketchup and salt to his fries, offered some to Delia.

"No, go ahead."

Between bites, Joe wondered how long she'd been playing pool, who had taught her, and if she was a regular customer here. Before he got a chance to ask her, someone nudged him on the shoulder.

"Hey," the guy said and began to sign, "I thought I recognize you. You look good. You been w-o-r-k-i-n-g out?"

"No. Just work c-o-n-s-t-r-u-c-t-i-o-n," Joe signed back. "T-i-l-e work with my brother. Busy all the time. What about you?"

"Same job, w-e-l-d-i-n-g." He looked across the bar area, then, from where someone was waving at him to come on. "Sorry, I have to go. Girlfriend r-e-a-d-y. Good to see you." He gave Delia a quick glance, and then told Joe, "See you later."

"You too." Joe turned back to Delia. "Friend," he told her, before finishing off his meal, taking a final slug of his beer to wash it down with, and then gave her a shy-like grin.

The bar was getting more crowded, and a new melody was coming from the jukebox.

"So, what kind of work do you do?" Delia asked.

Joe printed, "I work tile business with my brother Dominic."

"Ceramic tile?"

"Yeah. Some marble. Diff kind tile."

"Sounds interesting. Is Dominic older?"

Joe nodded, motioned he had three sisters and four brothers.

"Wow! Eight children? Your parents have been busy."

Joe chuckled. "Yeah. Busy all the time. Own beauty salon. Both work."

Delia gave a surprised look. "Your mother and father are both hair-dressers?"

"Yes. Both." Joe proceeded to tell her more. "Me and my brother Petro born deaf."

"Is either of your parents deaf?"

"No. Just me and my brother. He one-year younger than me."

"How old are you, Joe?"

"Twenty-two. You?"

Delia grinned. "How old do you think I am?"

Joe halfway shrugged, wasn't good with guesses, but knew she was older. "You tell me."

"I'm twenty-eight, soon to be twenty-nine."

Joe's eyebrows raised. He noticed the faded tan line on her finger, and decided to ask. "You married?"

"No. Divorced. Happily divorced."

"You have children?"

"Two girls—six and three."

Joe nodded. "What else?"

"What else, what?"

"What you like do for fun?" The dialogue and note exchange was a new experience for Joe. Aside from those with family or work-related questions, he was more accustomed to meeting girls from the deaf community, girls who spoke in sign. It surprised him that the exchange was not as awkward or uncomfortable as he might have thought.

"I like to shoot pool, and I read a lot. Mostly, I'm learning to speak five different languages. Oh, and my friends tell me I'm a bit of a hippie."

Joe laughed at her openness, imagined her sitting somewhere in a corner, barefoot; her legs crossed Indian-style, smoking marijuana with her hippie friends. "You speak five language? Really?"

Delia smiled and nodded. She seemed comfortable with herself, did not appear to be weighing her answers, or of what he might think of her.

"My mother speak French," Joe wrote. "Born Canada."

"Parlez-vous Francais?" Delia asked.

Joe gave a puzzled look.

"I'm sorry. That wasn't fair," Delia admitted. "I just asked you in French if you speak French."

Joe smirked. "No. Not me. Just sign. Where you learn shoot pool?"

"My ex-husband taught me. It was the one thing," she said, holding up her index finger, "the only thing we had in common."

Joe looked confused, passed Delia another napkin to write on.

"My ex had a big ego," she began. "When it came to pool," she flexed her muscles, puffed out her chest to describe the man, "after a lot of practice, I was beating him at his own game. That's why he left me." She held a straight face, a shrug of indifference.

Joe scowled questioningly, until Delia burst out laughing. She was kidding, of course. Joe could not help but notice the way her smile lit up her eyes like fireworks, the unpretentious way about her made her easy to be with. Communicating with notes and reading each other's lips was not as easy as signing.

It required time and patience on both sides, but Delia didn't seem to mind. There was suddenly a lull in the conversation. Folks were milling around, looking for an empty table in the over-crowded bar. It seemed the right time for Joe to make his exit. He reached in his back pocket to pull out his wallet and pay the bill. From the inside sleeve, he slipped out a small piece of paper and handed it to Delia.

She scanned over the images that were deaf signs of the alphabet. She seemed surprised, until she looked up again. "Thank you," she said. "It was nice meeting you."

"Welcome." Joe nodded, returning the smile. Not knowing what else to say, he gestured he was leaving and then headed toward the door.

On his drive home, he found himself thinking back over the evening. He liked meeting new people, getting to know their quirks and mannerisms, trying to figure them out just by watching and observing. People were funny. No two were exactly alike, and that included those he was related to. He enjoyed getting to know Delia and was glad she'd written her name down for him. It was one he'd never come across before. D-e-l-i-a. Admittedly, he never met a female who could shoot pool quite the way she did. The evening turned out to be a good one, and though he was glad to have met her, he had no illusions of seeing her again. He did not ask for her number, nor did she offer it, which was fine with him. It was better this way. His life was complicated enough, and even if it weren't, she was out of his league. As a mother of two small children, an educated, hearing woman—one who could not possibly understand the life of a deaf man, or that she would even want to, the idea of anything more than a casual acquaintance was not even worth entertaining. It took one to know one. Without that inexplicable likeness, one could not truly relate to the other.

CHAPTER 17

Joe crept alongside the tree trunk, a belly-crawl, easing his way carefully over broken branches and around the occasional stump. The matted leaves cushioned the ground, but also hid areas he needed to watch out for to keep from snagging against his splint that could potentially cause him another blackout. His mind leapt to areas of his past that he had long ago put to rest. Rather than shove it back away in a locked corner where it was best left kept, he used it as a means to keep from dwelling on the throbbing in his leg, a throbbing so brutal that nothing from his past could measure up to.

He could smell the fresh dirt now, wished he could quicken his pace, but knew that slow and steady was his best course of action. The trunk's roots were strung out everywhere in dry, mangled web-like shavings. As he rounded the grave-like hole from where the tree had fallen, he felt a sense of triumph—the thought of new life, from the dead and dying. He stopped moving, to rest a moment. He'd been going at it strong, and was tired now. He lowered his head, closed his eyes to take a break, and just like that, he was out.

"Get off your ass, and get to work!" his father blasted, surprising them all when he entered the kitchen. They thought he was at the salon.

It was Saturday, and the three of them—Joe, Petro, and Jeremy, their twelve-year-old nephew, who was spending the summer there from Tennessee to earn some money working with Dominic, were taking a lunch break. Dominic had agreed to spare Jeremy for the day to give the boys a hand to paint the exterior of their parents' home.

At the precise moment his father arrived, Joe stood at the kitchen sink, washing his hands. Petro was seated at the table, making himself a ham and cheese sandwich, while Jeremy was about to pop a frozen pizza in the oven.

"What the hell is going on here? You should be outside, painting!" he shouted, eyes dark and simmering.

The commotion caught Jeremy by surprise, caused him to freeze and then bolt for the nearest exit, taking his frozen pizza with him.

"Lunch time." Joe pointed to the clock on the wall that read 1:05 p.m. He stood there unflustered. His arms wide open, trying to figure out his old man, who was nearly a half foot shorter than he was. Joe had long ago come to realize the outbursts were unpredictable and could rear their ugly head at any point and time, and with no warning at all. His father mastered the role of intimidator, at least where his family was concerned, putting the fear in them since they were children. But Joe was no longer a child, and no longer frightened of him. He had stopped trying to please and impress his father to save himself from disappointment.

"What . . . problem?" Joe motioned, their eyes locked together.

When his father made no comment, Joe dried his hands, opened the refrigerator, pulled out the carton of milk and poured himself a glass. Petro completed the makings of his sandwich, and then took a bite.

Without another word, their father turned to leave, and then headed back out of the driveway.

"Where J-eremy?" Joe asked Petro. Neither of them saw him leave. After a quick look in each room, the two stuck their heads out the back door, to find their nephew, paint brush in hand, continuing where he'd left off.

Petro waved, cackling. "Come on in," he motioned. "Father gone." With his forefinger at his temple, Petro made a circular motion. "Grandpa crazy!"

Jeremy relaxed a bit, at least enough to go back inside. He returned to the bedroom just off the kitchen and retrieved his not-so-frozen pizza he'd hidden beneath the bed.

The boys, curiously watching him, hooted with laughter. "Why you hide pizza?"

"I don't know," Jeremy said, looking sheepish. "I didn't know what to do."

Joe stirred, half awake, didn't think he'd been out long and remembered the look of panic on Jeremy's face. He and Petro laughed about it at the time, but it wasn't the sort of feeling a grandson should have of the person he was meant to trust and look up to.

There were moments when his father had shown a different, more playful side, but for a three-year-old, it was impossible to know the difference. It was during one visit, following Micheline's divorce. Jeremy was sitting on the living room carpet quietly playing with his plastic toy animals. He held up a two-inch lion, examined it closely, when Grandpa sprawled himself out on his belly, watchfully observing him. Without warning, he leapt toward him with a vicious growl. Jeremy, who nearly jumped out of his skin, started wailing.

Micheline rushed through the doorway. "What happened?"

His father roared with laughter, but also hugged on Jeremy to show he meant no harm. "Grandpa scared me," he whimpered, wiping away the tears.

The following year, at the age of four, a similar incident occurred where Jeremy, oblivious of all others, was amusing himself on the living room carpet, again with his toy animals. Grandpa aimed to have a little fun with him, a repeat performance. He got down on all fours, crept towards Jeremy, his face all twisted, exposed teeth and a gritty growl in his throat. Jeremy froze when he saw him, fear taking hold, but just as quickly gave a hardy growl back, that surprised everyone. Jeremy still had the look of a frightened little boy, but when his grandpa and others in the room were laughing, Jeremy laughed too. "I scared Grandpa," he said proudly.

The sky above him, now black, was a canvas of glittering lights that reminded him of a time so long ago. He lay there, motionless, allowing his mind to float and drift, then settle to the time Micheline fell off the tractor, her leg caught over the lift bar, landing on her arm. Though he was young then, only seven or eight at the time, the memory stuck with him like a faded scar still visible to the eye.

"What the doctor say?" his father asked, irritated that the incident caused him to spend part of his weekend in the ER, waiting to see a doctor.

"It's not broken," Micheline said, her arm in a sling, looking tired and anything but relieved.

"Give me that Goddam arm," he told her. "I'll break it myself."

It was later, back at the house on the island, that he

complained it was a complete waste of time, when the x-rays proved the arm was sprained, and not broken. It was that night, Joe remembered, that Micheline chose to sleep outdoors with him, in the tent he pitched. When he asked her if her arm was hurting, all she could do was nod and swipe back the tears. To try and cheer her up, he turned on the flashlight, directed it toward the roof of the tent making animal shapes with his hand. Micheline watched for a time, saying nothing. After awhile, after tossing and turning, the two of them unzipped the front flap of the tent, scooted out to sit and gaze at the river. The brightness of the star-filled sky illuminated the thousands of tiny lights from the homes on the mainland. Joey noticed his sister cradling her arm. It was wrapped with a bandage from the edge of her knuckles to her elbow. There were tears rolling down her cheeks, as she stared off into the distance. Not knowing how to help her or what to say, he placed his hand on the center of her back, rested his head against her shoulder. Side-by-side, they sat for the longest time . . . just gazing at the river.

The memory served him well. And though there was no river now, no tent pitched to view it from; he knew that somehow . . . he would find the strength to keep going.

CHAPTER 18

Joe lifted his head, just long enough to remember why he set it down. He wasn't sure how much time had passed. For the moment, at least, the pain in his leg dulled, so long as he did not jar it, and his craving for water lessened. He wondered about the trailer, that he could no longer see the light. It gave him one more reason not to want to move. He rested a bit longer, his thoughts back to Delia, the one person he'd always been able to count on. Their chance meeting all those years ago, he never would have imagined the likelihood of a relationship developing, much less it coming this far. Though life, as he knew it, almost never turns out the way one might think it will.

It was ten weeks later, following the night they first met, when Joe spotted Delia at the bar. Their eye contact made an instant connection. She wore a blue and white striped blouse tucked into a thin-waist denim skirt, fringed at the bottom that fell just below the top of her cowboy boots. He wondered if she had a fondness for horses, or if they were just comfortable to wear.

She approached him, spelling the words quickly and perfectly, in sign. "Hi—how—are—you?"

Joe took a step back, he was blown away. His family, even, struggled with sign, those who still lived at home anyway and made an attempt to learn the language. His mother worked long hours at the salon, and when she wasn't there doing manicures or whatever, she was at home cooking and cleaning, any number of things. Rarely did Joe find her with idle time to learn the book of sign. Memorizing the alphabet was one thing, putting sentences and phrases together took work and practice, but at least she did make some effort.

"Wow, you can sign?" Seeing Delia again felt natural and as comfortable as when they first met. He didn't expect to run into her again, but he had thought about her. She was easy to talk to and he liked her sense of humor.

"My name is D-E-L-I-A," she spelled out, again effortlessly, and seemingly quite amused with his reaction.

"You learn fast," Joe told her, still blown away.

"I like learning l-a-n-g-u-a-g-e-s. I found me an A-S-L book at the l-i-b-r-a-r-y."

"How you know I speak A-S-L?"

"I asked around, and then saw an old school t-e-a-c-h-e-r one day. She has a f-r-i-e-n-d with a deaf child, and told me A-S-L is the most c-o-m-m-o-n."

Joe grinned, still tongue-tied. Delia was unlike anyone he'd ever met.

"It's been f-u-n. There's so much to learn though. It's not easy."

"You smart. Learn fast." They found them a table, shared a bit more about their week, their jobs, the upcoming holiday, and what plans they had in the works, with the help of swapping notes. Before he knew it, Delia checked her watch, said she had to go. When she stood to leave, Joe surprised her by asking for her number.

"You want my phone number? How does that work?"

"I have T-T-Y. Like phone t-y-p-e-w-r-i-t-e-r," he signed slower, to give her a chance at keeping up. "I type m-e-s-s-a-g-e. Someone . . . I mean . . . r-e-l-a-y . . . o-p-e-r-a-t-o-r tells you m-e-s-s-a-g-e. You talk back. I get print message."

"Oh! That sounds pretty simple. I don't need a T-T-Y?"

"No. If you have . . . more e-a-s-y . . . but . . . you no need."

It was how things got started. Soon after, the back and forth printed messages began. To avoid a misunderstanding of his intentions or have certain expectations of him he could not fulfill, Joe was straight with her from the start.

"I like talking to you . . . Delia. You not like other girls I know. Want know you better. But want be honest. I dont have much money for dates. Want save money and move out my parents home . . . find own apt soon maybe."

"I understand, Joe. Don't worry. With two daughters at home, I don't have the funds or the freedom to live the kind of lifestyle that other singles live. You know . . . concerts, late night parties with friends, things like that. I like spending time with you too."

"Yeah. I thought so. You learn sign. Make me feel good you want learn."

"I like to be challenged. Learning sign does that for me. I've always been that way. But I like getting to know you too."

"You different. I like that you different." Joe enjoyed the back and forth, not knowing what she might say next, feeling a stir inside.

"Maybe, if you want . . . you can come over some time, just hang out, or watch a movie. No strings attached, okay?"

"What mean . . . strings?"

"Oh . . . it means . . . I have no expectations. No pressure. Okay?"

"Sure. Same for me. No pressure. No strings."

"Okay, well . . . How about next weekend? You busy Saturday night?"

The first time he drove over to Delia's place, it was not anything like he might have imagined. She wasn't into girly things, had a relaxed sense of style, an odd assortment of antique furniture, with a child's playhouse in the living room, and a larger one out back. The place held a comfortable vibe to it, and the girls were already in bed by then, giving them time alone, with no distractions. He didn't know quite what to expect, had not told his mother, or anyone just yet, about Delia. There was no reason to, not when he still had some reservations about his involvement with a hearing woman, a divorced mother of two, who he feared might have a change of heart in the no-strings deal.

It wasn't until after that first evening together when they simply sat for hours, getting to know one another, that Joe felt those nagging reservations melt away. The give-and-take exchange was effortless, the conversation relaxed and natural, nothing was forced, that by the time he noticed it was well past eleven, he feared he had overstayed his welcome.

"Oh . . . sorry . . . late. I better go, let you go sleep." Joe stood, gave her a sheepish grin.

"It's okay, I needed this. It doesn't even feel this late, but the g-i-r-l-s, I'm sure, will have me up by s-e-v-e-n." Delia walked Joe to the door, and then turned to face him, her hand on his arm. "Thanks for coming by. I hope we can do this again soon."

Joe paused, picked up on the look in her eye, hoped that

MICHÈLE ISRAEL

he was reading her right, and then decided to just go for it. He leaned in to her, and she into him. The kiss was soft and tender, just like her lips were. He eased away gently, sensing the chemistry between them, which surprised him all the more.

"First time," he told her.

"First time you kissed a woman? No way!"

Joe gave a shy-like grin. "No. First time I kiss a h-e-a-r-i-n-g woman."

"Oh . . . and . . . ?"

"I like it."

"Me too."

Joe thought about that kiss on his drive home, tried not to read too much into it, but knew he would be seeing Delia again soon.

It was during his second time over, though, the topic of conversation got a little deeper.

"I like it when we're a-l-o-n-e like this, just us," Delia said, "no d-i-s-t-r-a-c-t-i-o-n-s like at the bar. When I'm home, at least until about 8 pm, I'm w-a-s-h-i-n-g dishes, giving the girls a b-a-t-h, picking up after them. I don't get much alone time, not like this."

"Me too. I get it. G-r-o-w-i-n-g up in a house full of brothers and sisters, no such thing as a-l-o-n-e time." He wondered then if she might ever want more children. It was not a topic he normally delved into, but something he felt strongly about, and better to clear the air now, rather than later.

"What are you thinking?" Delia asked.

"You want have more c-h-i-l-d-r-e-n?"

"No. I'm done having babies. My t-u-b-e-s are tied. What

♦ 150 ♦

about you?"

"No, not me. No want children."

"Oh?" Delia hesitated. "You don't like children?"

"No, I do like. My sister M-i-c-h-e-l-i-n-e has son, J-e-r-e-m-y. When he was little, I play with him, pull in w-a-g-o-n, give g-o-c-a-r-t ride. He older now, maybe ten, I think. Live in T-ennessee." Joe grinned, felt as if she was waiting for more. "I like children. Just . . . no want have baby."

Delia seemed content with his answer, did not press for more. From there, the relationship became more and more comfortable, their weekend nights more and more frequent. While Delia cooked them dinner, Joe made small repairs around the house. Other times, he'd pick up a pizza to give her a break or take them all out for a DQ. The girls liked that. The four of them, at times, would play a hand of *Steal the Old Man's Pack*, or a game of *Chutes and Ladders*.

After bath time, one night early on, Sarah padded her way back to the living room where Joe waited, her hair still wet with curly ringlets, her feet bare, wearing a pink nightgown with a rainbow on it. She handed Joe the book she held and then crawled her way up on the couch beside him.

"Sarah . . ." Chloe chided in her big-sister voice, "he can't read to you, he's deaf."

Joe understood, looked down at the book, its title: *Big Bird Says . . . A game to read and play.* He glanced to Sarah, who sat there patiently, smiling, waiting for the story to begin. Joe opened the book to the first page, and read the words to himself: *I know a game called "Big Bird Says," I'd like to play with you. Just follow me and read along. I'll tell you what to do.*

Big Bird says to touch your nose . . . Shut your eyes . . . Touch your toes . . . Touch the top of someone's head.

Joe pointed to Big Bird, began to flap his arms like a chicken. He then touched his nose. Sarah played along, flapped her little wings and touched her nose. Joe closed his eyes for a beat, and then opened them to find Sarah's were already closed. He lightly pinched her big toe, Sarah squealed with laughter, and then scooted off the couch to touch the tip of his boot. Joe patted the top of Sarah's head, and then lowered his own for her to pat his.

Chloe waved her hand to get Joe's attention. "She knows this story by heart."

Joe shrugged. He didn't mind. He flipped the page to continue on, enjoying the game, but Delia called for them, it was time for bed.

"Thank you for doing that," Delia said a few minutes later, after tucking the girls in. "Sarah loves being read to, and you h-a-n-d-l-e-d it perfectly. She loved it, but don't be surprised if she asks you again and again, even to read the same s-t-o-r-y."

Joe gave an easy smile. "I like story books too, when I was little. Even before I could read, I could understand the story sometimes from the p-i-c-t-u-r-e-s."

"I'm sorry about what C-h-l-o-e said."

"No problem. She no understand deaf have trouble talk, not read."

As time went on, Joe realized the more he got to know Delia, the more he saw that he liked. She was easy to hang out with, was not demanding or needy, did not complain if he needed to work, or even if he decided to do something with the guys, for a change. It became clear that the two of them wanted to spend more and more time together that Delia suggested he stay the weekend.

"You sure?" He asked, not wanting to get into the wrong kind of habit, make any promises he might not be able to fulfill, or feel obligated in any way to do so.

"Yes. It's fine."

"What your d-a-u-g-h-t-e-r-s think?"

"They're just kids, Joe. They're not going to j-u-d-g-e you," she teased.

This kind of longing for someone, it was all new to him, but he liked the way Delia made him feel about himself. She didn't take him for granted, always thanked him for even the little things he did for her, like replacing the broken hinge on the girls' toy box or smoothing down a drawer so that it would not stick. She would ask his opinion on newsworthy topics, remember what kinds of foods he liked, and she never made plans to include him without asking him first. Despite her not being a deaf girl, their different cultures, and the slight age gap, their relationship became as comfortable as the feathered pillows in the bed they shared. No longer could he deny the strong sense of belonging he felt, the deep understanding of one another, and that what they shared was all he needed.

Joe stopped at his parents' house to see Micheline, who was visiting from Tennessee. It was where she landed on her feet, with her son Jeremy, several years later, following her divorce. His folks were at the salon. Jeremy was spending the night with his cousins Kev and JayDog, leaving the house to him and Micheline.

"So . . . when are you getting married?" Micheline asked, getting right to the point.

Joe wasn't surprised that she knew about him and Delia. Since the time she left home, the few years during her marriage, they barely saw her at all. But after the split, she made annual visits back home, and was always one to write or call, and stay in touch.

"Never!" *Why do people always think marriage is next step?*

"Never?" Micheline repeated, looking puzzled now.

Joe shook his head, a sourly expression, and avoided eye contact. "No way!"

Micheline waved her hand to get his attention. "Why? You and Delia . . . together long time, two years, right?"

Joe gave a half-hearted shrug, focusing more on the paperclip he was toying with; his back leaned up against the counter. Her question made him uneasy. It was true that he and Delia were together for more than two years, and for the past ten months he'd been living at her place. Joe kept his eyes lowered, hoping for a change in topic, but he knew his sister was waiting for an answer. As much as he might have wanted to, he couldn't explain his reasons for feeling the way he did, any more than he could explain it to himself.

"Never!" he repeated. "I don't want get married, ever!"

"Do you want children one day?"

"No. Never!" He did not pause to answer; it was something he'd already thought through.

"Why?"

Joe shrugged. It was impossible to put into words a feeling, a desire, or lack of. Back in the old days, when his parents first met, their courtship was brief, and then the two were married. It was the way things were back then, when a wedding with someone you barely knew was more accepted than shacking up. Times are different now. It wasn't that he was knocking marriage for others, it was a person's right to follow their heart and hope that it didn't steer them in the wrong direction.

When Micheline did not press for more, Joe relaxed a bit. Maybe she sensed his reluctance to talk on the subject. He and Delia were happy with the way things were, it was all that mattered.

"What about you?" Joe asked, his lips forming the words with barely any sound at all. "You want more children?"

Micheline nodded. "I hope so. But . . . right now, nobody special," she hugged herself, "in my life. I don't want . . . baby before I get married first."

Joe understood. He knew she didn't have it easy, working two part-time jobs, in addition to the full-time one with the State. "You ever hear from D?" he asked, referring to her ex.

"No. But I keep in touch with his k-a-r-e-n-t-s." When Joe gave a confused look, Micheline scribbled on a piece of paper: *parents*.

Joe nodded, proceeded to show her the correct sign for a "P" verses a "K". He then positioned his right P-hand to his right temple, then to his chin to demonstrate the sign for *parents*.

"Like this?" Micheline made the sign.

Joe nodded, smiled, and then Micheline continued on. "Jeremy . . . visit . . . his grandparents every summer, and Christmas. They are good to us—me and Jeremy—it's not their f-a-u-l-t what D did."

"J-eremy see D?"

"No. Only his parents."

Joe was glad he wouldn't have to deal with those issues, glad he and Delia viewed things the same way. She'd already been down that road. They discussed it beforehand early on, to some degree, especially the subject of having children. It was something he knew with certainty he wanted none of his own. It was not a subject he went back and forth on and had nothing to do with the cost or responsibility involved, he simply did not feel equipped or paternal enough, and he knew that his parents, at least, did not have it easy raising deaf children. He made no apologies. When Delia told him about her tubes being tied, that there would be no more babies for her, he saw it as a match made in heaven.

CHAPTER 19

Back on course now, hoping the rest was enough to get him further, Joe kept his movements small, his head low, and to help shoulder the helplessness he felt inside, he kept his thoughts on Delia. Of all the people in his life, including family, she was the one who surprised him the most. When people say a committed relationship is not only work, but like a rollercoaster, with peaks and valleys and that adrenaline rush, he knew it to be true.

"Where is this relationship going?"

Joe froze. *What she mean, where it going?*

Delia stood in reverent silence a full ten seconds or more, before she spoke again. "Do you love me?"

"Yes," Joe answered calmly, but sensed trouble brewing.

"Then, why not t-i-e the k-n-o-t?"

The tying of a knot made him think of a noose around his neck. If that was what she wanted, to choke-hold him with a noose, she didn't know him as well as he thought she did. Things were fine the way they were. Delia had her job, he had his. He helped her pay the bills, mowed the lawn, repaired her car, what more did she want? It took him awhile to get adjusted, but her daughters were now used to having him around.

Sarah, the youngest, thought of him as more of a father figure, since her own was hardly in the picture. When Joe made no response, Delia opened her arms. Her demeanor was calm, but her eyes, full of questions, stayed on his face. He was beginning to feel backed into a corner, and he didn't like it. They had talked about this, hadn't they? So, what changed?

"I don't want get married," he told her finally. He saw the hurt in her eyes, the look of disappointment. "I love you. I am here for you. What's the problem?" Marriage was not what he signed up for. He made her no promises, which was why the subject never came up.

Until now, that is.

Joe shook his head, what more could he say? When Delia realized that was all she was going to get out of him, she turned on her heel, and without another word, she walked away.

Over the next few weeks, there was no more mention of marriage. *Good*, he thought. Things are fine the way they are. Why spoil that? But just as soon as he figured the matter was settled, Delia brought it back to the table.

"Joe, I want to talk and see where your mind is at with us getting married."

Why she want talk when I already tell her? Why she cause problem, make me feel bad—I never lie to her? Maybe someone put idea in her head. Delia didn't seem the marrying kind when he first met her. Her divorce should have been as clear as a huge billboard sign that marriage, more often than not, does not work. It was an old-fashioned concept that's been proven to fail over and over again, so what was the point? It only caused pain and bitterness in the end. This was not just him talking, but something his friend Jake told him one day, that one in three marriages end in divorce. A couple did not need to stand before a judge, recite some silly vows that sound good at the time, but then tossed aside at the first sign of trouble. And the cost of a diamond ring alone could set a man back for years. Joe was sure there were marriages that ended up failing long before the ring was even paid for. It was all some preconceived notion that a wedding ceremony was the expected happily-ever-after ending that was only true in Cinderella fairytales.

As far as Joe was concerned, he was with Delia because he wanted to be. It had nothing to do with an over-priced ring, a marriage certificate, or a sense of obligation. The important things were love and trust in one another, nothing more. He was only twenty-five, and yet he knew of half a dozen circumstances to back up his argument. Micheline, for one, after barely three years of marriage, was now raising her son alone, with no child-support or help whatsoever from her ex. He lied and betrayed her, and much worse, she said. She and Jeremy were better off without him in their lives. His true character became evident to everyone when he failed to even make contact with his son. Once he realized Micheline was done with him, when she stopped falling for his empty promises, his lies and verbal threats that he would harm her or someone in her family if she ever left, he gave up, moved on and made no further contact.

"Good riddance!" Micheline had said. Joe found it odd that she never blamed the *other woman,* that she wasn't even mad at her. "The blame is on him, not the woman he cheated with." Once she thought about it long enough, Micheline admitted that the other woman did her a favor. It was the final straw that gave her the strength and the courage to walk out of an abusive relationship, without a penny, without a job, or even a car to do it with. Where did her marriage certificate get her?

The more Joe thought about it, the more convinced he

became. Even Dominic, who was a baptized Jehovah's Witness since the age of fourteen, who took his vows seriously and married a woman of his faith, suffered years later at the hands of his then loony-tune-of-a-wife when she went manic psycho depressive on him. His divorce ended up costing him a hefty sum of money, a lot of heartache, and his dad's final words did not help the situation.

"I tried to tell ya, didn't I, she wouldn't go the distance?" Consumed with disappointment, Dominic gave a defeated nod. With a sneer of sarcasm, his father added, "The Lord works in mysterious ways," and with that came a hardy laugh.

Joe could think of many others who were burned by marriage. The one that stood out for him now was his good buddy Jake's Uncle Tom, whose bitter divorce left him drowning in debt.

"Between child s-u-p-p-o-r-t and a-l-i-m-o-n-y," Jake spewed over a beer they were having one night several months back, "Uncle T-o-m . . . ex-wife . . . m-a-x-e-d out credit cards, daughters' student l-o-a-n-s, car and health i-n-s-u-r-a-n-c-e— all on him!"

Joe asked, "How your uncle pay all that and his bills too?"

"Because N-e-w J-e-r-s-e-y law and some jackass attorney said so. My uncle wife was w-h-o-r-e around while he work his ass off, r-e-n-o-v-a-t-e their home, pay bills, and she only want spend—spend—spend. Get her n-a-i-l-s done, s-p-a treatment, shopping, trips to New York City, and go meet men like . . . like b-i-t-c-h in heat."

Joe had watched and listened, knew that Jake was hot over the whole mess. They became friends in their freshman year, in Trenton. He knew that Jake thought a lot of his uncle, that he was a good man, a good provider, and that he hated to see him getting screwed over like that.

"You think divorce s-e-t-t-l-e-m-e-n-t enough, right?" Jake continued. "But no, even after she marry again and happy, right . . . she take him to court—want more and more money. She lie. Greedy. Turn his daughters against him. She laugh and d-i-s-r-e-s-p-e-c-t him. She never be happy. Want r-u-i-n him."

"You think you ever marry, after that?" Joe asked.

"No way!" Jake paused a beat to consider the matter seriously, until his smirk gave him away. "If I meet beautiful woman, look like F-a-r-r-a-h F-a-w-c-e-t-t, maybe I change my mind. Don't let me do it."

"She old . . . almost f-o-r-t-y, I think?" Joe said, and then laughed. He wasn't sure how serious Jake was about not ever wanting to marry, but he certainly couldn't blame him if he didn't. Like his uncle, he was honest, worked hard, treated women with respect, and would never deserve what that woman put his uncle through.

The bottom line was that he loved Delia, he was good to her, and he knew that she loved him too. A lot of people don't even have that. Their relationship worked. He thought she agreed and assumed she understood. Only now, she was stirring up this whole business again. He was beginning to wonder if this was what all women did—they lured you in, agreed with your thoughts and ways, and then once you were hooked, they changed the rules on you. *Why she don't drop it?*

"What are you afraid of, Joe?" Delia asked, the creases in her brow more prominent.

"Look, you marry before, right? Look what happen!"

"Yeah, but he was a j-e-r-k! We never should have married. It's different with us."

"Yes . . . different . . . because we no marry. Better. We don't have to worry all that bullshit."

"Come on, Joe. It's not bullshit. It's what g-r-o-w-n-u-p-s do. It's called c-o-m-m-i-t-m-e-n-t."

"You not listen to me, Delia. Why you not listen? I told you, I don't want marry!" He blurted the words out as plainly as he could, his jaw squared, his body tense, and then he turned to leave, shoving the door open on his way out.

It was not until after Delia was in bed asleep that he returned home. He hoped that by now, she would have cooled off as he had, and leveled her thinking. She was a smart girl, and he liked that about her. Smart people could be reasoned with. Surely, she would see that he was right. Marriage was over-rated and old-fashioned, and when things did not work out, it made it that much harder to walk away, too many pieces to pick up, and then having to start all over again, while overcoming a sense of failure.

The next morning, Delia showered, dressed, and left for work. She never so much as looked his way. Joe pretended not to notice, pretended not to care. She would get over it, of that he was sure.

That night for dinner, Joe ate alone, and the one after that. Maybe, he thought, she needed some help to take the edge off. It had been a full week, after all.

He could feel the heat of her skin through her thin nightgown later that evening, when she lay beside him in bed. Their bodies were not touching, she made sure of that, though her presence enticed him in a way he could not deny. He thought of moving his foot to touch hers, to test her reaction, but knew her feet would be cold and run chills up his spine, and not the good kind. Instead, he rolled over onto his side, faced the back of her head and could smell the strawberry shampoo she used to wash her hair. He wanted to touch it, run his fingers through it, but resisted the urge. Instead, he eased himself an inch closer, remembering the time she asked him if there was a pocketknife in his pants or if he was just happy to see her. He didn't get the joke at first. There were some things that hearing people said in humor that flew over a deaf man's head. After she explained that a pocketknife, once open, doubles in size, in comparison to him being *happy* to see her, he laughed out loud. Until the time, that is, she got all twisted upset over him leaving his dirty clothes on the bathroom floor and his beard shavings in the sink; he used the joke on her to change her mood.

"Calm down," he told her, "if you want play with my pocketknife later." He thought the joke would be funny, because it was, but her stone-cold stare told him otherwise.

By now, Joe was so close to her body, he could feel her steady breathing. Gently, he slid his hand over her waist to scoot her up against him, but her body tensed up, stiff and unresponsive. He could tell she was not sleeping, nowhere close, but when he nudged her shoulder, she shook it away.

Fine! If this was what she wanted, he would never beg for her affection, not even for sex. He turned over, adjusted his pillow, and went to sleep.

For the next few days, they kept their distance. Joe too could be stubborn, and he was not budging, not on this issue. Delia didn't get to change the rules of their relationship just because she wanted to.

Finally, it was Saturday evening when Delia cooked them a nice dinner, a sit-down kind of meal, just the two of them. The food smelled incredible. He could see her through the kitchen door, taste-testing the gravy. She turned toward him with a smile that all was forgiven.

"Oh good, you're home," she said, and then leaned in for a kiss. "Dinner will be ready in twenty minutes."

Joe knew then that everything was going to be all right, feeling more relaxed than he'd felt all week. He showered out of his dirty clothes, made sure to place them in the hamper before slipping on a clean pair of shorts and a white T-shirt. When he saw the trash container in the kitchen, he scooped out the bag, tied it in a knot, and then replaced it with a new one. It was one of the simpler things he knew would make the rest of the evening go well. He dropped the full bag in the outside trash bin and then remembered to change the burned out light bulb from the motion sensor.

After putting the ladder away, careful not to get dirty, he hurried back inside to wash up. His timing was just right. The table was set, and Delia was transferring the steaming hot, mashed potatoes into a ceramic bowl.

"Where C-hloe . . . S-arah?"

"With my mom. It's just you and me."

Joe took his seat when he noticed for the first time she'd gone all out. There were grilled steaks and mushroom gravy, corn-on-the-cob with melted butter, all of his favorites. The crispy hot rolls were fresh out of the oven and the tossed salad was sprinkled with cucumber and diced tomatoes from their garden.

"Wow!" He brushed his hands together, ready to dig in.

Pleased with his response, Delia passed him the salt, knowing he liked to add some to his corn, while she preferred hers without. For several minutes, they ate in silence, while sharing the butter knife for the rolls or the dressing for the salad. Joe could not remember the last time he'd had a meal this good, where everything was hot and ready at just the right moment.

"This good!" he motioned, more with his eyes than anything else. He was busy chewing and savoring the taste. It was not often that she splurged on steaks when the cost alone was enough for them to have two nights' worth of chicken or meat-loaf for the four of them. He liked that she did not mind cooking, even with her full schedule and the kids. On his own, he could boil hotdogs or do burgers on the grill. That was about it, unless it came out of a cardboard box with instructions.

They chatted a bit about his day at work, keeping the conversation light and easy.

"The girls are spending the night with Mom, so we have the house to ourselves."

Joe raised an eyebrow, he knew what that meant. They could do it anywhere, anytime, and be as loud as they wanted.

When their bellies were full, Delia cleared the table, filled the kitchen sink with hot sudsy water to let the dishes soak, and then motioned for him to sit on the couch. Joe wondered if she wanted to watch a movie, and let their meal settle first. He reached for a toothpick from the stove, looked to see if she'd picked up something from Blockbusters, but the moment she sat down, he got the feeling something else was on her mind.

"Joe . . . we need to talk." Her expression turned serious. "First, let me say that I love you. That is not going to change. Please understand that I want to spend the rest of my life with you."

Joe listened, quietly. There was more she wanted to say, a lot more, he could sense it. She spoke calmly and gently, and yet he felt tightness in his chest grab hold of him.

"I know that you love me. It's not about that. I just need to feel that this relationship is going somewhere . . . toward a c-o-m-m-o-n g-o-a-l. I don't want to be forty-years-old one day and still have a live-in boyfriend."

Joe's heart sank.

"I don't want to fight about this. I just want you to think it over. Either we get married, or maybe . . . maybe it's best if we both move on and go our separate ways." Her eyes were clear and sobering, the most tender he'd ever seen them, and yet they were tearing him apart. But more than anything, he was stunned speechless. It was the last thing he expected her to say, today, or any other day. "You don't have to say a-n-y-t-h-i-n-g," she added, "just think about it."

CHAPTER 20

Joe awoke, gasping, as he lifted his head from the stench of sewage. He searched about, expecting to see what . . . that he was in bed, at home, with Delia beside him, sound asleep? But Delia wasn't there. No one was, just an empty grave-like hole in the solemn forest.

The moon had shifted lower, shedding light on the dirt-covered roots that were twisted and sprung out in every which way. There were gnarled remnants and jagged stumps in the hole, rocks and driftwood stained from the marsh. His heart raced when he remembered his insistent crawl along the length of the tree trunk, until finally he reached its end. He was cold now, so cold that he wondered if the temperature dropped into the thirties, despite the prior evening's forecast. It would not be the first time they'd gotten it wrong.

His fingers were numb, his elbows sore, and his shoulders ached deep within the rotator cuff. He rolled over to his back, rested his head on his rifle case. At least the damn thing was good for something. The sky was now a muted deeper blue. He wondered if he would be awake to watch the sunrise, or if there would even be any sun. He could barely move, but to keep from freezing to death, he used the edge of his knuckles to pry open his fingers, hold them, and then close them again. They were rigid from non-movement. To get the blood flowing he made a fist, held it tight, and then counted to ten.

He opened again, spread his fingers long and wide, lengthening the muscles from within. The moon provided just enough light that he could see his hands were caked in crusty filth. He made a fist again and then opened wide. With his hands near his mouth, he began to blow, while rubbing them together vigorously. With flattened palms, he repeated by blowing deep, long breaths over and over. He kept at it until a simmering of heat circulated and the blood flow returned, rolling his wrists around and around and then reversed the direction.

It made him think about the times he did warm-ups in PE, more than thirty-years ago. He loved participating in sports, whatever the season called for, but the warm-ups seemed to delay what he loved best. When Coach was not looking over his shoulder, Joe would skim through and fast-forward the stretches in order to spend more time on the important stuff, the stuff that got his adrenalin going. The stuff that gave him a natural high, like his long jumps, his shot-puts, and his javelin throws. The more he focused and practiced, the better he got. Until one cool morning after a long jump, Joe landed in the sand pit, doubled over from a sharp twinge in his leg. Coach came over to check out his injury, had him bend his knee, stretch out his leg, and then roll his ankle to make certain nothing was broken. The problem, Joe pointed out with a pained expression, was behind the thigh area.

"You pulled your h-a-m-s-t-r-i-n-g," Coach said. It was later that night, when Joe was icing it, that he recognized he had not been warming up his limbs enough. Cutting corners resulted in an injury that also cost him the ability to perform. Coach had been right about that, too.

With his fingers and hands now more pliable, Joe stretched his arms above his head and back down again. He opened them wide this time and then crossed them in front of his chest to hug himself. He repeated the process several more times, over his head, out, and then hug. Each set, he counted to ten. The heat stirred within him with each repeated cycle. When his upper body thawed, he proceeded with his lower limbs. So not to jar his injured leg, he carefully took hold of his left thigh, pointed and flexed the foot, and then moved it from side to side until he could roll the ankle slowly. He pointed and flexed, pointed and flexed again, over and over, and kept at it until his limb came alive.

Finally, he felt ready to get back onto his belly. The light from across the field, the one that guided him, was long gone now. Without it, he could no longer see the point from where the trailer stood. What he did see, just beyond the forest trees, was a dark muted shadow where the barn stood. Beside it, hidden, would be the bed of his truck, an estimated fifty or sixty yards away. That is, if he were able to go in a straight line, which up until this point was not the case. He began to snake his way around the stump pocket, the distance of a standard size trampoline, his bum leg dragging behind him like a hollow, deadened tree trunk. Attempting to move too quickly risked excruciating pain, when the splint he made would snag at objects along the way. The leg pulsated at times, slowing him down to a halt. Getting out of the woods was the ultimate goal, but losing his leg in the end was not an option. Realistically, he knew some of the dangers of putting off treating an injury such as the one he sustained. He'd seen the shattered bone tip protruding from his shin. The splint he fashioned to keep the leg straight allowed him the ability, in short increments, to crawl his way out; though with it cost him increased pain and random blackouts. There was bleeding, and no telling how much blood he'd lost. The amount of time he spent cold, wet, and dirty, created a higher risk of infection. He didn't need a medical license to know the seriousness of his situation. The leg had begun to swell immediately following the fall. Deprivation of water or any other kind of fluids merely compounded it all.

To get back on course, he blocked those thoughts now. He could not control the outcome any more than he could have controlled his tree-stand from collapsing. He was getting closer and closer to the edge of the forest, and once he got there, he would then find a way to make his way home to Delia.

Since the ultimatum, Joe had spent the past few weeks on edge, trying to figure out what he should do. The tension between him and Delia became unbearable. He understood, finally, the meaning of having *an elephant in the room*. That something so big and stifling stood between them, making it hard to breathe or think of anything else. Despite his convictions, he was torn. Did he want his cake and eat it too? He didn't think so. Micheline had said as much about her ex.

"What you mean . . . cake . . . eat it too?" Joe motioned the words, with an odd expression.

"It means he wants to be married," she pointed to her now ring-less finger, "and be single too."

"What you mean . . . he eat cake?"

"It's just a saying, that's all. Not a real cake. It's an expression," she spelled out on a scrap piece of paper. "He wants a wife (cake) and a girlfriend. He can't have both! If you eat the cake, the cake is gone, right? You don't have it anymore. That's why you can't have your cake, and eat it too."

Joe chuckled, made a circling motion with his finger at his right temple.

"I know it sounds crazy. Do you understand?"

Joe gave a light shrug; he wasn't sold on the part of the cake.

Micheline found a notepad, began to write: "It just means he wants both—to be married with all the benefits that come with marriage . . . and to date or sleep with other women. He can't have both."

"He tell you he want both?"

"No. He tells lies. He said he loves me. He wants only me. He can't live without me. He cries and wants another chance. Blah... Blah... Blah... All lies. And then he told his girlfriend lies too."

Joe got it. Her ex was a cheat.

He thought about that conversation now, knew he did not want to lose Delia, but marriage . . . marriage meant forever, a locked in sentence of *for better or worse*. How was he to know if what they shared now would remain the same and sustain them? What if Delia went psycho on him like Dominic's first wife, and how does one measure one's love for another person? These questions were a constant battle that he dealt with. Never would he have imagined it would come to this, an either-or ultimatum. He should have known that things were too good to be true, that nothing stays the same. That even in the midst of springtime, when the sun is plentiful and the temperature just right, a day would come when the clouds roll in, lightning would strike, and a storm would wreak havoc. Though true to her word, Delia allowed him time to think it over. She made her position clear. There was no room for negotiation and no room for compromise. She would have it her way, or they were done. He thought about it every day, while he sawed and hammered at work, his drives to and from, when he showered and even when he slept. He was no longer setting tile with his brother, and even if he were, it was not a topic of conversation he would ever share with Dominic. He knew what his advice would be, that the Bible was against couples living together, *fornicating* outside of marriage. While he believed that Delia had a right to what she wanted, he did too, and he was not going to be pressured into something he felt so strongly about.

Still, he felt the most conflicted when he came home at night. When he lay in bed beside her and throughout the night when he tossed and turned in a restless sleep, and felt the rise and fall of her breathing, the thought of losing her left him with an empty feeling inside. The girls looked to him as a father figure now, and he looked to them as part of his life, his family, and more than just a package deal. He didn't know why marriage, all of a sudden, was so important to her. Or that the act of the ritual, more than love and trust, suddenly became more of a guarantee of commitment, security and safety. All that *bullshit* she'd once called it, was now a deal-breaker.

Was he supposed to know at twenty-five how the rest of his life was to be mapped out? Could they not just enjoy being a couple and allow life to take them where it was meant to, naturally? Did falling in love and living together have to lead to a public display of husband and wife? Had he made a mistake by moving in, created a false sense of hope that ultimately led him to this either-or decision? If he was thirty-one, a single parent with two daughters, would he see things differently? But how could he when he was not those things? And why did everything have to be so complicated?

Agreeing to Delia's terms felt like a death sentence. The outcome of telling her 'no,' also felt like a death sentence. It was what he deliberated with for weeks. Back and forth his mind went. There were moments when he leaned more one way, and the next he was right back to the other side, where he started. He tried to picture his life without Delia in it. It was like losing a best friend in a fatal accident. Someone you grew to love and trust and depend on. Someone who had your back and understood you in ways your own family didn't. When he tried to picture himself as a husband, an image of a noose came to mind. His reality, though, was that he needed to make a decision. The back and forth was driving him up the wall, and he could not stand the thought of yet another day of the suffocating *elephant.*

"Okay," Joe finally told her, as they were getting ready for bed.

"Okay, what?"

"We get married."

"Really?" Delia's face lit up, her eyes did a little dance. She hugged him tight, kissed him on his cheek, his nose, his neck, and then, square on the mouth.

Joe laughed. It felt good to see her relaxed and happy again, damn good to have her in his arms, with an overwhelming sense of relief that he finally was able to make the decision that lingered between them for far too long.

"I love you!" Delia said, kissing him again. "I love you so much."

"Love you too." The words came straight from the heart and Joe meant them each and every time he said them. This would be a day he would always remember, one that would seal the fate of their future, the two of them together, with the girls. He was glad she hadn't poked and prodded him for an answer, so for that, he would have to own up to whatever the future held. Right or wrong, he wanted to believe that his decision was made for the right reasons.

But as he held her in his arms that night, after their

love-making, he could not shake the nagging feeling that it was all wrong and that he'd just sold his soul.

Joe stopped by the house to tell his family the news. His mother was alone in the kitchen, peeling potatoes; his timing just right.

"Me and Delia. . . marry soon."

"You are?" His mother smiled. "Congratulations!"

Joe smiled too, not really knowing what else to say. The news would get out soon enough. He wanted her to hear it from him first.

"Have you set a d-a-t-e?"

"No. Not yet."

"Do you want to tell your father . . . or want me to tell him?"

"Okay," he shrugged, "you tell him."

"Do you want to stay for dinner?"

"No. Want tell you news. What you cook?"

She paused a moment, proceeded to sign: q-o-r-k c-h-o-q-s

"What?" Joe made a face.

"Wait a minute. How do you make a 'P'?"

Joe showed her, with three of his fingers on his right hand.

"Oh, that's right. I get them mixed up." She tried it again, spelling p-o-r-k c-h-o-p-s.

Joe grinned, and then hugged her bye. He needed to go; said Delia would be expecting him.

During the next few weeks, Delia was busy making plans. She seemed to be on a fast track, as if the clock was ticking and time was running out. She found a justice of the peace, discussed available dates, food for the menu, a cake, and everything else women did to prepare for a wedding.

"Do you want a t-r-a-d-i-t-i-o-n-a-l white w-e-d-d-i-n-g cake?" Delia asked him one evening during dinner. "Or maybe c-h-o-c-o-l-a-t-e with c-r-e-a-m-cheese i-c-i-n-g?"

"Whatever you want . . . fine."

"I thought we could have something small here, in our b-a-c-k-y-a-r-d, just friends and family."

"Okay." Joe took another bite of his meatloaf, his gaze directed at the food on his plate.

Delia tapped the table. "When do want to go pick out rings?"

"I don't want ring. Just one for you."

"Why?"

"I don't like j-e-w-e-l-r-y, you know that. Did I get m-a-i-l today?"

"No. Just j-u-n-k, I think. It's on the c-o-u-n-t-e-r."

Joe finished off his plate, placed it in the sink, before sorting through the store coupons, the advertisements, and then he sliced open his car insurance bill to locate the premium he was expecting.

"Anything i-m-p-o-r-t-a-n-t?"

Joe frowned, and then signed. "My car i-n-s-u-r-a-n-c-e go up eighty-five dollars."

"Why?"

"My c-o-m-m-u-t-e to work over twenty m-i-l-e-s. New a-d-d-r-e-s-s here change."

"You can always do a price check. Or I can call my i-n-s-u-r-a-n-c-e and see what they would charge. Hey, guess what? After we marry, we can be on the same plan. Did you know they give d-i-s-c-o-u-n-t-s for married c-o-u-p-l-e-s?"

Joe dumped the junk mail in the trash, when Delia motioned for him to stop.

"Hey, save those c-o-u-p-o-n-s!" She told him, and then followed with a barrage of questions and assertions, reflecting her excitement of a bride-to-be. "What do you think about a t-h-e-m-e for the w-e-d-d-i-n-g? I need to buy i-n-v-i-t-a-t-i-o-n-s. Should we d-e-c-o-r-a-t-e the b-a-c-k-y-a-r-d? We don't have a lot of chairs. What if it rains? This house is too small to fit more than ten or twelve people c-o-m-f-o-r-t-a-b-l-y. I need to check on maybe r-e-n-t-i-n-g some f-o-l-d-i-n-g chairs."

Joe said nothing. She seemed to be having a good enough time all on her own. Whenever she asked his opinion about something, he felt annoyed by it. He wasn't trying to spoil her fun, but this was her idea, not his; she might as well pick out what she wanted. Choosing invitations, decorations, or the flavor of the cake, she could handle those things. And as for a *theme* or whatever the heck that was, he could not care less about. It was just a wedding, after all, not Mardi Gras. What he did wonder about, though, the one thing that bothered him now, was his lack of interest in the whole affair. Shouldn't he be excited right along with her? Was he not supposed to feel some sense of pride when his friends high-fived him with congratulations? Instead, he felt like a phony just going through the motions. Like a caged animal, he felt trapped. There were moments he cursed himself for getting suckered in, that he caved in like a cheap tent for the sole purpose of not losing her altogether. With a wedding happening, there would be no losing her or moving out, so what was his problem?

He should be happy that someone like Delia was choosing him to be married to, in spite of her first failed marriage. She didn't seem to be worried about repeating a mistake, so why was he? Even if he were to change his mind, did he want to move back home with his parents? No way! Besides, he made the decision so not to lose Delia. Brooding, worry, and second-guessing would accomplish nothing. He made his choice, he was stuck now. There was no turning back.

CHAPTER 21

The shadow of the barn loomed closer and closer, and so did everything else. The trees, the sky, the forest, the air—all of it was closing in on him. The mold and smell of the rotted wood seeped in through his nostrils, his mouth, and his ears. The gunk caked under his fingernails made it impossible to rub his eyes or pinch his nose to block out the stench. He started to cough, the rancid odor stuck in his throat, over and over again. His body shuddered, and then pain so piercing it was as though a nail gun were being used inside his leg. Joe cringed, prayed for it to stop. His eyes began to tear and his nose leaked fluid. He swiped at it with his sleeve, when it dripped to his lips, the taste of a coppery substance, the taste of blood. He rolled over to his back, pinched the bridge of his nose, rested his head and waited. To steady the drumming in his chest, he took in deep, slow breaths through his nose, blowing air out of his mouth. He could no longer guess how much time had passed, his thoughts were blurred and his fear bone-deep, it made him irrational. Time was running out, and he knew it, like a ticking time-bomb staring him in the face.

Tick . . . Tick . . . Tick . . .

The swelling of his leg against the ties of his splint caused immense pressure. He wanted so badly to loosen them, but to do so would risk having them break apart, endangering his situation further. The area was saturated with bloody, crusted mud that even if he could loosen the ties and stomach doing so, the end result could be disastrous.

He lay there for what seemed like a long time, having slept some. His eyes were wide open now; the sky in focus was looking down at him, soothing and caressing like a mother cradles her newborn. He was no longer sleepy and for the moment the throbbing lessened, so he took it as a sign to keep going.

While owning the pain, overcoming it, he placed one elbow forward and then another, one stroke at a time, like a master of self-will and discipline. Attempting to move too quickly could cause him another blackout. It was not just a matter of will to keep moving, but one of good sense and logic to pace himself. He worried that next time he might not wake up, that there may not be a next time where he would see the light of day. His truck was up ahead. *A little closer now, isn't it?* He inched his way, used his battered, achy arms and his good leg to do all the work. The inside of his left knee and thigh were noticeably raw and chafed from the rubbing of his wet trousers. The cold and stiffness of the material each time he stopped moving and then started up again was like grinding salt into a rug burn, causing it to blister and bleed over and over. If only he could shift his weight somehow, change his position, relieve some of the strain and pressure that resulted from the same repetitive movements, it might help. But short of reaching his destination, there was no other way of accomplishing that. There was no point in torturing himself endlessly with *if only* . . . his regrets of what he could have or should have done, had he known. So he dug in and kept on. All the while he pleaded for strength, begging for his body to keep going, imploring his mind to hang in there and not fail him. In his head, he talked himself through it.

There was no way to know how much longer he needed to

go, or at what point the moon shifted. He didn't stop to check, just placed one arm in front of the other, his left knee bent with his leg at an angle, he pushed, and he slithered, pushed and slithered again in slow, repetitive movements, his useless bum leg being dragged along. Until . . . something changed . . . his mind began to clock out . . . and his body stopped responding. He had enough sense left, just barely, to know what was happening. It was all he could do to keep from bursting into tears, but even that took strength that he did not have. There was a time to work and a time to rest. He'd had the good sense to know the difference, but that was before, and now his brain would not compute the message.

Where my truck?

What happen to light?

He could no longer see through the misty fog, a fog that just suddenly appeared. The shadow of the barn vanished, swallowed up by a fierce, dusty wind.

Something wrong.

I can't see.

What happen to me?

He didn't want to stop, didn't want to believe it, but his mind and his body and all the nerve endings in his fingers were shutting down, like a thunderclap taking out the power. No longer was he in control. His faculties were being stripped from him and his head was now flooded with people's faces, pixilated pieces flashed, both near and far.

You can do this! Coach said.

Delia was looking out the window, scowling.

Jester and Prince scratched at the door, wanting to be let out.

A set of white headlights passed by so fast that the air pressure changed.

A pair of bald eagles flew off in the distant.

His tree-stand collapsed beneath him.

Delia exploded through the door. *Where have you been? Keep your eye on the prize!*

His mother shouted: *Stop! Go back!*

His body tumbled into a free-fall, from a cliff, into a river, and then landed in a hole-like grave, in the middle of nowhere.

The scene changed when his family trickled in to a darkened room full of people. His mother and father were speaking to some of their relatives Joe had not seen in a very long time, a good thirty-some-odd-years or more. His brothers and sisters congregated in hushed whispers, all with solemn faces and reddened eyes. Uncle Willie and Aunt Carol were there. He recognized some of his cousins from Canada, though he could not remember most of their names. There were so many people, work buddies and friends, neighbors and acquaintances, some of them crying. Joe arrived late so he was clueless. He looked around for Delia. They must have driven separate cars.

Someone die?

He followed the line of people, though no one approached him or seemed to notice him. They were all too busy, too absorbed in their own private conversations to even acknowledge him. Even those who looked his way were too lost, too upset to even say, *Hey, how ya doing?* Instead, they seemed to look right through him. But maybe now was not the time for idle chit-chat and catching up. There would be time enough for that later.

Eventually, Joe reached the front of the line. With the others having cleared the way, he saw the open, padded casket. There, inside the coffin lay his body. He was dressed in a dark suit and tie, which struck him as odd. He didn't even own a suit. His face and hands were clean and unblemished, not a single scratch on him. Someone, he suspected, had put what looked like make-up beneath his eyes to cover the dark circles.

Stunned and speechless, Joe wanted to shout.

This mistake!

I not dead!

I rest. Take break.

I pace myself.

Don't you know by now I not give up?

I never give up.

This mistake.

Stupid, stupid mistake!

Wait!

I not dead!

Oddly enough, the scene changed again. Joe was back in the woods, his body light as a feather with nothing to hold him down. He floated from a slight distance away, watched the shell of a man work his way along the murky ground with its purposeful gait, a nearly dead man crawling. The sight of him made the hair on the back of his neck rise. His movements were slow and restrained, painful to watch, until he stopped and ceased moving altogether. All at once, patches of fog appeared, thick and wet that made it difficult to see. Joe wanted to pick up the motionless man, carry him to safety. But when he reached through the hazy mist to find him, no one was there.

Tick . . . Tick . . . Tick . . .

It was late and long after the girls were put to bed and the TV turned off that Joe lay beside Delia, unable to sleep. The room was dark, all but the light from the full moon that seeped in through the open window. It cast a hue of dark blue against the walls that moved about, when the slightest breeze flickered at the curtain. It was what caught his attention and relaxed him finally, after he tossed and turned, trying to get comfortable. Delia, too, had a twitch in her leg. One moment she hogged the covers, the next, she flung them off as if she were burning up. On any other night, Joe might have asked her what was wrong. If anything, she should be sleeping soundly. He was the one whose life was about to change, *for better or worse*. It was a turning point he never saw coming and could not have possibly predicted. Though as much as he tried, he could not shake the sinking feeling of regret.

The lamp beside Delia was suddenly switched on. When no other movement was made, Joe turned to see what was up.

"You don't really want to get married, do you?"

Afraid to respond, to say anything, Joe wondered what caused her to ask the question. He was afraid it was one of those trick questions that either way he answered would develop into an argument. To be safe, he said nothing, nothing at all.

"Do you s-t-i-l-l love me?"

Joe brushed his fingers through his hair, took in a deep breath, and then nodded. Of course he loved her. It was the reason he agreed to get married in the first place, the reason he was with her now. His feelings toward her in that respect had not changed. But not knowing what more to say, he waited for her to continue.

"I don't want you to feel you have to marry me. I can tell you're just going through the m-o-t-i-o-n-s, I can feel it."

He watched as she drew a long breath. She was sitting up now, her foot curled beneath her and her fingers caressing the little black hairs below his navel.

"It's no fun being the o-n-l-y one who's excited about this w-e-d-d-i-n-g." He saw the sadness in her eyes, no tears, just sadness. "I don't want to lose you, Joe. And I love you too much to force you into something you're not r-e-a-d-y for. So be honest with me, okay? You don't really want to get married, do you?"

Joe felt a knot in his chest. She was being honest with him, completely and utterly honest. She deserved the same from him. Without a word, he took her hand in his and felt its softness, and then he slowly shook his head.

"Then we won't do it."

Joe's hand ceased moving. It was not what he expected her to say, not the Delia he knew. *She serious?* Was she letting him off the hook?

The burden he carried for weeks lightened, but not by much. He thought he would feel like a million bucks, but he didn't. He wanted to take her in his arms and kiss her, but he couldn't move.

"I hope . . ." Delia began, "one day you'll change your mind and want this as much as I do, because I do love you, Joe. I always will." She leaned over, kissed him lightly on the lips, and then switched off the light before laying back down again.

In the dark, with nothing more than the flicker of the curtain from the nighttime air, they cuddled closer, with Delia's head nestled between Joe's arm and his chest. It was the answer Joe was searching for, the perfect solution. And yet . . . he could only wonder what just happened?

CHAPTER 22

The sleeve of his double-layered thermal pullover was being torn to shreds, exposing his arm to the cold. Teeth so sharp they ripped at his skin, tearing a chunk of his flesh. The attack was so sudden that it jerked him to his senses, prepared to defend himself. His fists thrashed about like a madman, pounding against the sides of the wolf's head, causing it to retreat, at least for the moment. Had he seen them coming, Joe would have had his gun out of its case, ready to pull the trigger; it was what he saved his bullets for. But these were red wolves, and there were two of them. They were thickly built canines with a massive head and chest, their legs long and sturdy enough to seize upon whatever they set their mind to. On a good day, Joe was no match for either of them, not without a weapon to give him half a chance. He kept his eyes on them while he inched his way to his rifle, relieved to have some form of protection, but the strap was caught on something beneath him. With his free hand, he attempted to locate the problem when they hovered over him again. The two of them growled. Their upper lip pulled back in a sneer, baring their purplish gums and yellowed fangs. Joe froze, ceased what he set out to, his chest knotted and hammered away.

Don't show them fear. It was a rule he knew. If he were able to run, they would take him down in seconds and make a meal out of him. If he moved too fast and they felt threatened, they would attack him on the spot. To ease back and make no movement at all, while keeping them within his line of vision was his only shot at survival. It would buy him time to get control of his rifle. If he made a move to shoot, his aim had better be good. Even so, he could kill only one of them at a time. The other would be quick to seek vengeance. Joe watched them with a steady gaze and wondered if once they got a real good look at him, his scent alone would make them reconsider. He was, after all, covered in mud and day-old dried up blood and sweat, and could only imagine that he smelled anything but human.

As if they were assessing this odd-looking creature before them, the wolves backed off a bit, curiously probing the scene. One circled around him and then stopped to sniff and prod at his splinted leg.

No . . . God, please . . . don't let him do it.

Would the smell of blood entice them? Joe winced at the thought. And then the second wolf joined in to sniff at his boot, his old broken laces, and within the confines of his splint. If they were to suddenly claw at his leg, he would want to be put out of his misery sooner than later, but he was not ready to die. The thought of making even the slightest wrong move, Joe could barely breathe.

He knew little about wolves, not enough to guess their next move, anyway. But he knew enough not to take any crazy chances by shouting or swinging his case at them to get away. They were in charge. To undermine them or underestimate their capability would be foolish. He figured that one of two things would happen. They would either make a dead man out of him or they would turn and go away. He was hoping for the latter, but prepared for the worst. Preoccupied with their sniffing and frolicking, a sort of tribal dance, Joe shifted an inch, maybe two. He reached his right hand back, searching blindly for the zipper of the case that was lodged beneath his hip. Readjusting his weight could cause too much movement, enough to threaten the wolves further. For the time being, they seemed complacent, he didn't want to change that. They appeared to be at a crossroad—go in for the kill or move on to what they normally sought after. Maybe he was not worth their trouble. Then again, how much trouble could a crippled man be? If the thrill of the hunt was part of the conquest and the challenge itself was what drove them, was it possible that his life could be spared? Time stood still and his heart continued to race. His gaze never left their sight when he lifted his hip, just enough to dislodge the strap. He eased the case alongside him, in slow, microscopic movements, and then swallowed the saliva that formed in his mouth. It was strange, their behavior, not at all what he might have expected. He was not about to question why they were stalling, or what their intentions might be.

Wolves, for the most part, hunted smaller, ground-dwelling animals such as rabbits and raccoons. The red wolf was also known to travel in packs, in order to hunt deer. Thumbing through a *National Geographic* one day, Joe noted they were regarded as the tenth most endangered species in the world.

The female wolf nipped at the other to get out of her way. But when the male growled back, Joe realized he was dealing with two dominants, which made his predicament all the worse. Without steering his eyes away, he began to unzip the case, with barely enough movement to draw their attention. But at the sound of metal, he supposed, the female ceased what she was doing, her head jerked towards his hand. Ears ramrod, darted up, she growled. Adrenaline rushed through his veins. Joe froze. His hand was halfway into the gun case when the male wolf came sniffing and clawing to get at what was inside.

He needed to react now, and fast, before it was too late. With his free hand, he located a small block of driftwood, slung it as far as he could, to distract their attention elsewhere. Their heads snapped to the area it landed, intrigued enough to ease away. It was then that Joe made his move. He whipped out the rifle, shoved his finger inside the lever, and aimed the barrel at the two.

The wolves stopped to look back, their snarling jaws frothing at the mouth as they changed their direction. Joe struggled to steady his aim, to focus his blurred targets, first for the male, the larger of the two, and then to the other that got in the way. He could not afford to miss his mark. He needed to get it right. And then something peculiar happened, that caused him to wait.

The female wolf sat on her hind legs, her head and ears pulled back, her snout open, aimed at the sky, she began to howl. The male joined in with her, their eyes closed, the two of them wailed.

Joe now had a clear shot, he could shoot one and then the other, but his chest pounded a word of warning. Were they trying to make peace, or was it just wishful thinking? He could no longer think straight, and there was something else too, he didn't know what, but it kept him from pulling the trigger. The barrel of the gun wavered slightly, his hand shook, hesitated . . . when it came to him. He remembered now, reading something about the howl of wolves. It was a way for them to communicate with others of their kind, possibly when in distress, or . . . was it when they lost track of one another? It was long ago, though the reason why was not important. Not enough to miss his chance of freeing himself before it was too late. It was a gamble, and he knew it.

The persistent howls continued. They were in their world now, ignoring him altogether. Joe aimed at the head of the male and then pulled the trigger hard. Only, it misfired. Without hesitation he quickly re-chambered the round, aimed again, when he felt a slight tremble in the forest, a shifting of air, and then he saw them . . . the approaching stampede of wolves. His chest hitched, but he went for it and pulled the trigger, firing twice. First at the male, and then at the female, the two slumped to the ground. But the charging lot was closing in on him, and he was down to one remaining bullet.

Joe braced himself for what would happen next. Within seconds, he would either be trampled to death or eaten alive. Their opened jaws rushed at him all at once, eager to devour him limb by limb. He screamed an anguished cry, begged a silent plea, and with his final thoughts of Delia, he pointed the barrel of the gun toward his own chest.

Weeks passed since the turning of the tide, the presiding pressure and weight of it all, with Delia's sudden change of heart. At first, Joe thought it too good to be true, to be given a pass just like that, a *Get Out of Jail Free* card. The question was, for how long? In the days that followed, the weight of doom slowly dissipated, and life continued on as it had before. The subject matter was not mentioned, not since that very night. At the time, Joe feared that Delia, in her own way, would hold it against him, look at him differently, become bitter, and make him feel guilty. For the first several days, Joe spent much of his time in a funk, trying to figure out how long this reprieve would last. His stomach cramped at the very thought of her bringing up the topic of marriage again. He loved their life as it was. He didn't want to lose Delia . . . or her daughters. He remembered the time, early on, when he caught Sarah washing her doll's hair in the toilet, suds floating over the top of the bowl, a near empty shampoo bottle on the floor, with water everywhere.

"Nooo!" Joe scolded when he found her. Sarah stopped immediately, a frozen expression, her lower lip quivered and tears welled up in her eyes. He didn't mean to scare her, nor did he want her running off squalling to her mother. To reassure her, he squatted down to her size, and with a hand towel, he wrapped it around his head like a kerchief, holding the ends together beneath his chin. He blinked his eyes rapidly, gave her a cockeyed grin. Sarah giggled, and then tried to pull his makeshift head-wrap down over his eyes, but Joe flipped it off and placed it gently on top of her head. She pinched the bottoms together with her tiny little fingers, blinked quickly to mimic the way he'd done. The two of them burst out laughing.

"What is going on?" Delia asked from the doorway. "Oh my God, what happened to your baby doll, Sarah?"

Sarah picked up the forgotten doll, its tangled hair in disarray, clothes wet and sopping, and handed it over to her mother. She then removed the hand towel from her head and in a feeble attempt wiped up the water from the floor.

"She s-h-a-m-p-o-o doll in toilet," Joe told Delia, "should be clean now." He smirked, handing her the near empty bottle of strawberry fragrance.

Joe smiled at the memory. Whether or not he was cut out to be a dad was not the issue, he came from a family with a history of problems, and not just deafness. His parents later learned, well after the birth of their eighth and final child, after he and Petro were tested and diagnosed, that Jena, too, born the year prior to them, lacked hearing in her right ear. It was not until his high-school days that Joe sought out answers.

"Mom," he motioned, "why we deaf, me and Petro? You and Dad not deaf."

His mother pondered a moment before answering, perhaps surprised at the question that never came up before, at least not where he was concerned enough to ask for specifics. She reached for a notepad and printed the words carefully in block letters: WAARDENBURG SYNDROME. "Go to the library," she said, "you can read and understand better."

It was there that Joe learned that one in forty-thousand people was affected by Waardenburg syndrome. The most common side effects of Type I and Type II were wide-set eyes with a disturbance in the iris of the eye, bushy eyebrows that connected in the middle, a patch of white or premature gray, and either partial or permanent hearing loss. It was considered genetic, usually inherited; in most cases the affected person had one parent with the condition.

One parent? Joe pondered the matter while mentally forming an image of his mother and father, and then his brothers and sisters. Micheline and Dominic shared none of those symptoms, and as far as he could tell, neither did Alanzo and Stefano. He was never told of a family history of deafness on either side, none that anyone was aware of.

Later that evening, with all of them at the dinner table, Joe concentrated more closely on his mother's features. Her skin was of fair complexion, dusted with freckles across her cheeks and nose; her eyes were brown and her eyebrows ordinary. At the age of forty-four, she showed no signs of graying. Susanna and Jena, sitting side-by-side across from him, bore remarkable similarities to one another, unlike their mother. From their somewhat shorter, stout stature to their thick, connecting eyebrows and wide-set eyes, even their fingers were exactly alike. It was then Joe became aware of Susanna, who at eighteen had a tiny forelock of white hairs in her bangs. One might have thought she'd carelessly swiped it with a brush of paint, and yet until now, he never noticed it before.

Joe reached for the bowl of mashed potatoes, took a generous helping before setting it down again. Inheriting certain traits of his parents, such as eye and skin color, features of the nose, ears, and bone structure, were to be expected. It was also reasonable to believe that when a certain disease ran in the family, even one of a skipped generation; it increased his chances of contracting it at some point in his life. But to share a *syndrome* with a specific name and type that laid out all the details, to learn of it now, with no explanation what caused it, other than a case of bad luck, a one-in-forty-thousand chance, where four of the eight children having symptoms, three of them having partial or total deafness increased those odds significantly. There were rarer types, as well, Type III and Type IV, that caused changes in skin pigmentation, abnormalities in upper limbs, even life-threatening symptoms that required surgery. The list went from bad to worse, and yet there was always a worse scenario, and for that, Joe considered himself on the not so unlucky side of things. He could not miss what he never had to begin with, nor did he see himself as being handicapped. Those kinds of words were merely labels that hearing people came up with to identify those different from themselves. Being deaf was no more of a handicap in the hearing world as a hearing person would be in the deaf community. Living in silence was his norm, which came with some advantages—advantages that a hearing person could no more identify with than he could in their world of noises and sounds. To have never experienced things like sky-diving or parasailing, traveling to Italy or Greece or the Grand Canyon, a person could only go by what they read in magazines, watched in videos or on TV, or of what they were told by someone who had. It would be like trying to describe a rainbow to a blind man who is only familiar with shades of gray. Color had no more meaning to a blind man than sound did to the deaf.

Joe picked at his food when his father said something to his mother. Not until she answered, did he know what exactly.

"Yes, there's cake, do you want some?"

When his father nodded, his mother retrieved the upside-down pineapple cake from the dishwasher, the place she used to store their breads and other treats. Since the time they moved to the new house, eight years earlier, it was never used as its intended purpose because it would increase the water bill, his mother would say. But Joe was not thinking about that now. He all but forgot his half-eaten plate of food, the dessert that would come after, or what anyone may be saying or doing. Instead, he studied the finer details of his father's features. Aside from the fuller cheeks that held pockmarks, his connecting eyebrows and wide-set eyes matched his own. At the temple, there was also a patch of gray he assumed up until now was a sign of aging. He must have been staring a little too conspicuously.

"What you looking at?" his father snapped.

"Eyes," Joe said, and then pointed to his own.

"What about my eyes?"

"C-o-l-o-r," Joe spelled out in sign.

"What's he saying?"

Having understood the question, Joe, with the use of his thumbs and forefingers, stretched open his eyes and stared directly at his father.

His father set his fork aside, curled his lower lip down and his tongue upward over his top lip, mimicking the face of a baboon, while also spreading his eyes wide open, exposing a set of bulging pupils to the point that everyone laughed.

Joe laughed too, but more importantly, he saw and understood finally. His father's eyes were not of the same color. One was a pale shade of blue. The other held a patch of brown in the iris.

Before telling his mother the news, Joe waited a few weeks before doing so. Not due to uncertainties of the change in plans, but to put off the questions he knew would follow.

"We cancel w-e-d-d-i-n-g," he told her.

"Why . . . what happened?" His mother's expression was serious, more one of concern, but he was glad that no one else was around. She could fill the others in later.

Joe scratched the back of his neck, not having given it much thought what he would say, though he wanted to be honest. "I not r-e-a-d-y." He gave a brief shrug, not wanting to go into all of the reasons, or admit the possibility he may never feel differently.

"Oh." His mother gave a sober look. "Is everything okay?"

He nodded, before lowering his gaze. His mother's eyes searched his own; he could feel her watching him, trying to read him. She placed her palm on his arm, gave it a squeeze.

"D-elia want marry." He paused. "Not me." He motioned with his hand that he did not know why or how to explain it.

"Are you happy?"

"Yes. Happy. I love D-elia. Just . . . I don't know."

"It's okay. You're still young. Twenty-five is young."

"How old . . . you and Dad . . . marry?"

"Umm...," she grinned. "I was twenty-one. Dad, twenty-two. That's too young."

Joe agreed, and then took in a deep sigh. "You sorry . . . get marry?"

"No." His mother looked away briefly and then came back. "I wanted to be married and have lots of children," she said thoughtfully, "but I was very young too. Too young."

Joe felt there was something more she aimed to say, or perhaps was thinking, but he could not be certain. It was no secret that his father was not an easy man to live with. His mood swings could catch you off guard at any point and time, and yet, his mother, not to him anyway, ever said a bad word about him. If she complained to anyone at all, he had no knowledge of it.

"Take your time," she assured him. "You'll know when you're ready."

CHAPTER 23

Eyes snapped open like switches in a fuse box, hard as steel. He was drenched in sweat, his chest pounded like an African kettle drum as he twitched and jolted awake, his white-knuckled fists swung about in a wild frenzy as he fought to protect his face.

Several moments passed before Joe realized he was alone. His reaction to whatever spooked him caused him to wait and scan his surroundings. One can never be sure in these woods. When all seemed clear, his anxiety settled, and his heartbeat came slowly back to normal. He shifted to his side, rested his head against his left arm, the right one he remembered now had been mauled by the wolves. Their teeth were long and razor sharp, with all intent to kill. His shirt sleeve, however, was no longer torn. He felt for his rifle then, still there, zipped up inside the case. His battered leg, the one they tampered with, was also no worse than before. The nightmare, so incredibly real, was the worst one of his life. Worse even than the past twelve hours or more when the start of his actual nightmare began. He wondered how much more he would have to endure, how much longer before the suffering was over. After his pulse rate settled, he dried his face with the edge of his collar. Despite the cold, the touch of his skin felt hot and clammy, a sure sign of fever. He recalled now witnessing his funeral. There were stories of people having had an out-of-body experience before, but Joe wasn't convinced of those tales. They fell in the category of hallucinations or having the ability to communicate with the dead. The idea of it was too weird and creepy, impossible to imagine without experiencing it firsthand, which he hadn't, not really, unless the dream counted as if he had. But the details of the wolves especially, left him trembling. He turned cold, very cold, and still his forehead was again covered with sweat.

Joe boosted himself up to a halfway seated position, and then looked across the wooded area. The images of trees wavered, forcing him to close his eyes and lay back down again. It all remained so vivid, the red wolves and their heated snarls. The two of them howled, and then the others in a pack charging towards him. There could not possibly be a worse way of dying than to be eaten alive. If he were to die here in these woods, if there was no other way around it, he would rather drift off to sleep and not wake up. It was clean and painless. Nothing could be more horrifying, for Delia or a member of his family, than to be forced to identify his body or rather his ravaged remains. It would haunt them for the rest of their lives.

A strange sensation came over him then, as if someone tapped him on the shoulder. He bolted. Eyes wide open, and saw the sky was now a milky gray.

Moments passed.

He recalled floating through air, a lazy-daisy kind of float, as a bystander watching a dead man's race. It was his own image, of course, that he'd seen, an exhausted, broken down image, he knew that now.

As the early morning hour came into focus, the treetops stood watch, branches that were still and bare. If he didn't know any better, he would think he was having yet another dream, one that resonated much clearer. Daybreak would soon settle in.

Attempting to lift himself up again, he needed to get back on track, and could finally see the outline of the barn up ahead. It must be five . . . maybe five-thirty, there was still work to do. His head throbbed, but the pain in his leg was now bearable, so long as he didn't move it too quickly. He sat up straighter, examined his ties, and could feel fresh blood oozing through the open wound. It trickled down his shin, and then lowered to his calf. He needed to see a doctor, fast, get to Delia, hail a passing vehicle, something! But before he could do those things, he needed to keep going and get out into the open where he might be spotted by someone in the vicinity.

Delia would be pacing about by now.

Today . . . Saturday, no . . . Sunday.

Folks that went to church would not even be up yet. No one would be stirring around at this hour.

Flip the script.

Stay positive.

Every minute counted. But first, he needed to wait and figure things out. He'd always thought of himself as one who liked to work things out, alone, in his own head, rather than seek advice from others. It took him years to even begin to open up to Delia, the kind of soul-baring you don't entrust to just anyone. She taught him the importance of communication, and in some ways, he taught her to respect his boundaries, that there would be times he would need space, that he was still a work-in-progress. The more he shared about himself, his family, and more specifically his father, the more intuitive she became.

Since relocating to North Carolina, Joe agreed to work for his parents who, once they sold the salon and retired, started up their own home rental business. From the bursting seams of Jersey to the little town of Williamston, a mere speck on the map, where the people are full of *Bless your heart* and good intentions, the two locations were about as different as night and day. Both came with pros and cons, it was just a matter of what a person was looking for. For his father, at least, it was a profitable move where he was able to buy a home outright at a fraction of the cost of what it would have up north. It allowed him to begin purchasing fixer-uppers that would later be rented out to tenants. Where his father had the cash and the vision of a lucrative business, Joe had the skill, the know-how, and the strength to do the work. Whether he was gutting out a room, installing sheetrock, spackling, or just doing cosmetic repairs, Joe set his own hours and worked at his own pace.

When Dominic and his new wife, Deanna, moved down, they too became involved with some projects of their own, in addition to Dominic running his own *Tile Mechanic* business. Years of dedication, doing volunteer work with the *Witnesses*, building kingdom halls in remote locations and developing countries, exposed them to many different vocations that greatly benefited them, both in the rental industry and the business world, a diversity of trades that Dominic was only too happy to share with his brothers. But unlike Dominic, Joe preferred to work alone.

Joe's instinct was now telling him to clear his head and leave it alone, but his mind kept going.

"Why you finish my job?" Joe fired off, his hands flailing, something that startled and troubled Dominic.

"Dad didn't want to w-a-i-t for when you would be back.

He told me to finish it. Did I do something wrong?"

It irked Joe that Dominic was usually the one his father turned to first when things did not play out to his way of thinking. It wasn't Joe's fault he was born deaf, or that his father never bothered to learn sign. Dominic was often sharing one of his stories from his travels abroad, what he'd seen and done, the wonderful people he'd met. The retelling of his experiences was full of details, exuberant storytelling engaging anyone within earshot. At times he would stop to sign or explain what he could for Joe and Petro's benefit, having to spell some of the words or use pen and paper, despite it slowing down the story. When others chimed in, asked questions, or started a story of their own, much of it was lost on Joe, leaving him to feel like more of an outsider.

"Leave it alone!" Joe told Dominic. "I don't like you finish my job," he added before storming off.

In hindsight, he thought about his relationship with his brother. Working together, on and off over the years, for some reason, made Joe tense. Dominic was accustomed to running his own business, being in charge, delegating certain tasks, explaining what needed to be done and how to go about it. In some ways, Joe admired his organizational skills, his ability to manage several projects at one time, and his foresight of what to do when problems arose, or who to ask if he didn't know the answer. His brother seemed happy and content with his life, his wife, and their steadiness as *Witnesses*, his relationship with his parents. And still, at times, Joe felt annoyed by Dominic and could not pinpoint why.

"Where were you today?" Dominic's note began, the one left on Joe's backdoor. "I needed your help. Are you okay? Are you sick? Please call or come see me."

Joe didn't know how to explain it, he simply wanted out from working with his brother. He took an extra day to mull it over, while finishing up another project for a friend. By the time he made it back to the worksite a couple days later, he found someone else, an older black man, completing the brick work, the job Joe was hired to do. It was the final straw. Later that evening, he sought Dominic out.

"Why you give my job away?" Joe confronted him.

"I haven't heard from you. I called and even left you a note. What happened?"

"I was busy . . . work another job."

"Joe, you have to communicate with me. I have c-u-s-t-o-m-e-r-s who r-e-l-y on me," Dominic said; his signing had much improved over the years.

Joe stood there, on edge, anger brewing. He didn't know how to tell him that he wanted to move on, and that he didn't want to have this conversation.

"What are you thinking, Joe? Talk to me."

"I feel . . . you don't trust I do good job alone, you no r-e-s-p-e-c-t my work. Feel f-o-o-l-i-s-h you give my job away. You think I little Joey. You think I not smart because I can't hear you talk."

"No, that's not true. I think you do e-x-c-e-l-l-e-n-t work, that's why I hired you. I want us to work together. You're my brother, and I love you. I do appreciate your help, Joe, and your i-n-p-u-t." When Joe said nothing, Dominic went on. "Remember when you s-u-g-g-e-s-t-e-d removing the b-r-i-c-k-s and redoing the roof on the b-o-i-l-e-r room? I liked your idea. We put our heads together and now look at it, it's a m-a-s-t-e-r-p-i-e-c-e! Your idea was a good one."

Joe shifted uncomfortably, looked down, then back up again. "I feel f-r-u-s-t-r-a-t-e. You no share i-d-e-a-s with me."

"I'm sorry. I don't mean to f-r-u-s-t-r-a-t-e you. If you have questions about anything, ask me. I am not u-n-w-i-l-l-i-n-g to share my thoughts. It takes me awhile to explain, though; I am slow to sign and sometimes I talk too much before making my p-o-i-n-t and then . . . you get i-m-p-a-t-i-e-n-t with me." Dominic took a breath, looking drained. He puffed some frustration air out, waited for Joe to say something, but when he didn't, he went on. "Look, Joe. . . I m-a-n-a-g-e many different p-r-o-j-e-c-t-s now, I have a lot of r-e-s-p-o-n-s-i-b-i-l-i-t-i-e-s and some of them are tough to handle. For us to work together, I need you to communicate with me. Please don't be upset. Try to understand."

The exchange was more than eight years ago, before Dominic sold two of his fixer-uppers and moved four-hours away, near Charlotte, to build a home for him and Deanna on the lot beside her parents. He often commuted to Williamston, where their parents and much of the extended family lived now. By this time, his parents owned and managed a dozen rental properties that Dominic helped them with, more and more, since Joe had eventually moved on, to work on his own.

Joe's visit that one Sunday was less than a year ago, the day before his father was to have knee replacement surgery.

It was a few months later that Joe became curious enough to check out the home Dominic was building for their parents.

Dominic seemed surprised to see him and was eager to show him around. The place was so big, Joe wondered what his parents would do with so much space.

"I wanted to build Mom and Dad a d-i-s-a-b-i-l-i-t-y friendly home," Dominic said, "near Mom's family, in a s-a-f-e neighborhood. The full a-p-a-r-t-m-e-n-t upstairs is for anyone who wants to visit, or maybe a live-in a-i-d one day. The heated floor I added will warm the T-r-a-v-e-r-t-i-n-e tile. What do you think about the tile I found?"

"Looks good. I like it. Where you find?"

"I had it shipped from Florida. I n-e-g-o-t-i-a-t-e-d a good deal since I was able to buy so much."

"I like wood doors. Look expensive."

"Aren't they nice? These are good q-u-a-l-i-t-y doors, but I like to shop around. I found them at H-a-b-i-t-a-t for H-u-m-a-n-i-t-y. The large framed doorways are for h-a-n-d-i-c-a-p access. Dad's shower, too, has wheel-chair access."

"Dad have wheelchair?" Joe figured he would be mostly recovered from his surgery the previous winter, up and walking better than before.

"Not yet, but maybe soon. He stays in bed a lot."

"Dad stubborn, no like exercise. He should walk."

"M-icheline told Dad he doesn't have to walk up and down the road. He can walk up and down the staircase at home. Dad made a face: 'I'm not doing that!'"

Joe laughed, and Dominic joined in with him.

Joe thought back to that day and the ones that followed. Dominic said he could use an extra man, if Joe needed the work.

"A-lanzo is coming down to help with the e-l-e-c-t-r-i-c for a few days, maybe a week. Petro and his friend E-m-e-r-y are coming from F-l-o-r-i-d-a to do the s-h-e-e-t-r-o-c-k." All that help coming enticed Joe to make the decision that he would help too.

For two or three weeks, he put in what hours he could, grouted the tile walls in the shower, installed base trim, trimmed out the kitchen cabinets, and assisted Petro and Emery with hanging the drywall, using a board lift due to the nine-foot ceiling. During that time, his father seemed to lose interest in the project. The one or two brief times that Joe even saw him, he barely said a word to any of them, just viewed what was going on with a frown, and then wanted to go back home again. His gait was slow and unsteady.

Joe figured he would be looking forward to moving into his new home, happy it was nearly finished. The place looked like a palace, he thought, compared to the others they lived in.

"What wrong with Dad?" Joe asked Dominic one afternoon. "He no look good. Look sad."

"Dad is d-e-p-r-e-s-s-e-d."

"What for? Should be happy."

"Last year, Dad *was* happy. He wanted to be involved with all the decisions for the house. We discussed everything together: the b-l-u-e-p-r-i-n-t-s, the s-e-p-t-i-c, the foundation, the c-o-n-c-r-e-t-e, the framing, the roof and siding. Mom and Dad came to visit many times each week, stayed for several hours."

"So, what happen?"

"After Dad's knee surgery, he stayed in bed mostly. He only

got up to eat and check on his s-t-o-c-k-s. When he heard on the news his s-t-o-c-k-s took a dive, he called me: 'Dominic, what should I do, I just lost a ton of money?' I told Dad, 'Don't do anything. The s-t-o-c-k m-a-r-k-e-t will b-o-u-n-c-e back. It always does.'"

"What happen, he take money out?"

"Yup. He sold off all his s-t-o-c-k . . . and took a big loss. He thinks he's poor now. He's not poor, just u-p-s-e-t with himself, I think. He should have left his money alone. The s-t-o-c-k m-a-r-k-e-t went up again, but it was too late."

CHAPTER 24

An aura of nostalgia illuminated everything, even the matters that pained him the most. It was an ongoing inner-battle of self-awareness Joe tried to make sense of.

In a conscious decision to put it out of his mind, he hitched up his rifle case, slipped the strap over his head to keep it from falling, and onward he set off in his usual awkward manner, pushing off with his left foot, slow and wary, so not to snag the branches that held his right one straight. He searched for strength to keep going, reached deep from within for a thought or a memory, anything to grab hold of that would help shoulder the pain and the helplessness he felt inside. His movements were small, they had to be; it was all he could do to keep from blacking out again. Bit by bit the edge of the lot drew him nearer, egging him on like a dangling carrot that represented life.

He'd once been a strong competitor, a hardy beast in his class. Not just as a teen, but later on into his twenties and thirties when he competed in outdoor wilderness sports in the deaf community during their annual retreats. There were solo and duo events that involved a range of equipment, tug-of-war team events, as a test of strength. In the *Two Man Bucking Saw* comp, using a six-foot crosscut lance tooth saw that was popular in the late 1800's and remained common with wildland firefighters until the mid-70's, he was nicknamed

Lumberjack Joe, taking first place sawing through blocks of wood in the least amount of time. For each comp he participated in, it cost him an entry fee. Any winnings he earned did not amount to much, not after his out-of-town incurred expenses. But it wasn't about the money or about upstaging anyone else; it was about the camaraderie among his teammates, all of them on the same playing field, that gave him a sense of belonging and acceptance. Win or lose, it was about performing to the best of his ability, giving every ounce of gumption that he had, and then coming away feeling good about it. All of it served him a purpose. A purpose he could not articulate into words, but sustained him in the way food did to the hungry or water did to the thirsty. It nourished his mind and fed his soul, and that meant more to him than any prize money ever could.

That time period, so long ago, the way he remembered it, he could still go through the motions in his sleep and somehow come out on top. Joe latched on to the thought and the memory and pretended to be Lumberjack Joe again, only this time he was competing in a new event, a sort of marathon. There was no partner to be paired with and no team to battle, but in this challenge, unlike all the others, winning was everything, and losing would be the end of the road for him. He advanced a single stroke and then another, bit by bit, his eyes half closed to keep the image alive. And then out of nowhere, Coach knelt down in front of him, looked him straight in the eye. *This here is your Olympic race*, he said, *the one you never had. Go for the Gold, Joe!*

No sooner was Coach there, he was gone again. And then it was Mickey, Rocky's coach, speaking from outside of the ring, his black knit cap on his head. *"Get outta here! Will ya? This is like fighting in a zoo! People die sometimes when they don't wanna live no more. I'm gonna stay alive and watch you make good."*

There were others too, male and female, young and old. Some of them he didn't even know, watching and cheering from the sidelines. As the morning turned lighter and brighter, his focal point drew nearer and nearer. He'd covered half, maybe more, of the remaining distance when a stinging in his leg burned and the ache in his muscles deepened. He stopped and laid his head to rest, not wanting to lose his rhythm. Mickey flashed back. *"If you wanna blow this thing, if you wanna blow it, then damn it I'm gonna blow it with ya. If you wanna stay here, I'll stay with ya. I'll stay and pray. What do I got to lose?"*

The crushing thought of losing, of giving up, of checking out, it was a different kind of pain than what the rest of his body was fighting. It was all too much, too soon, and it terrified him. With nothing more he could do, he rested, and then he prayed. There were no memorized passages or scriptures from the Bible, just straight-talk.

He spoke no words and there was no need to sign, just his pure deep thoughts that would register just the same.

Please God, don't let me die. I want live. Want keep going. But I hurt. Really hurt. So tired, God. I want stop pain. Please . . . stop pain. My leg kill me. Like . . . slow death. My head dizzy. Make me feel crazy. I don't want quit. I never be quitter. Please God . . . help me. I want live.

Moments later—how many, he didn't know, but when he lifted his head, the spell was broken. There was no Mickey, no Coach, no Delia, and no fans. Good thoughts were all that he had, so he clung to them like a floatation device in a Class V rapids riverbed. To get himself back on track, he focused on the clearing of solid, dry land, where he'd be able to move a little more quickly. He managed a few more yards, rapid breaths puffed through his cheeks as he rested his head, encouraged by how much closer he was. If he could just hold out a little longer, he would somehow find a way to climb inside his cab, and then turn on the heat to get warm. His fingers were so cold that he thought they might break.

He was not sure why, but he sensed he was being watched and looked around to see who was there. He could have sworn that someone made a quick dash from behind one tree to another. He was in no mood for games, but was someone even there?

He waited, blinked hard, and then waited some more. When he looked up again, he saw no one, yet every nerve ending was on high alert. Even in the midst of it, even while the images and shadows ricocheted through his skull, with his final thoughts of Delia, he could feel himself slipping away.

It was springtime of 1995, more than seventeen years ago. Joe was on his way home from a worksite. He'd taken a different route that day, due to increased traffic and road construction. Delia was gone that week; she'd been taking courses to become a sign language interpreter. It was something that completely floored him the moment she mentioned it.

"What a-b-o-u-t your job?" he asked her.

"What about it? It's just a job. It's not something I'm p-a-s-s-i-o-n-a-t-e about."

"What you mean?" Joe grimaced. "I thought I was your p-a-s-s-i-o-n."

Delia fixed him with a long, careful, searching stare that was not devoid of sarcasm. "You know what I mean. I want to feel like I c-o-n-t-r-i-b-u-t-e to the world, ya know? Provide a s-e-r-v-i-c-e that's important. And I think I'm good at signing. I enjoy it!"

"You not good . . . you great! But . . . won't you have to go back to school . . . you thirty-six . . ." Joe hesitated, "or maybe thirty-seven now?"

Delia ignored the question. "So? Are you saying I'm too old to learn, to go back to school?"

"Nooo." Joe chuckled. "I mean . . ." He tried to think how best to say it, but then Delia went on.

"It'll be a lot to handle for a while. I'll have to work days, do school at night."

Joe had to hand it to her, he knew no other woman with as much ambition. It was not until later in the course she explained just how much work it involved and the challenges that came along with it.

"Learning A-S-L is much more than just being comfortable in the language or being a good listener. It requires an a-n-a-l-y-t-i-c-a-l mind, having a good grasp of both English and A-S-L, before I can hope to offer a good interpretation."

"You interpret good. What is a-n-a . . . ?

"A-n-a-l-y-t-i-c-a-l? It means having the mindset to analyze a deaf person's thoughts, what they say, how they say it, and what they mean."

"Yeah. You can do that."

"Look here." Delia pulled a sheet from her text book. "There are three different kinds."

Joe read the page that described the three major forms of sign language currently used in the United States: American Sign Language (ASL), Pidgin Signed English (PSE), and Signed Exact English (SEE). He was somewhat familiar with all three, but more accustomed to ASL. It was all in the way the interpretation was delivered, either word-for-word, or just the basics.

"Today, we were told that only thirty-eight p-e-r-c-e-n-t of people that take the exam will pass."

Joe raised an eyebrow, but did not want to discourage her. "You will pass . . . you will." He liked to take credit for having chosen a great girl to be with, but in truth, it was Delia who set him straight and reminded him more than once that she was the one who chose him. They joked about it after she'd come clean.

"I was watching you from across the l-o-u-n-g-e," she said, "when you circled the p-o-o-l table. I noticed the way you carried yourself, the way your shirt fit nicely inside your belted jeans, your slim hips and your broad s-e-x-y shoulders . . . the way you handled the c-u-e s-t-i-c-k, with smooth, easy j-a-b-s, and I knew right then I wanted to meet you."

Embarrassment played across his face, drawing color to his cheeks. "So you don't want j-u-s-t beat me at p-o-o-l, you want pick me up too?"

"Honestly? Shooting pool was j-u-s-t an excuse. I wanted you for your body." By this time, Delia was laughing and enjoying the look on Joe's face.

"You h-u-s-s-y!" he teased.

Joe smiled at the memory, as he steered his truck through the back roads, swerving to avoid a scampering squirrel. It was Delia's favorite time of year, with the weather just right, freshly cut lawns that were green and plush. Azalea bushes were in full bloom and the sky was an even shade of blue. He felt especially good today, and there was no wonder why, as he passed a farm with the faint smell of cattle behind a barbed-wire fence. There were horses grazing in the field and a golden retriever playing catch with its owner. What caught his attention, more than anything, was the row of Magnolia trees that ran along the edge of the property. There were a dozen or more, beautifully placed, full of chalice-shaped flowers, pearly white in color. Had it not been for Delia, he would not have known the likes of a Magnolia tree. It was her favorite and what lured him to pull over and stop.

There was no one behind him and enough room on the shoulder to park. He stepped out of the vehicle, taking in the two-story log cabin, a two-car garage and what appeared to be a workshop out back. It was a fine-looking place. There was no telling what something like it would cost, let alone the property taxes, the maintenance and upkeep. He soaked it all in, wishing Delia were there with him. Not that they could ever afford such a place, they lived a very modest lifestyle, after all. He was fine with that, but a man could dream, couldn't he?

Joe watched as the owner waved for the dog to come, tossing the Frisbee into the bed of a red pick-up. The golden retriever, unaware she was being watched and admired, hopped in after it. The tailgate was closed shut, and then the man drove them up a path along the property, out of sight. Joe could see that the land went up a ways, and knew that Delia would have loved to see the Magnolias. He'd seen one before, but never in such a spectacular arrangement. It was like comparing a bouquet of freshly cut flowers and a botanical garden.

Joe wondered if Delia would be home yet, she'd been gone for five days, the longest they'd been apart. The workshop she attended was in Albany, a three-hour commute from their home in Jersey. She was expected back by dinnertime, was what she told him the morning she left. He missed her more than he expected he would. Not that he enjoyed the break apart, because he didn't, he liked coming home to her at night. No matter how her day went, she was always happy to see him, always smiled when he walked in the door. He liked that. And he liked the feel of her warm body close to him at night when they slept. In light of the fact they were both independent, different in some ways, not so much in others, their relationship worked well. He considered himself a lucky guy, and for the first time, could not imagine his life without her in it. It was hard to believe that eight years had passed since their first meeting at the bar, even harder than his having turned thirty the previous winter. In some ways it felt like he'd known Delia all his life.

During the time they first met, when he lived at home with his parents, so young and naïve about the world and the pressures that came along with it, had someone told him then that he'd wind up with a woman who was not deaf, a strong-minded divorced woman raising two young daughters, he would have laughed himself silly. He would not pretend it was easy. There were moments and bouts when he wanted to just hightail it out of there. But after calming down, the incident would blow over. As a young boy, there were conflicts with his sisters and brothers, it was part of the process, he supposed—growing pains, immaturity. Delia's girls were older now and used to having him around. Though they hadn't learned to sign like their mother, they found ways of communicating their wants and needs. As much as they needed steadiness in their lives, Joe needed it too. He never wanted them to feel he was only there temporarily or that he might abandon them one day. That was never his plan. By now, they surely knew him well enough that he was there to stay.

Reluctantly, Joe pulled himself away and got back behind the wheel of his pick-up. As he fired up the engine, he caught sight of the thousands upon thousands of butterflies that fluttered from all the Magnolias. Their sudden appearance took him back to the time Sarah marveled over the orange and black spotted butterfly that landed on the knuckle of her hand. Afraid to move, she remained still, sitting on her bicycle.

"Look, Mommy, look!" After several moments passed, Sarah slowly lifted her hand and spoke to the butterfly as if it might understand. "You're pretty," she said. "Really pretty." When it still didn't move, she kissed it lightly, watched it flutter off and then land on the tip of her nose.

Joe laughed. Delia told her to be still, ran to get her camera, but when Sarah tried to catch it, it was too late, the butterfly slipped through her fingers, flew off and away. It was during that same time that the ultimatum was put to rest. There were moments when Joe wondered, if Delia had not relented and he'd gone through with it, would he have held it against her? Even now, he couldn't say for sure. What she said to him, though, how she said it and the look in her eye, was something he couldn't forget. To Delia's credit, not once did she begrudge him or throw it in his face. It was something that surprised him over time and was no longer a concern.

Joe shifted the truck in gear with Delia still on his mind and followed the road that curved around a bend. The property of the Magnolias to his right led to a canopy of trees up ahead that lined both sides of the country road. He reached for his pocket watch, the one stored in his ashtray. It seemed a good place for it, since he never smoked a day in his life. He saw then it was after six, surprised to have lost track of time, returned the watch to the ashtray, his eyes back on the road when he saw it—a swirling object soared between the trees in mid-air to the other side of the road. By the time he realized what it was, the golden retriever lunged out directly in his path.

Joe slammed on the brakes, turned the wheel sharply to

the left, skidding within inches of hitting the dog, who just managed to clear his frontend. He pulled off to the side to catch his breath. The incident happened so fast that when someone knocked on his passenger window it startled him. The man walked around to his side of the truck.

"You okay?" It was the same man at the Magnolias playing catch with his dog.

"Yeah." Joe nodded, relieved to have stopped in time.

"She knows better . . . run . . . road . . . sorry." He rattled off an apology. ". . . truck okay?" The man removed a piece of cloth from his back pocket, proceeded to wipe his brow. "Come here, Sam," he called the dog over, who was now holding the Frisbee in her mouth. The man seemed to be speaking some to the dog and some to Joe.

"Deaf," Joe said, pointing to his ear.

"Oh. I'm very sorry. Samantha, sit!" She did as she was told, still with the Frisbee between her teeth. The man rubbed her head.

Joe extended his right hand through the open window. "Joe." He was relieved that no one was hurt. "Nice dawg."

"Hi, Joe! I'm Rick." The two shook hands. "You live around here?"

"No." Joe gave a wave to the other side of town. With a grin, he reached his hand toward Sam, having understood her name.

Sam gave a quick glance to her owner. When he nodded a go-ahead, she took a step closer to the truck, her head tilted upward.

Joe took hold of the Frisbee, and Sam released her grip on it.

"Good dawg."

Sam responded in kind and woofed a greeting.

"She likes you."

Joe allowed her to sniff his fingers, and then gave a pat and a scratch behind the ears. When there was no more to say, he handed the Frisbee to Rick, and then started up his engine. Rick thanked him again.

"Bye, Sam." Joe waved and smiled at the dog, gave a thumbs up to her owner, and then headed on his way.

A few miles down the road, he eased off the gas when he entered the city limits. At the traffic light, he came to a stop, and then waited for the pedestrians to cross the road. The woman out front caught his attention. She wore a crimp flowery skirt down to her calves, a simple white blouse and a pair of ankle-strapped sandals, her hair the same shade and length as Delia's. She held a notebook in one arm and a handbag made of macramé on the other. There were many similarities—the way she moved, the way she carried herself, she could almost pass for Delia.

Joe found himself staring, watched her reach the curb, and wondered again if Delia would be home yet. He was only ten minutes away and would soon find out. He expected her to be tired from the drive and doubted she would feel up to cooking. He could pick them up a pizza on the way; their favorite place was right up the road. But when the light turned green, Joe hit the gas and drove on past Vinnie's at the next corner. Maybe they would eat dinner out for a change, a nice sit-down meal. The girls were with their grandmother for the night. Entering their neighborhood, there were teen-aged boys throwing a football in the street. A man walking a beagle reminded him of Pogo, his parents' new pet. After Tonto passed away, a stray came to their door looking for scraps to feed on, and they decided to keep him. At first, Joe was surprised to see they let him stay in the house, even through the night. It made him want a dog all the more, a Lab of some sort or part Shepherd, maybe two to keep one another company when no one was home. Dogs weren't like cats. They needed attention and caring, training and discipline. One day soon, he would go to the animal shelter, maybe with Delia, and take a look.

Joe pulled into their empty driveway, disappointed she wasn't yet at home. He checked the time again to find it was six-thirty. Delia's workshop was scheduled to end at three. He sat there a moment, hoping that nothing went wrong. Not that he should worry. Delia knew how to change a tire, if it came to that. He'd shown her the first year they were together. When she asked for a quick lesson, it didn't surprise him, and was something that would come in handy one day. He showed her where to position the car jack, how to work it, and how much to tighten the lug nuts without stripping the thread. It was a service he taught his younger sisters as well. Delia was no different in that way. Her mind was like a sponge, always eager to learn and try new things. Joe made sure, too, that she kept a working flashlight in her glove compartment and a set of jumper cables in the trunk. He gave her car regular oil changes, checked the fluids, the air filter, the tire pressure, and cleared the battery cables of corrosion, but it didn't hurt for her to know a few things should something go wrong on one of her road trips.

Joe eased the key from the ignition, paused a bit longer before getting out of the vehicle when Delia's blue Pinto pulled up behind him. It was strange; even after all this time, she still did it for him. He felt a stir inside, that made it feel more like weeks than days since he last saw her. From the front seat of her car, Delia waved out the side window, and then held up a large square box, from Vinnie's. It was crazy how their minds worked alike.

Joe opened her door, took the box that was still hot from the bottom, and set it on the roof of her car. Delia stepped out, grinning. They were eye-to-eye, the two of them close to the same height. Her smile alone reminded him why he missed her so much. He took her in his arms, hugged her in a way he usually reserved for the bedroom, and then kissed her full on the mouth with a longing he hadn't expressed in a good while. They were often busy with one thing or another, tired after a long day, time spent with the girls that did not allow for privacy, and on top of it all, Delia was often immersed with her studies.

"Wow! That was nice. Maybe I should leave more often. Is every t-h-i-n-g okay?"

Joe nodded, unable to contain a mischievous grin, or begin to explain what had come over him. He grabbed her suitcase from the backseat, reached for the pizza, and motioned for them to go inside.

The moment he set the bag down and the pizza on the table, he turned to her and realized again just how much she meant to him, how she fulfilled his life in a way that only she could.

"You look different. What is it?"

"I miss you." Joe's insides suddenly knotted up. He was not big on words or a show of emotion and until now did not feel the need to do so.

Delia gave a nervous smile, tried to read more into it. "I missed you too. Are you sure everything's okay?"

Joe nodded, his hands wrapped loosely around her waist. The pizza was likely beginning to cool, but he couldn't wait to say what he wanted. Remembering her words again, he played them in his head. *I hope that one day you'll change your mind and want this as much as I do, because I do love you, Joe. I always will.* He was staring into her warm brown eyes that were now looking back at him in that puzzled way. She was everything to him, more than he could have ever hoped for.

"Joe?"

"I love you," he said, and then he placed the palm side of his fist over his chest and heart and made a few circular motions. "I'm sorry." He choked back the urge of losing his composure, needing to state what he was feeling. It was something that didn't come easy, that made him nervous and unsure of himself, and he didn't know why. He swallowed hard and went on. "I'm sorry I hurt you. I d-i-s-a-p-p-o-i-n-t you . . . I was dumb." He gave a little knock against his skull. "You make me happy . . . make me smile every day . . . make me laugh . . . I feel l-u-c-k-y have you in my life. I'm sorry . . . take me long time to tell you." His walls were finally down, the reservations he had suddenly seemed trivial. This was where he belonged and with the woman he was meant to be with, for years and years to come, however many they were fortunate enough to have. The only thing holding him back, he supposed, was his own insecurities, of maybe not being good enough, or even trusting that what they shared was for the long haul. But life, as he knew it, came with no guarantees. He understood that now. There was nothing more for him to say, than to just say it.

"Will you . . . marry me?"

Delia drew a slow deliberate breath and then froze. Her expression was one of disbelief, a lack for words, and there were tears in her eyes. Fresh, raw tears that Joe hoped were tears of joy and not that after all this time, she would change her mind. The thought of that happening never occurred to him. Since that first day, there had been no one else—not for him, not for either of them. Delia covered her mouth, and was crying now, but there was something else too. She was nodding her response as the tears spilled over and ran down her cheeks. Joe pulled her close, kissed her salty lips gently. She was smiling finally, her face flushed with happiness.

"You want pizza now, or later?" he asked, an undeniable *look* in his eye.

Delia was almost giddy, seeing the sudden change in him altogether. She, more than him, was the spontaneous one of the two, so her answer came as no surprise.

"Pizza . . . what pizza?"

Joe lifted her up in his arms, carried her off to the bedroom.

It was a bright, sunny day in May, five weeks later. The marriage took place in their backyard, a casual affair with their closest friends and family. They agreed to keep it simple so not to leave them strapped with debt. Joe's parents took the afternoon off from the salon to make the two o'clock service. Micheline sent her regrets from Tennessee, along with a card and gift that she would miss their big day. Jeremy's high-school graduation was scheduled that same weekend. There was no date suitable for everyone, Joe knew, but he was sorry that his oldest sister and nephew would not be able to make it. His mother later told him that Jeremy would be leaving in a few months for the Air Force. Joe didn't know when he would see him again. It didn't seem so long ago that he was still a child, a frightened twelve-year-old boy who had hidden a frozen pizza under a bed. It was hard to believe he was grown up now, enough to join the military.

Of his remaining siblings, all but Jena, who was living somewhere in Louisiana or Texas, he didn't know, were able to attend. Uncle Willie and Aunt Carol were there, Uncle Sal and Aunt Rose, several others on his mother's side of the family, his friends Phillip and Jake, and a dozen or more cousins. From Delia's side was her mother Florence, her grandmother Margaret, two of her closest friends, and of course Chloe and Sarah.

Delia wore a cream colored, sleeveless, two-piece dress that fell just below her calves. Joe suggested she might wear her cowboy boots, the ones she wore when they first met.

"That's tacky," she said. "I'll save those for the h-o-n-e-y-m-o-o-n." She gave him a look that made him grin. Instead, she found herself a modest pair of flats to match her dress. Her hair was left long in its natural state, the way Joe liked it. She wore a headpiece with an arrangement of daisies and baby's breath to compliment her bouquet.

Surprisingly, Joe was about as calm and relaxed as he could have hoped for. There were no cold feet for either of them. He'd done his bride proud and wore dark gray slacks and a white, short-sleeve polo shirt. He felt a bit over-dressed, given the backyard affair, but it was his wedding day, after all.

After the brief ceremony, there was plenty of food for everyone, and lots of good natured joking. The children played badminton and volleyball. The adults sat in the shade, and caught up on the latest family news and gossip that eventually led to another beer or a second slice of cake. Later that evening, after everyone was gone, and the two of them were alone, Delia opened a bottle of champagne, poured them each a glass, and handed one to Joe.

"To my husband, my best friend, my rock, my lover, my forever and ever, I will love you always!" She extended her left pinky.

Glad that it was just the two of them, Joe didn't want to

share this moment with anyone. "To my wife . . . my best friend . . . my soft p-i-l-l-o-w at night—" he added, with a grin. "I love you always." He linked his pinkie with hers, as the two toasted their future.

CHAPTER 25

Joe hugged his body to draw in heat, bent his left knee upward to drag his heel to and fro and ease the shivers. He'd been out for a while, long enough for the cold to set in. He stretched his arms to release the tension and then rubbed his eyelids and temples to clear the cobwebs from his thoughts. When he opened his eyes again, he saw the palest of blue skies above the treetops, and with it a sign of hope. It was a new day. Darkness was over. To be sure he was awake, he propped himself up on his elbows, waited and watched, until he witnessed the sun coming up, just a sliver seeped between the trees. Toward the edge of the woods, he caught a glimpse of his tailgate, no more than twenty yards away. Despite the bouts of nausea and hunger pains, he wondered if there was a bottle of water in the truck, some Gatorade, anything at all. Even the slightest possibility gave him an ounce of something more to look forward to.

His competitive edge kicked into gear. Though slowly at first, he was back at it, his insistent crawl, telling himself there was no pain. With each onward stroke, his breaths came out as gusts of steam, a burst of energy from some unknown place, that killer instinct that some fighters get during the fight of their life. It almost seemed as if someone was helping him, as if he was no longer doing the work alone. The edge of his truck drew him nearer and nearer. He was not going to die.

Soon, it would all be over. There would be no more blackouts, no more wolves or hallucinations, no more nightmares. His leg was taking a beating as he dragged himself along, a little quicker this time, propelled on as if he'd been slipped a dose of speed. Within minutes, as if he'd suffered a blow to the side of his head, it brought on a massive headache, but he was almost there. With his vision blurred, he kept going. It was a straight shot until finally, he reached the clearing. There were no more detours around fallen logs or weaving to avoid jagged stumps and sinking holes. No more wet and soggy leaves or stench filling his nose. He kept his head low and managed to place one arm in front of the other. Every so often, he would open his eyes to reassure he was getting there and then closed them back again to pacify the migraine in his head.

There were two kinds of people in the world, doers and slackers. It was not about winning or losing, but about exerting the effort to break out of one's shell, discovering an inner strength you didn't know you had, so not to derail the natural order of one's potential. Joe knew that he was damn well going to cross that finish line, or die trying.

When he reached the edge of his truck, everything in him relaxed. He lay there, dog-tired, his chin against the cold gravel. With his fingers, he grasped a handful to feel its texture and to affirm how far he'd come. He released the gravel and clutched it again and again to reaffirm. Minutes passed until his mind became lucid and calm, even the headache began to dissipate. In these moments of rest, an image floated through his mind of that nine-year-old boy crossing the river, with an oncoming *Empress*. He'd made it then and was sure going to make it now.

There are some who believe when a person dies, it is their time to go, that our days are predestined, regardless of what we do, how we live, and at whatever age. But Joe wasn't buying it. His belief was that people were held accountable for their choices in life. Just as it was his choice not to tell Delia or anyone of his plans the previous day, or when he plunged to the ground, injured and afraid, he chose to fix what he could, keep going, and strive towards a way out.

Having come this far, he propped himself up, brushed off the gravel still stuck to his chin, and then supported his back against the rear tire. It felt good, so good, to be sitting up straight, and with it, the sliver of sunrise from across the way was like a waving white flag during a NASCAR race, with only one lap to go. From where he sat, he scooted his bottom over a few feet to align himself with the edge of the driver's door where he would make his next move. He contemplated first how to go about it. With the light of day, he checked his wound through the branches of his splint, tore open the hole in the fabric of his pants, and saw the puss oozing, surrounding the tip of exposed bone. Fresh blood pooled the area of the old dried up crusty blood. He forced himself to look away when saliva gathered in his mouth in a choked sense of desperation. His heart began to race, so he took in a deep breath and then another, eager to get on with it, but allowing the nausea to pass and not rush his movements.

With the driver's door to his side, he reached up with his right hand to unlatch the handle, but when he did, his fingers slipped. He rubbed his hands together to draw in heat, wiped his fingers against the dry areas of his clothing before trying it again. This time, the handle unlatched to where he was able to pry open the door. Pausing then, about to slide his gun case across the seat, he decided instead to use it for leverage. With his back still up against the side of the truck, he shifted his bottom and his legs over to align himself with the step ledge of his cab. With the use of both palms, he placed one on each side of him, on the step, slid his left foot in towards his bottom, and then summoned all his strength, pushing himself up enough to seat himself on the ledge. Everything in him felt shaky and unsure. He couldn't risk a mishap, cause a fall of any kind. With his right hand he steadied himself on the arm rest of the door, using his left one to grip the cased rifle end, and between the two, he gritted his teeth through the hideous pain and with all of his weight on his left leg, he stood to an upright position.

The second he was up, there was immense pressure throughout his lower right limb—a heaviness and oozing of more blood, and a wave of dizzy. He lowered himself onto the cab seat, placed his rifle out of his way, before scooting himself back along the seat, until his bum leg was completely inside. Only then was he able to move it sideways, onto the floor. With his left hand, he closed his door shut, rested his head against the window, and let out a deep sigh. There was a buzzing sensation in his head, the insides of his ears burned, his body shivered.

He reached in his pocket for his keys, shifted to neutral, and then turned the ignition key. The engine turned over and died. With his hands, he positioned his bum leg out of the way, used his left foot to pump the gas pedal, and then tried it again. This time, the engine roared and the vibration made him feel safe and alive. He switched the heater on high, tilted the air vents to blow directly on him, and then scanned the floor and cubbies for something to drink. After coming up empty, to alleviate the pressure, he lifted his bum leg and laid it across the seat. With his back against the door, his head resting against his forearm, he allowed the growing warmth to soothe him.

He was anxious to be on his way, but first he needed to thaw out his limbs, get the shakes under control, and rest his head a bit. Driving the truck would be his next big hurdle, and to do so, he would need a clear mind and his wits about him. As the cab grew warmer, Joe knew it was time to reposition himself behind the wheel and somehow drive home. For the first time, he wished, even imagined it, that he could be lying in the back of an ambulance so that he could just drift off to sleep, while they got him to the hospital. From there, they could call Delia for him. His wallet and ID were in his back pocket. Everything would be all right, then. But he needed a plan first. The truck would not drive on its own.

With his eyes closed, the warm air blowing against him, filling up the cab, he relaxed and thought about how to go about it. With a useless right leg and his left one needed for the clutch and the brake, he was a leg short to work the gas pedal. He was thankful, though; so very thankful, that his heater was working, that he'd made it this far, and that in a few moments, he would be on his way. The warmth felt so incredibly good, and the padded cushioned seat was the next best thing to a bed. It was the most comfortable he'd been all night. Just a few minutes more was all he needed to complete the final stretch.

A BOOM exploded, rocking the house, the lights shutting down instantly. It was nighttime, his mother was not at home, only his father. Joey looked out his bedroom window, saw nothing but flames. The highway was on fire, and there was smoke billowing everywhere.

Someone grabbed him by the arm, his father, who led him

outdoors where his brothers and sisters were gathered in the dark, and then set off toward the front yard where the flames swelled even higher.

"Wah happen?" Joey motioned to Micheline, who was holding Alanzo and Stefano's hand. At eight-years-old, Joey didn't need any hand holding.

"Accident," she said. "A big, big truck turned over and caught fire."

"Where Mom?" Joey motioned.

"I don't know. I just got home."

It was then his father returned with Tonto on a leash. There was no way to exit their driveway, where the truck in flames lay on its side, so they walked in the opposite direction, through the body shop lot, and around to Main Street. Tonto seemed skittish, kept yanking on his father's arm. Hundreds of people gathered outdoors, from their homes and nearby stores that lined the street. The workers at the corner gas stations were huddled in groups with flashlights. The center part of town was without electricity, even the street lights were down. The area looked more like a ghost town, and the growing flames and the smell of smoke made it all the more frightening.

Fire trucks approached the scene, police cars, rescue squads and paramedics. Joey followed the others through the intersection, when he saw the eighteen-wheeler tanker on its side. It lay there, engulfed in flames against the railroad tie re-taining wall that supported the property of their home. Traffic came to a halt with cars lined up from every direction. Folks were leaving their vehicles to get a closer look. Joey wanted to stop and watch with the others, worried their house might be in danger, but his father hurried them along. The heat from the flames grew hotter and hotter, when he wondered if the driver was trapped inside, or already dead.

The cab grew stifling hot, to the point that Joe, in his weary state of mind, consciously switched the knob down to low. There was pressure against his leg, so much pressure that the pain brought him back.

Eyes flashed open. With a jolt, he sat up, stunned to see that his gas tank needle hovered just above the empty line.

No!

His plan was not to fall asleep, but to warm up and figure what to do next. He doubted there would be any drivers on the road at this hour, not this far out. When he eyed his gun case, the idea came to him. He would use his rifle to work the gas pedal. He knew once he lowered his right leg again, the pressure would intensify, but he needed to get moving now before his gas ran out. If only he were able to drive from this same position, with his leg elevated. At some point he would have to readjust himself and get going, deal with the pressure, and pray—pray—pray he could hold up a bit longer. He didn't come this far to crap out now. He was glad, at least, that Delia would be home. Sundays were her off days. Unless . . . unless someone called in sick. Even then, the store didn't open until noon, which meant Delia would be home.

Joe unzipped the bag, pulled out the Winchester and cycled the lever three times to empty the magazine, double-checking the chamber to be certain there were no remaining bullets. He took in a deep breath, lowered his right leg down again and adjusted himself behind the wheel. With his left foot he held down the clutch, shifted into first gear, and then with the butt of the rifle against the gas pedal, he eased off the clutch. The truck moved forward. He kept it in first until he was back on the road, headed south toward Greenville, before letting off the gas and quickly shifting into second without the use of the clutch. He'd read and known about power shifting and quick shifting, but never till now did he have a need for it. There was a right way that required shifting quickly enough to avoid grinding the gear. When he was well on his way, he let go of the gas, shifted to third, until finally he was able to pop it in fourth gear.

Off to a good start, he was twenty-five minutes away, and with any luck at all, he'd be home in less time than that. Delia would be there, it was closer than the hospital, and easier that way. He followed NC-903, held the end of his rifle in his right hand, while steadying the wheel with his left. His plan was to not brake or shift any more than he had to. All he needed to do was to keep his eye on the road and steer the truck home. He knew enough about the area in the ten years since moving there that he would find no gas station open, not on this route. With Williamston to his back and Robersonville to his right, he was in what was known as tobacco country. There would be no stop signs until he reached the center of Robersonville, and none again till the center of Stokes, where only a meager four-hundred in population resided.

The truck shuddered as Joe rounded the curve. Just as he suspected, there were no other vehicles out. Even the homes he passed showed no sign of life. The churchgoers, too, were likely still in bed. Having the road to himself gave him more freedom and liberty should he cross over the line. With a straight shot, the road flat and open, he bore down on the accelerator till the speedometer rose to sixty, in a forty-five mile per hour zone. For the first time ever, getting pulled over would be a welcome infringement. But even at this hour, a cop could die of boredom, waiting for a traveler to come along. The odds of one being in the vicinity were about as likely as his truck sprouting wings.

His grip against the rifle made his hand and arm vibrate to the point it grew tired fast. Without realizing it, his speedometer was back down to forty. He rounded another corner, weaved over the center line, when the butt of his rifle slipped off the pedal. It was then that he noticed the light lit up on his dash, the one that told him he was scraping the bottom of his gas tank. There would be no stations open, not till he reached Greenville, anyway, and by then he would already be home. He took hold again of the gas pedal, bore down, and to preserve what little gasoline there was left, he switched off the heater with a finger on his right hand and steadied back at sixty.

Several miles later, when he entered Stokes, he was forced to come to a stop. The sharp right turn would not allow for anything else. He let go of the gas, pumped the brake, quickly downshifted from fourth to third, and then finally to second, when he was able to complete the turn with a semi-rolling-stop, before giving it more gas and power shifting up again. Each time, he held his breath, but the truck was old, so any grinding was the least of his worries.

With less than ten miles remaining, his chest hitched and his leg throbbed, but he was more than halfway there. His mind wavered, so he blinked hard to stay focused, hoped to God that his remaining fuel would hold out. In the summertime, he often kept an extra can on hand when he mowed lawns, but in December, there was no need.

Joe eased off the gas, long enough to downshift and complete his turn, foregoing the stop sign. When he picked up speed, he quickly shifted up and then gunned it on the shoulder of the road to avoid a dead carcass and the crows feasting off the blood-coated guts. He gripped the barrel of his rifle, pressed harder to make up for lost time, when out of nowhere the angle of the sun suddenly blinded him. In a fit of desperation, he eased off the gas again, pumped the brake, downshifted with a grind in the gear, and could no longer tell where the road was until he felt the front tire run off the pavement. To keep from winding up in a ditch, he swerved left, back onto the road, and then straightened himself up again. Still, he could barely see anything through the windshield of his truck. Judging by the angle of the sun it had to be 7:00 a.m., or close to it. With his speedometer leveled at forty, he lifted his left knee long enough to steady the wheel with it and flipped down the visor. With only a few miles to go, he was counting on Delia to be up and ready. She was normally an early riser, and he would need her help to take over. His hand on the rifle quivered, he was losing it again. He blinked hard, blinked again, and then slowed down the truck. If he blacked out, he would never make it home. This was not going to happen. Not again. Using his left knee to steady the wheel a second time, he quickly rolled down the window to let the cold air in. His breathing grew heavier, his chest pounded. The truck zigzagged before he straightened it again. If he had an extra hand, he would dry off his face with his sleeve to keep the sweat from dripping to his eyes. Just a couple miles more.

Drive... Drive... Drive...

Joe was in his final stretch when the floaters from his right peripheral vision surfaced. Distorted and shaded in color, the blotted shapes bounced along, up and down, one after the other, like fake ponies on a merry-go-round. There were two larger ones in size out front, oddly shaped, followed by three, four, maybe five smaller ones behind. He kept his eyes on the road, veering away just long enough to spot the gas needle falling parallel to the empty line. The one and only time he'd ever run out of gas was before he reached this point. A mile, maybe two from the intersection, Joe grew anxious and punched it, focusing his attention back to the road when everything became more distorted and the floaters grew in size. He blinked hard to force them away, released the wheel long enough to swipe at his brow, when he saw them—the herd of deer fled across the roadway directly in his path.

CHAPTER 26

Joe dreamt he was floating, slow and lazy, through the silkiest river water. Surfaced, he floated, glided down and then up again, in and out, with everything warm and light and easy. He was at it for what seemed a very long time, so long that it made him think of a distant, yet certain conversation he'd had with Phillip.

Their friendship developed during high school in Trenton, and then a few years later in the mid-eighties, they reconnected at Muscle Beach Venice in Los Angeles, California. It was there, after enjoying the afternoon being entertained by the world-class adagio and gymnastics training and performances that they went for a bite to eat at some hole in the wall burger joint, away from the crowd, to catch up on their past few years since graduation. The two shared an easy, down-to-earth kinship where they could be totally honest with the other without the worry of judgment.

Joe admired Phillip's relationship with his father, the supportive role model he portrayed. The two were so close, in fact, that Joe was surprised to learn that Phillip was not his biological son and that his father was really his step-dad. "He marry my mom when I was three," Phillip told him. "He good dad, love me and my mom."

Where Joe suspected that Phillip had everything in a father that a boy could want, Phillip, at times, felt something missing as an only child. Had it been up to him, he said, he would have liked to have a large family, with brothers and sisters, like Joe had. Phillip's life and his own were about as different as any could be, yet each held a certain amount of curiosity about the other. It was there, at the burger joint that Phillip opened up to him about his father's struggle with cancer.

Having met the man only once, Joe still felt as if he knew him well, from all the stories Phillip shared over the years. It was easy to see that Phillip respected his dad enough to seek out his advice and guidance, and even when that advice was not always followed, and he later regretted it, his dad would tell him it was all part of becoming a man, making your own decisions and then learning from your mistakes. They shared the kind of rapport that Joe, at the time, wished he could have with his own father.

"Sorry about your dad," Joe said. "What kind c-a-n-c-e-r?"

"P-r-o-s-t-a-t-e," Phillip told him. "H-e-r-e-d-i-t-a-r-y. Both his father and brother die from c-a-n-c-e-r, but they live longer, seventy, maybe seventy-two. I think slow grow c-a-n-c-e-r, no s-y-m-p-t-o-m-s, only when advanced."

"Oh, I didn't know."

"Yeah . . . my mom say important to get check-up after forty. Dad always think he fine. When he see doctor, was too late." Phillip took a bite of his burger, kept his eyes lowered to his plate. It was one of those awkward moments, Joe thought, when you felt that something more needed to be said, but you didn't know what. At the age of twenty-one, Joe had no experience with these matters. *Grandpapa* died before Joe's fifth birthday, he didn't even remember ever meeting him. Grandma Barone suffered a stroke when he was seven, and then *Grandmaman* when he was eleven.

He fixed his eyes on Phillip to see if he wanted to talk more

about it, not wanting to pry into his thoughts. As the two finished up their burgers in silence, Phillip swiped the ketchup
from his lip with a napkin, took a long swallow of his Mountain
Dew, and then looked up at Joe. "I watched him die, ya know."

"Your father?"

"Yeah. They give him c-h-e-m-o for six months. Make him
sick and tired all the time, all he do was sleep." The agony in
Phillip's eyes was raw—so much so that it was as if his father's
death had been more recent than a year ago. "T-r-e-a-t-m-e-
n-t make him feel weak, sick, he don't want to eat, food don't
taste good." Phillip paused. "That year . . ." He paused again,
rubbed his hands against his jeans to somehow make it easier
to go on. "That year was long one . . . m-i-s-e-r-a-b-l-e . . . I
never see no one s-u-f-f-e-r like that before. But . . . Dad never
complain. He no feel angry. He hope for c-u-r-e. We all pray,
hope for c-u-r-e."

Joe nodded, somewhat uncomfortable, somewhat pained
by what Phillip's father went through, but also how awful it
must have been for Phillip and his mother to stand by and witness, knowing what the outcome would be.

"Then . . . after no change . . . test show c-a-n-c-e-r grow . . .
grow . . . grow . . . Dad say, 'No more!'"

"He stop c-h-e-m-o?"

"Yes, he want stop. And then one week later, he better.
Feel like . . . c-h-e-m-o want kill him and not help him. When
he stop, he was better. He look good, like before, healthy."
Phillip's eyes lit up, his face relaxed. "He get strong and more
strong, happy to live, ya know? We walk together . . . play basketball . . . play chess at night. I think . . . maybe . . . maybe
c-a-n-c-e-r go in r-e-m-i-s-s-i-o-n. But then . . ." Phillip's eyes
went sad again.

Joe already knew the outcome of the story. It just made it

tough to watch his friend relive it. If there was something he could say or do to help, he would. But Phillip sighed heavily and went on.

"Those ten . . . maybe . . . twelve weeks were g-o-n-e fast. Each day after that was bad a-g-a-i-n. Dad stay in bed all day . . . sleep most time. His last day . . ." Phillip laced his fingers together, looked down, as if contemplating what next to say.

"His last day, what?" Joe knew that Phillip witnessed his father take his last breath, but maybe there was something more he wanted to share.

"He look old. You don't recognize if you see him. They give him m-o-r-p-h-i-n-e, ya know? He don't want eat for many days, he r-e-s-t, look peaceful. Before he get this bad, he tell me he proud o-f me and he ask me to take care my mother for him." Phillip told him. "That last day . . . my mom and me . . . we sit next to his bed and wait. There was no more talking. Nothing. J-u-s-t wait. When he open his eyes . . . he reach for my hand, and he tell me: 'Son . . . I ready to go now'."

Phillip's brow wrinkled, confused like. "What do you mean? Where you want to go, I ask him. Dad tell me he ready to die." It was the first time his father even spoke of death, Phillip said. "Dad want to live and grow old with my mom . . . see me marry one day . . . spend time with his g-r-a-n-d-c-h-i-l-d-r-e-n. Dad want to travel, ya know, to Europe . . . and take Mom in hot a-i-r b-a-l-l-o-o-n one day. I never know that. He want to be there for me too," Phillip said, "when I need him. I ask Dad: 'Why do you say you ready to die? You have pain? You need more m-o-r-p-h-i-n-e?'—"

Joe felt as if he were there, with Phillip and his mother, watching the scene he described. He blocked out the other people around them, focused only on what Phillip was telling him that his father struggled to keep his eyes open, struggled to sign with his shaky hands.

"—'No pain,' Dad tell me. 'J-u-s-t tired. Like when you drive alone from J-e-r-s-e-y to California. No stops. No breaks. O-n-l-y for gas. Exhaustion takes over. Your brain begins to shut down. You s-t-r-u-g-g-l-e to keep your car on road, s-t-r-u-g-g-l-e to stay between lines. J-u-s-t a few more miles, you think, before you can be there, and let go.' I understand what my dad was saying. He have no more f-i-g-h-t left, no more e-n-e-r-g-y. Even when he l-a-y there in bed, j-u-s-t breathe, was too hard, too much work." Phillip, at first, admitted to Joe he didn't know how to respond to what his father said. But then he thought about it through his father's way of explaining things, and asked, "You a-f-r-a-i-d?"

His father managed a slight curl of the lip intended as a smile, and then shook his head. "Nothing to be a-f-r-a-i-d of, Son. Nothing."

Those were the last words he spoke, Phillip said. "I think he want us to know he was going to be okay, not worry . . . not feel sad. Mom and me . . . we love him so much. We miss him . . . but . . . we know he love us too. Death don't change that."

It was not until now, twenty-seven years later, that Joe wondered if he was on his way to that same place. The lightness of his body floated in and out, up and down. There was no pain, no hot and cold, no achiness or discomfort. If this was dying, then folks had it all wrong. There were far worse things, far worse . . . than dying. From what he could tell, it felt like taking a nap in an old wooden rowboat, the anchor dropped to keep from drifting away. When a ship passed, the waves would follow, rocking him to and fro.

Slipping in and out of consciousness, Joe could no more tell if he was still among the living than he could his whereabouts. There were blurred faces looking down at him, faces that could be real or imagined; strangers mostly. The last thing he remembered was . . . yes . . . making it to his truck. But where had he been?

It was cold, very cold.

There were wet leaves and dirt, no water or anything to drink.

Something happened. Something terrifying.

A fall.

His leg exploded on impact. Indescribable pain.

Some of it was coming back to him, bits and pieces, in no particular order.

The truck was warm inside.

The night grew darker.

He was alone, afraid.

Delia could not come.

The light from the trailer guided him, until it dimmed and disappeared.

The nighttime stars, in their own way, brought him comfort. Never before did the sky ever look more beautiful.

He prayed to keep going, weaved in and out of his lane, through foggy vision and a trembling body. His leg, at times, was on fire. The gas needle dropped to empty. His chest pounded and his mind struggled to keep up. There was a blow to his head that flashed pain, flashed lights, and then . . .

It was strange, he thought, that he felt no pain now. No pain at all.

CHAPTER 27

Summertime, there was no electricity, no TV or running water, but with it came the freedom to explore and dream and imagine the world through the eyes of an eight-year-old swinging from a tire that hung from an old farm oak tree.

It was a fine day for climbing trees so that he could reach the best green apples, fill up the edge of his shirt until it grew too heavy, and then toss them down for Petro to catch. Micheline would later bake them an apple cobbler for dessert when they visited *Grandmaman* on the mainland. Afterward, Joey ran barefoot to the river's edge, the apples all but forgotten, and began to bait his hook with a worm he'd dug up moments earlier, to catch him a smallmouth bass.

Susanna laughed at him, like she always did. "You won't catch a fish like that. Not from the shore. You're just wasting your time." Whether it was true or not, Joey paid her no attention, the fun was all in the trying.

When he tired of fishing, he joined in with Petro, Alanzo and Stefano, who were covering their bodies in mud. His mother stopped what she was doing, the building of the rock wall to keep the land from receding, to run and get hold of her camera. By the time she returned, she waved and called to them to look her way. The four of them grouped together now, resembled muddy swamp creatures. They posed with flexed muscles, beneath their seaweed covered chest, with some hanging out of their swim trunks, all of them laughing, and long after their mother snapped a picture.

Joe remained on the brink of consciousness. In and out, he floated, drifted, slept hard, and then as if he were about to wake up. There were glimpses of his surroundings—starched white hallways, bright lights, x-ray equipment, blue scrubs, technicians in their colorful smocks, doctors and nurses who spoke in hushed whispers, as if he might hear them. He slept through part of it, but remembered the ghastly look on their faces when the splint was first removed and a vague memory of shots that were administered to numb the leg, and then the washing of his wounds. He was given water to replenish his fluids and an IV drip in his arm. At some point, what lingered through his mind were their troubled gazes, their inability to look him in the eye for more than a few seconds at a time.

Did he only imagine it?

Joe tried to center his attention that he must be in a safe place now. Delia, he could have sworn, told him some of what the doctors said. But how? And when? He'd lost enough blood to cause the leg to hemorrhage. They would need to restore the blood, pump him with fluids and antibiotics, in hope of fighting the infection. There were portions of shattered bones that were now gone, twisted shards of remaining bone and torn pieces of ligaments that broke through the skin. There were multiple risk factors at hand—dehydration and cardiac arrest were at the top of the list, but what really caught Joe's attention, what made him cringe and lingered helplessly in his mind, was the question whether his body could fight off the infection so not to face an amputation. Not when, but *if* the fever goes down in time, could they even address the issues of the breakage.

"You're very lucky," Delia said.

"Where am I?"

"I-C-U, in the hospital."

Joe tried to stay alert, to understand all of what she and others were saying, but his mind kept searching for answers of how he'd gotten there. It was like one ongoing nightmare after another, with twists and turns and fuzzy patches along the way.

Lucky?

"You could have died out there. The leg, they said, is in very bad shape." Her eyes, Joe could tell, were saying so much more. She was worried for him. More worried than he'd ever seen her. He was conscious enough of what the doctors said, but more specifically, what they didn't. "Is he going to be okay?" Delia had asked. The doctors, however, dodged an answer. "Wait and see," was all they offered, before turning to leave the room.

Joe didn't want to think about that right now. All that he knew was that somehow he'd made it. He was warm now, finally warm, safe and unafraid. But more than anything, he needed sleep to give his body time to heal.

Whether it was minutes or hours, even days, Joe didn't know. He struggled between real and imagined, past and present, with flashed instances when he opened his eyes just long enough to see Delia still sitting there. There were snapshots of his past, troubled times that seemed to surface and resurface, with no clarity. Things he would just as soon forget or not face at all.

Joe completed boarding up the front doorway of the vacant rental. The new door had yet to arrive, and the remnant of a category three hurricane was on its way. After driving in his final nail, he turned to find his father watching him.

"Where the hell have you been?" he grumbled. "You're late!" He wore the same, dissatisfied look of disappointment. Why did it matter what time he arrived? He wasn't there to punch a time clock, wasn't hired for a specific set of hours with standard lunch breaks or time-and-a-half when exceeding a forty-hour week. Those jobs usually came with perks and benefits, and if you were lucky, a retirement pension.

Joe eyed his father, pointed to his wrist. "Why matter?" He was tired of his damn nit-picking and complaining. Did his father think that he didn't know about the times that he turned away and shouted his irritations to his mother and others that eventually got back to him? Did he think he was too stupid to see and get the gist of what he was saying?

"Banker's hours!" his father said.

Baker hour? "Wah?"

"You," his father pointed, "work. . . bank. . . hours. BB&T opens at nine o'clock."

Joe was fed up with this ongoing complaint. Would he ever get off his back? *Damn pain in the ass.* He yanked out a slip of paper and a pen from his pocket, handed it to his father. "Wah time... you... want me... work? Write down," he pointed to the paper. "Wah time?"

His father, at first, stood speechless. These moments were rare: him silent, his jaw slack. A good ten seconds passed before he took the piece of paper, scratched the side of his head, pondered a bit longer, and then told him, "Up to you." He pointed to his wrist. "Same time every day."

Joe opened his arms wide, exasperated. "No matter."

When his father said nothing further, Joe waved him off and went on his way.

Why was it impossible for his father to just, for once, be happy that he did a good job and that he got the work done? Why was he always sneaking up on him, watching him, looking for something, anything, to gripe about? Joe knew for certain that his father would never have gotten away with treating his employees at the salon this way. He must have been respectful for them to want to stick around as long as they did. To his customers, it was always a friendly "Good morning" or "Good afternoon" with a smile, and "Have a good day." He would joke around with them, be flexible when they were late, but with his family, it was always "Where the hell were you?" and "What took you so long?"

After his parents sold the salon, moved down south, and started up their home rental business, he and Delia later joined them. The affordable cost-of-living there allowed them to purchase their own home in the country. Joe accepted the role of working for his parents, though the hours and jobs varied from week to week. They needed someone to renovate the fixer-uppers, do maintenance and repairs, and he liked that he was able to be that person. Delia was signing professionally by then, and with his ongoing projects, there was enough to pay their bills, put money in his pocket, and allow them to live the sort of lifestyle they wanted, away from the rat-race of city living.

When other family members on his mother's side retired and moved to the area, they too joined in with buying and renting out homes. This allowed Joe additional hours of work, and he was surprised too, to be offered more money per hour, without asking for it. But when his father got wind of it, he set out to put an end to that.

"Hey, Joe," his aunt Lisa said, "I have a new rental and would like to hire you to tile the kitchen, maybe a bathroom in another house. But your father said we have to ask him first."

"What you mean, ask him first?" Joe formed the words with his lips, giving off a confused look.

"Your father said no one can hire you to do work, unless we check with him first. Did you know?"

Joe shook his head, feeling the heat begin to rise and then simmer. He left there, headed straight to town to pay his father a visit.

After parking his truck, he huffed his way up the porch steps, his keys in hand, and entered the kitchen. His father was sitting at the table, reading the newspaper, his mother stirring something on the stove. The moment Joe entered, his father looked up.

"I almo forty-ye-ole!" Joe blurted. "Work my-self!" he pointed to his chest, his gaze directed at his father.

"What's he saying?"

Joe began to explain it all to his mother. There were words muttered, mixed in with sign, back and forth pointing, and a note he scribbled out for clarity.

His mother looked sheepish and uncomfortable now, after reading the note. "He said you told the family they couldn't hire him for work without checking with you first."

"I did! He works for me. If . . . "

"Noooo!" Joe interrupted, shook his head. "You no own me! Work f-o-r my-self!" The two were in a heated stare-down with Joe standing near the table and his father remained seated. His mother froze, saying nothing at all.

Silence permeated the air between them. With nothing more to say, Joe turned and headed out the door.

CHAPTER 28

Joe pried open his eyes, enough to find the room dark, all but the familiar blinking monitors, some green, others white and yellow. He closed his eyes again, drifted off to a peaceful place—a place that once, so long ago, was his getaway, where he could think things through.

Black River had scenic views, winding trails, handmade rock paths, peaceful waterfalls and babbling brooks.

The pine forest with its unpaved trails led to wooden bridges that in some areas overlooked one of the oldest water-powered mills in New Jersey—Cooper Gristmill, built in 1826. It was the one place, the only place, just below the dam, that Joe seemed to rid himself of whatever troubled him. It was also where he took up fishing, at least on a more serious level. Folks who were there kept to themselves, and he liked that. Fishing was a sport of leisure that allowed him to reflect, to cool off—it was a sort of therapy to pacify his mind and calm his nerves.

He was sixteen when first introduced to Black River, a few miles from home in Chester Township, within walking distance. Once he discovered the perfect spot for fishing, he used his time there to unwind after a long day working at the Public

House, washing dishes. A sort of haven, compared to a busy kitchen full of people coming and going. As a job-starter, he worked there one season on the weekends, until Dominic offered him something better.

"How's the job going at Public House?" Dominic asked.

"Okay." Joe shrugged, nodded. It was far from his dream job, if he was ever to have one. Not working in a hot, stuffy kitchen, people peeling potatoes and carrots, dropping off buckets full of dirty dishes for him to wash up.

"What do they pay you there?"

"M-i-n-i-m-u-m wage."

"How would you like to work with me, setting tile? The jobs change from week to week. Some are small, only takes one day. Bigger ones . . . maybe a week. I can teach you and pay you more than minimum wage. What do you think?"

Joe raised an eyebrow. "How much?"

"How does ten dollars an hour sound?"

Ten dollars an hour? It was more than twice what he made washing dishes. "Okay. When do I start?"

At the onset of summer, the weeks varied from project to project; some locations were further than others. Working a few days a week was great. Joe not only liked the extra money, but also what he was doing, using his hands to create something artistic rather than as a dishwasher. It also allowed him spare time to do other things too. In tiling kitchen backsplashes, showers and bathrooms, Dominic taught him how to spread mud, align and cut tile with the wet cutting saw without chipping the corners, adjust laying the tiles, grout and cleanup work. Joe caught on quickly that Dominic was organized. He laid out the ground work, showed by example, even how to read and understand his written contracts.

By the second month, the jobs seemed to multiply, and the

days grew longer to where Joe felt himself getting more and more agitated, more and more impatient, until finally, one day, he couldn't take it anymore.

At Black River that afternoon, hoping to catch some trout, Joe replayed in his head what happened with Dominic that morning. He'd worked a full day the day before, and the two before that, staying up late afterwards. By the time he'd fallen into a deep, restful sleep, it seemed no sooner did he feel something pulling on him.

"Hey, wake up!" Dominic said from the foot of his bed, having given his leg a shake. When a startled Joe lifted his head, he saw his brother standing there. "Time for work."

Joe was hung-over from lack of sleep. He'd been reading a magazine on the newest muscle cars, until well past midnight. It couldn't possibly be time to get up, he thought, until he saw who had awakened him.

"Come on, Joe," Dominic pleaded. "I don't want to be late. Get up. I'll wait for you downstairs."

Joe waved him away, watched him leave the room with an eye half open. When he worked at the Public House, he always worked the afternoon or evening shift, which freed up his mornings to sleep in as late as he cared to. Those set of hours suited him well. This sudden change to the schedule he had gotten used to was getting to be a real pain. To make matters worse, Dominic was always so upbeat and cheerful, talking about what projects were lined up, before Joe could even adjust himself to the light of day. He didn't understand why they needed to be at the worksite as early as seven, which meant being up an hour or more before then. He thought of asking for some time off, but he needed the money more, to save for a car. If he ever decided to take a girl out on a real date, he'd need a set of wheels first. Just the thought of it made him think about Brandi. She was employed at the Public House, and though she was twenty-one, Joe had caught her watching him whenever their paths crossed.

"Hey, Joe." Brandi waved, smiled, and then approached him, in her almost too-tight hostess worktop.

Joe blushed, smiled a friendly hello at the way she stood there right in front of him, her head tilted upwards, grinning, her long silky hair draped down her back. But then she boldly placed her hand on his bicep, feeling his muscle, and promptly moved it to his shoulder for more touching.

"Wow! You must work out a lot," she said. "Your arms are like steel. Watch out, *Lou Ferrigno!*"

Joe blushed again, flattered, but also feeling funny inside, until she was called back to her post, allowing him to get on with his evening shift in the kitchen.

He hadn't seen Brandi since quitting the Public House, and hadn't thought of her all that much . . . until now. She was a pretty girl, though not quite his type, a hearing girl, several years older than he was, and he was sure she already had a boyfriend anyway. Girls that looked like her usually did, they didn't waste time on sixteen-year-olds. And guys like him knew better than to think that they did. Brandi was friendly, that was all, a little flirtatious maybe, nothing more than that. The time he caught her staring, though, looking him up and down . . . even checking out his butt, he felt both embarrassed and turned on at the same time.

Again, more pulling and shaking. Joe jerked his head up, annoyed by the intrusion. "Wah?" He growled.

"Why are you still in bed?" Dominic snapped back. "We're already going to be late. Come on, Joe. I don't have time for this. You need to get up now. Hurry up! You have five minutes, or I'm leaving." Dominic left the room again.

Joe felt the blood rising to his face, the heat in his chest seething, about to explode. He threw the covers off, yanked on his jeans from the day before, a pair of clean socks that didn't match, and then shoved on his work boots without tying them. He snatched a clean T-shirt from the top of his dresser where his mother washed and folded them. After a quick dash to the bathroom to pee and splash water on his face, he stomped his way downstairs and through the kitchen. Dominic and his mother were seated at the table.

"Happy?" Joe fired off, hands flailing. "Big b-o-s-s man!"

"You're mad at *me*?" Dominic questioned, but Joe ignored him, already headed for the door. Dominic touched his arm, to stop him, but Joe jerked it away, flung open the door where it clunked against the counter. The screened metal door was shoved open. Joe made his way to Dominic's van, got in and slammed the door so loud that Dominic waited before approaching the vehicle.

"Come on!" Joe retorted, throwing up a hand. "Big b-o-s-s man, les go!"

A full twenty seconds passed before Dominic opened Joe's door. "Come on out, Joe."

"Wah's pro-blem? Late. Les go!"

Dominic made no move. Joe directed his hard gaze forward, crossed his arms against his chest, his back slumped against the seat, and ignored his brother altogether.

"Look at me, Joe," he waved a hand to get his attention. "I need to tell you something."

Joe wasn't having it. He closed his eyes, shutting his brother out. There was no sound and no visual. Moments passed, what seemed like minutes, when Joe opened his eyes again.

"Get out of the van, Joe. I cannot take you to the j-o-b-s-i-t-e like this. You can go back to bed if you want."

Joe leapt out. Anger brewing to the point Dominic took a step back. Joe's fists were balled up and ready.

"What, you want to hit me? Calm down, Joe. You still b-l-a-m-e me for what Dad did? It wasn't my fault."

Joe stood there, seething, ready to throw the first punch if he needed to.

"Look, I'm not going to f-i-g-h-t you, okay? But if you really want to hit me, if it will make you feel better . . . than go ahead." Dominic stood there, his arms at his side.

Joe made no move to strike, noticed his mother approaching, and then Dominic said he needed to go. "I'm sorry, Mom, I have to leave. I can't work with him like this."

"Are you firing him?"

"Mom, I cannot have someone like that at the worksite. This isn't working out. I'm sorry. I have to go." Dominic drove off in his van.

Joe flung the end of his fishing line out into the river, mulling over the blowup. He wasn't proud of the way he acted, and didn't know why he got so angry at times. It was like a switch went off inside, something out of his control. He liked laying tile, learning the trade, and it paid well. But the early morning hours, the commute with Dominic, being told what to do when he already knew how to go about it, and then getting home after six most nights, made for a long day. There were other things he wanted to do, and when he did them, he was late getting to sleep.

But more than that, he was still angry at Dominic over what happened the previous fall, wishing he could erase the incident from ever occurring. He hated having it replayed again and again in his mind, and he didn't want to hate his father or stay mad at Dominic. Joe knew that he was not without blame, that he could have handled things differently, but when Dominic showed up and intervened, was something he could not forget.

"What the hell you doing, watching TV," his father lashed out. "Those damn sports again? Turn that crap off!"

"Wah prob—?"

"What . . . you still moping around over your shot at the Olympics? Is that what's the matter? Well, get over it. You think you have it so tough here, don't you? You don't know what tough is."

Joe could see his father was in one of his moods, and decided not to respond. He kept his eyes on the game. Bottom of the 8th inning, the score was tied, and the Yankees were up at bat against the Athletics.

"Hey! Did you hear what I said? Get off your ass and turn the TV off. I'll smash it, you don't turn it off."

Joe made no move, just sat there, halfway paying attention, the other half glued to Reggie Jackson, who was up to bat.

"Don't ignore me . . . I'm talking to you." His father moved in closer. "You want to waste your life over some stupid baseball game? It's all bullshit. What'd you do today, huh?"

Joe tried to block him from his view, not to react, to continue watching the game, but when his father stepped in his way, leaned over to nudge him on the shoulder, it made him tense up. "You think you can just ignore me? I told you to turn that crap off."

"Waaah? Leev me alooone!"

But his father wouldn't be brushed off. He nudged him

again, this time at the head. Joe bolted from his chair, fired up now, poked and prodded for the last time. He tightened up his fists, squared his jaw, ready to show his old man he was no longer a child he could just push around. He was tired of the way he was being treated, the way he was talked down to. School was out. It was Saturday. He was trying to watch the game, an important game, what the hell was his problem?

"What, you want to fight me?" His father looked stunned at first, but then raised his fists and took a pose.

Joe waited. He wouldn't swing first, but if his father touched him again, he might have to. The two were a few feet apart, each of them weaving slightly, like boxers in a ring, sizing up their opponent.

Dominic entered the living room, froze in his tracks, a bewildered expression. "What's going on?"

"He wants to fight me," his father said.

"No . . . Stop it! This isn't how we do things. Dad . . . Joe . . . This is wrong."

The two of them moved about, neither of them backing down, when Dominic positioned himself behind Joe, grabbing hold of his brother from behind, pinning his arms back to keep him from throwing the first punch. During the scuffle, his father broadsided him with a right hook, straight to the jaw. Joe lost his footing when Dominic tried to overpower him to the floor, and the two of them went down. He fought to free himself, when a swift kick came to his side, and then another to his ribs.

"Stop it, Dad. Don't!" Dominic cried out. "Leave him be."

"That'll teach him to raise his hand at me . . . the Son-of-a-Bitch."

Later in Joe's room, Dominic sat on the edge of his bed. Joe was nursing his bruised jaw with an ice pack, another one to his ribs, wanting nothing to do with him at all. He pretended not to listen, pretended not to care what he had to say.

"Joe . . . I'm sorry. I didn't know Dad was gonna do that. But I couldn't let you hit him. He's our father. The Bible says to h-o-n-o-r our parents. I couldn't let you hit him. And what do you think he would have done to you? Listen to me, Joe. Dad grew up in a bad neighborhood. He learned to s-t-r-e-e-t fight. When Dad was b-u-l-l-i-e-d as a k-i-d, he told his father, and you know what Grandpa said? He told Dad to find the biggest b-r-i-c-k that he could find and beat the b-u-l-l-y with it until he was b-l-o-o-d-y. And then he told Dad: 'So help me God, L-e-r-o-y, you come home with a black eye, I'm gonna blacken the other one for you. You let them make a p-u-s-s-y out of you, it's a r-e-f-l-e-c-t-i-o-n on me. So you kick his ass first, teach him some r-e-s-p-e-c-t. You hear me?'" Dominic told him. "I'm sorry, Joe, but I couldn't let you hit Dad. I just couldn't."

CHAPTER 29

B lack River was most beautiful in the fall, with its many shades of reds, oranges, coppers, and golds. It was a day in late October when Joe found himself mulling over what his mother had told him the night before.

"Why don't you talk to Dominic. See if he will give you your job back. He told me you do good work. He likes working with you, and the customers like you too, he said. But you have to get up early, that's part of the job. And you can't get angry, no fighting. That's not the way we handle things. You talk things out, be calm."

"Wah . . . like father talk calm?" Joe quipped.

"No, not like Dad. He gets mad too, but he's already grown. It's harder for him to change. You're still young. Find a better way to e-x-p-r-e-s-s yourself. Try to work it out with Dominic, he wants to help you."

Joe thought about her words, replayed them in his mind. It wasn't easy for him to admit he screwed up. He never meant to really fight his brother.

One evening, a few months after the blowup, Dominic stopped by after dinner. When he approached Joe, it surprised him.

"Hey, Joe, how you doing?"

"Okay," Joe nodded, and wondered if he came to give him his job back.

"Listen," Dominic began, "I've been really busy, lots of work and c-u-s-t-o-m-e-r-s calling me. I need help. It's too much for me to do alone. I was wondering . . . do you know anyone . . . a deaf friend maybe . . . that needs a job and would be interested working with me? I like working with the deaf and I don't mind teaching someone with no experience. Do you know anyone?"

"What about me?"

"You want to come back and work with me?"

Joe nodded.

"Well . . . you know what happened last time. And . . . I don't want—"

"I know . . ." Joe was quick to say. "I work better. No get mad. Be ready early. I need job, like work tile. Sorry about before."

"Okay. If you're sure, I'd like that."

Fishing continued to be a favorite pastime, and for Joe, there was no better place than the one he'd found and adopted years earlier just below the dam. He stood, one foot on a large flat rock, the other one off beside it, as he watched his line drift slowly with the current of the river. It was after graduation that he thought more seriously of getting a place of his own. Petro was a senior, and the way things were looking, it wouldn't be long before he too would be seeking a way out. It was no wonder to Joe how his brother felt, but for Joe, at least, he wanted no roommate, no little brother tagging along. It was nothing against Petro, just something he needed to do alone.

Joe reeled in his line, threw it out even further, as he thought of the look on Petro's face, and the one of his father.

"Why do you want to go to college?" his father asked.

"Why? Find good job, make a lot of money," Petro motioned.

"Oh yeah? Who told you that?"

"My teacher."

"Is that right. Your teacher told you that?"

Petro nodded.

"Does your teacher make a lot of money?"

Petro pondered the question a moment, and then laughed. "No, not a lot."

"See! Don't listen to what everyone tells you. People say stupid things. You want to go to college and wind up stupid?"

Petro gave a blank look, didn't respond. He shot a glance to his mother, to Joe, and then back to his father again, waiting for the punch-line, when none came.

Joe shook his head. There was no figuring out his old man, and the odd ways about him, both before he became a *Witness* and since he stopped attending meetings altogether. From all his preaching that the end was near, that studying *The Truth* was the only way to become part of the great crowd and live on a paradise earth, his father suddenly took a turn, and a change of heart against Dominic when he told them he was leaving for New York City to work for the *WatchTower* Society.

"You're making a big mistake!" his father argued. "Why move there? Stay here and preach."

"Dad, I've already committed myself. It's what I want. I need to make my own way now, and what better way than to serve Jehovah?"

"You're not gonna make no money there. You'll be putting money in their pockets."

"It's not about the money, Dad. You know we don't worship money. It's about serving Jehovah. Living there covers my room and board, my food. I'll be learning different trades, while serving Jehovah. If I need any money to travel or come home to visit, I can find work on the side, that won't be a problem."

"You should stay here, help out."

Dominic gave a solemn look. "I'm sorry you feel that way. I thought you'd be happy, proud even that I want to do this. Most people don't get this opportunity."

"You call leaving your family an opportunity? I call it a stupid mistake. You want to be stupid, then go! If you stay, you can get your hairdresser license. Maybe even take the business over one day."

"Dad . . ." Dominic wore a sorrowful look. Joe could see he didn't want to disappoint his father, but he could also see that Dominic's mind was already made up. "I'm sorry, Dad. I'm an adult now. I have to make my own decisions. This is the right one for me. I hope you can understand."

But his father didn't understand, and when Dominic left a few weeks later, Joe saw a change in him—his short-fuse became even shorter.

CHAPTER 30

Joe's mind floated and surfaced, floated and surfaced some more when it landed somewhere during his early high-school days when he tried out for the junior wrestling team and made varsity. Dominic had his driver's license, his own car by then. The two of them were on their way home from Sunday's service at the Kingdom Hall.

"I want to make a few door-to-door stops on the way," Dominic said.

"Nooo. Go home!" Joey opted to go with his brother so that he wouldn't have to sit in the back of the Suburban, waiting for his parents who were still chatting with the Nelsons.

"I need to finish my hours of service. It won't take long. Okay?"

No, not okay, Joey thought. Had he known ahead of time, he would have waited for his parents. But they were headed out the parking lot now, and rather than argue, he sat there, arms crossed, stewing about it.

"Hey," Dominic stopped the car and nudged him. "Just a few homes, okay, and then we can get us a D-airy Q-ueen—my treat."

The mention of a DQ was all it took. Joey relaxed, agreed, and soon after, they were at a nearby neighborhood, parked at the curb.

"We'll c-i-r-c-l-e the block, and then we'll be done."

Joey gave a nod, and then realized the original *few homes* were now more like a dozen. It was already noon, he was hungry and thinking what kind of Sundae he would choose, the creamy caramel or the hot fudge syrup—he liked them both.

The first few homes, there was someone to accept a copy of the *Awake* magazine. The next few, with no car in the driveway and no answer at the door, Dominic slipped a copy in the latch of the handle or door knocker. By the time they made it back around the block, with only two homes remaining, they approached a metal-link fence with a wooden glider swing set out front.

Joey unlatched the gate, admiring the lawn glider with the canopy top. It was something he could see himself making one day. This one was old and worn, the wood unpainted and mildewed, but the style was similar to one he'd seen before, only with a wooden roof instead of a canopy. Surrounding the glider was plenty of scattered debris in the yard: a broken sandal, an assortment of Styrofoam cups, a rusty can full of water and floating cigarette butts and a hodgepodge of dried-up dead plants. He noticed then an old woman peering out the screened-in door, chewing on something. The way her jaw worked it reminded him of Zeus, Little Freddie's nanny goat. She spit into the cup she was holding, and then called out to someone from inside the house.

They were halfway up the walkway, with Joey in front when the woman opened the door and out blasted a mangy looking mutt the size of a full grown Shepherd, its upper lip bearing sharp fangs. He growled a vicious bark that warned them he meant business. The encounter was so fast, before either of them could prepare for what to do. The old woman, in her nappy cotton housedress, remained behind the screened door.

Within two feet of the barking-maniac, Joey froze, his hands out in plain view to show he was not to be feared, but the sixty-some-pound brute charged at him with hot rage burning behind his snarl. Nowhere to escape and nothing to protect him, Joey did the only thing he could do. He struck repeated blows, knuckle-punched the right side of the dog's head, then the left, again and again, until the dazed maniac scampered back to the porch, its droopy tail between its legs.

"Get off my property 'fore I call the police!" the toothless nanny goat hollered, waving a baseball bat in the air.

Joey and Dominic hauled their butts on out of there, back to the car, breathless, and foregoing their final stop. "Wow! You gave that dog a beating!" Dominic said, halfway laughing, halfway scared out of his mind. "I thought he was going to bite your head off and then mine."

Sitting on the edge of the dock, his bare feet dangling above the water, Joe stared at the images reflected by the sun, waiting for the fish to bite. It was a warm day, the tenth in a row without rain. The pond at Gold Point was a wide open, peaceful place, empty of random fishermen, owned by his parents and reserved only for family to enjoy. His father was funny that way. Concerned that if the word got out to neighbors and friends, the fish would all be caught, leaving none at all for them.

A pond without fish, Joe thought, his father might starve to death. He didn't even fish out here, at least not anymore.

Joe saw the tractor across the way, a glimpse of the man riding it, on the other side of the property. The farmer was one of their renters who tended the land, though he didn't know him by name. The scene, however, triggered a memory of his childhood. Not just of the farmer, but the waterfront surrounding him, taking him back to when he was just a boy fishing at the edge of the river. A time when he slept in a pitched tent under the stars, catching lightning bugs in a jar, huddled around a campfire at night, pretending to believe somebody's ghost story.

It was during those summers that he ate strawberries straight from the vine, roasted marshmallows on a stick, walked barefoot in the sand, catching minnows with his hands. Each morning was a new day to wake up to. To run free, climb trees, scuff up knees and act silly. It was a time when he had no bills to pay, no responsibilities at all, and could let his imagination run free, be whoever he wanted to be, and dream of what the future might hold.

The line tugged, bringing Joe out of his daydream. He braced himself against the pull, began to reel in his catch.

The trees were tall and green, the mountains a hundred times bigger. It was near midnight and the sun was still out. Joe drove and drove, around one curve and then another, until the road narrowed, the pavement turned first to gravel and then to mere dust.

Had he taken a wrong turn? This couldn't be the way, he thought. He slowed to read the upcoming sign: Road Closure. Keep Left. He continued on for yet another mile until he reached a fork in the road. The left side was barricaded. Keep Out. Danger. The right side was open.

Why sign say, Keep Left? He must have read it wrong. With the right fork his only option, he pressed the accelerator, anxious to get there, steered the pick-up through the park area when the road turned to pavement again. Surrounded by enormous pine trees, the ground full of needles, picnic tables evenly spaced apart, Joe watched for bear. He continued down the one-way path with barely enough room for his vehicle. Finally, up ahead, he saw the light of the opening where the trees would clear. But as he neared it, the sun at just the right angle, blinded him. His truck kept moving, though slower, his hands tight on the wheel, sweat on his brow, when he felt the bottom break away. The road ended. The truck took a dive in midair. He was falling . . . falling . . . falling . . .

Joe bolted, arms thrashing about. Two doctors hovered over him in what appeared to be an operating room. One doctor looked at him with sorrowful eyes; the other one held a power-saw. The room was so bright it hurt his head and scorched his eyes, but soon enough he was back to total darkness.

He shivered cold one moment and was burning up the next. There were glimpses of Delia's face and horrified looks. Portions of normal seeped in to the craziness he experienced over and over like a twisting tornado that rocked anything in its path.

Did they give me something to sleep or to take pain away?
You could have died out there!
Blood clots in the leg that may travel to the lungs.
Breathing problems . . .
Fever . . . stop the bleeding . . .
You could have died out there!
How many fingers am I holding up?

Your leg is in very bad shape . . .
Wait . . . what power-saw for?
You could have died out there!
Foggy patches of floaters drifted nearer and nearer until . . .
Deer.
Delia drew back the curtain as she stood at the window,
a snarled expression, her arms crossed in front of her chest.
Is he going to be okay?
Wait and see.

CHAPTER 31

Joe awoke to find he was alone in a room full of medical equipment. The shades were drawn, with the only light a fluorescent bulb overhead and the ones from the monitors tracking his vital readings.

His first thought was that he didn't just dream making it out alive but that he was in fact in a hospital bed. His second, when his gaze landed to his right leg, the one elevated and packed with ice, was that it was still whole, and a part of him.

Joe made no attempt to move. It all happened so fast, and yet so slow, like a clogged up drain makes its way through the pipes, that he could barely trust in what he was seeing. Without moving his head at all, he allowed his eyes to roam and scan his surroundings until they landed on the container of water on the rolling tray beside him. He remembered being thirsty for so long, that he could not help stare at the pitcher. Trying to make sense of it all, to understand and come to grips with what happened, there were still too many unanswered questions. Too many blurred patches and missing links that he could not be certain that his nightmare was over. He closed his eyes again, tried to force his way back, when he had been driving . . . driving . . . driving . . .

Had his nightmare ended or just derailed temporarily? From the looks of it, he was still a long way from where he needed to be. He tried to remember what Delia told him before going into surgery, but his mind was a muddle of confusion. There was no feeling, no feeling at all in his right leg, as he gazed at it now. And where . . . where was Delia, had she gone back home?

"Good morning." His thoughts were interrupted when a nurse entered the room, her smile a bit too cheery, a bit too forced. She was a plump woman with dark eyes and even darker skin, wearing a pink smock covered with miniature poodles that made him think about Jester, Dingo and Prince. He'd not seen them in so long. His eyes closed and then he slept some more.

"Sit!" Joe signed to Jester, hooking the first two fingers of his right hand over the extended two fingers of his left, and then slowly moved them downward.

When Jester failed to comprehend the command, Joe helped him out by pressing down on his back-end, and then thought of an even better idea. He clapped for Prince and Dingo to come over. With the three in front of him now, Joe gave the command.

Prince and Dingo immediately complied. After a moment, Jester followed the others' lead, and sat.

"What are you doing?" asked Sarah, who had just returned from school.

"Teach," Joe said, pointing to Jester. "Where C-hloe?"

"In the house. You teaching him sign?"

Joe nodded.

"Can I help?" Sarah had not been home during the times when he taught Prince and Dingo, though she knew and understood the commands.

When Joe agreed, she set her book-bag down on a lawn chair, and stood beside him. Joe motioned for Prince and Dingo to *Stay*, and then snapped his fingers for Jester to stand. He gave Sarah the go-ahead, watched her give the command to sit. Without hesitation, Jester sat.

Sarah giggled. "This is easy."

"No easy," Joe said. "Smart." He rubbed Jester's head.

Sarah was called into the house to do her homework. Joe proceeded to finish what he started, motioned for Jester to get back in line with the others, and then gave the *Stay* command by folding back the three fingers of his right hand with only the thumb and pinkie pointed forward in the shape of a Y. He held it in front of his chest, while firmly moving the palm downward to signal them to stay in place. Joe turned to begin walking away, when he looked back and saw Jester following him. He set him straight again, pointed him back in line with the others. *Stay*—he signaled, and then tried it again. By the third time, Jester caught on. He was a quick learner, Joe decided. He'd already taught the others from day one the basic commands: to fetch, speak, roll over, come, lie down, sit and stay, without uttering a word. They came to understand early on that Joe could not hear sounds the way others could. When someone knocked at the door, they knew to alert him by leading him to that area. If only humans were able to adapt as quickly, he thought, to a different language, he'd have a much easier time of it.

Joe squatted to their level, gave them each a pat and a scratch behind the ears. "Good boy," he told them, and then fed them each a treat.

Joe shivered. The four walls, the soft bed, the meds going through his veins did little to ease the torture going through his head. In and out of sleep he went.

You can do this, Coach said. *This is your race. The one you never had.*

Delia and others cheered from the sidelines. *Come on, Joe!*

But then the sleeve of his thermal pullover was being torn to shreds, exposing his arm to the cold. Teeth so sharp ripped at his skin, tearing a chunk of his flesh.

His fists thrashed about like a madman, pounding against the sides of the mangy, maniac dog's head, causing it to retreat, at least for the moment. The dog turned wolf then. There were two of them now—red wolves.

He reached for his gun case to unzip the bag, when the sound of metal caused them to snarl, their jaws frothing at the mouth.

He thought he would die there, right on the spot, could barely move nor breathe. But when he braced himself for what would happen next, a stampede of wolves rushed at him all at once, eager to devour him limb by limb.

CHAPTER 32

By the time Joe caught sight of the herd of deer, they were halfway across the road. His body tensed, and then his reflex reaction took over. He slammed hard on the brake, gripped the wheel with both hands, swerved left to avoid hitting them, causing the backend of his truck to fishtail out of control where he spun into a U-turn, skidding off the shoulder of the road, and then stopped when the engine died. His head slumped over and his chest about to explode, several moments passed before he relaxed his white-knuckled hold on the wheel. Sweat dripped down his face and onto his neck as his body shuddered. He nearly missed them all, felt the thud just before the doe's hind legs bottomed out and she was thrown toward the ditch. The strike, however, was not strong enough to keep her down. Just as quickly as she'd fallen, she got back up again and ran off to join the others. It all happened in a blur, and was a wonder the truck did not flip over.

To verify and assess the situation, Joe peered over his shoulder to find them all gone. Not a single one was left in sight. He steadied his breathing then, reached for his rifle that was now on the floor, and got his nerves under control. His truck was now facing in the opposite direction, and he feared he might not have enough gas to start her up again. A half mile away from the intersection, and just beyond it was his home; he relaxed a bit, closed his eyes, the crisp cool air feeling good to him now. He rested his arm and his head against the window pane, wiggled his fingers, and knew he still had a chance.

But he waited some more, not eager to test the limits of his empty gas tank. With enough time passed and the engine still warm, he pressed the clutch and turned the key to feel the engine jerk and chug. He gave it a little gas, not too much, and then went to shift from fourth gear down to first, but the gear was either locked or jammed. He tried for second and third, but remained stuck in fourth. He jiggled the stick to and fro and then side-to-side to somehow jar it loose. Finally, he managed to get it in neutral, where it remained stuck again. To keep from panicking, Joe let his foot off the clutch, and relaxed a moment. The problem was more than likely a worn clutch or a damaged transmission part. The truck was eleven-years-old with more than a hundred and forty thousand miles, making either of those the probable cause.

With the engine still idling, Joe pressed the clutch again, held it down to the floor and tried to shift to any of the gears. He could feel the hold and grind, so he let off a beat and then tried to pop it in reverse. His chest hitched when the stick moved. He held it there, as he thought of what he was about to do next. With the barrel of the rifle back in his hand, he gave the pedal some gas, eased off the clutch, and set off to back his way toward the intersection, halfway looking over his shoulder, keeping centered in the road. He kept it steady at twenty-miles-per-hour when he saw up ahead the traffic light turn yellow. He would need to stop at the intersection of US Route 13. The timing of the light was configured to allow the highway the right-of-way for several minutes, while vehicles exiting from secondary roads were limited to a twenty-second timer. Within the past year, Joe timed the wait and knew that, if he stopped, he would have several minutes of idle time before the light turned green again. It was what caused him to make his decision, not to stop and keep going. As the light went from yellow to red, Joe proceeded to cross over six-lanes of highway—three that were headed east, three headed west, with a divider on each side. He was counting on the timing of the light change to give him the advantage of making it over safely, at least to give others fair warning as he backed his way over.

There were two vehicles to his right, with one driver giving a stupefied expression, his arms in the air. The other one from his left, a white Honda Civic, coming at him screeched to a halt, the back-end weaving, as he came to a stop to avoid colliding. Clearing the highway, Joe kept it steady, as he entered Brigham Road. This was it, he thought, his nightmare was over. He passed an empty parking lot on the right, a daycare center on the left, two neighbors' homes, and then backed his way into his driveway, angled directly in front of the bay window of his home before killing the engine.

The curtains were drawn tight, so he pressed the horn and held it down to get Delia's attention quickly. Seconds later, the drapes were yanked open. Delia was there fully dressed, her arms crossed in front of her. She was mad, alright, steaming mad.

With his arm out the window, Joe waved for her to come on out, but in stony silence, lips pinched tight, Delia held her ground. Again, Joe waved his arm higher, bore down on the horn again until finally she came barreling out—furious, shaken, with sleep-deprived, red-rimmed eyes.

"Are you trying to wake up the whole neighborhood?" She reached around his side of the truck, and upon a closer look, her face transcended to worry. "What's wrong?"

Joe sat there with dazed eyes, pale skin bruised and

feverish under his dazed eyes, with beads of sweat covering his forehead. At first, he said nothing. There were tears in his eyes and a thousand choked-up words he could not speak. He opened his driver's door, shifted his body and then pointed to his splinted leg. The branches were lopsided now, with blood prints everywhere—against the door pane, the seat, the steering wheel, even his scalp trickled with residue. His clothing was wet and moldy, his pant leg torn in places. He could only imagine the horror picture it painted.

Delia gasped. "Oh my God, Holy Jesus, what happened?" She clasped a hand over her mouth. "Oh my God! We need to get you to the hospital!"

"You drive."

"Can you make it to my car?"

Joe nodded, told Delia to pull alongside him, and then waited for her to run inside to get her purse and keys, and return moments later. By the time she was lined up beside his truck, he felt a wave of nausea rock through him. Delia ran back around, opened her passenger door, pulled back the seat to allow for more leg room, and then turned to Joe, who was doubled over with dry heaves.

He was home now, finally home. He had made it, but needed to hold on just a bit longer. Joe stepped out of the truck with his weight supported on his good foot, though it was barely able to hold him. He felt it coming again, that foggy buzzing sensation in his head, but he used the door and Delia to steady himself. When his knee went to buckle, he pushed through it and managed two small hops before he was able to lower himself into her vehicle. Once he did, his world went black again.

CHAPTER 33

There was a draft in the room, an airiness that caused Joe to open his eyes. A nurse had uncovered his right leg. His foot was supported and braced in a flexed position, bandaged with only his toes exposed. An overwhelming sense of relief overcame him that the leg was still whole. Though with it now, came a steel pin the size of a Phillips screwdriver, inserted through the heel of his foot. Attached at both ends of the exposed pin was a black steel-cased rod that ran up the front of his shin and connected to the tibia. Joe relied on the doctors to work their magic, but in the meantime, he wondered how long he would have to wear the odd-looking contraption that would require him to sleep flat on his back. He tried to wiggle his toes, but either he couldn't, or he was afraid it would cause pain, so he closed his eyes again, swallowed hard and then cringed at the soreness of his throat. The IV-drip was still hooked up, and the pain meds left him relaxed.

He wondered if his vitals were back to normal now, if his worst fears were behind him, and how long before he would walk again. He didn't want to burden Delia with more bills. She was already working way too many hours, and he barely saw her as it was.

"Hi, how are you feeling?" Delia signed, her smile bringing tears to his eyes. He didn't see her walk in the room, and it wasn't until she touched his hand that he opened his eyes and saw her. He remembered now the worried look on her face. Maybe it was just before going into surgery. Anything prior to or after that was still distorted. His memory of how he got there was also hazy. Delia was wearing a different set of clothes, he was sure, and she'd washed her hair. He could smell the scent of her shampoo when she leaned over to kiss him. He knew that he'd be lost without her, and would need her help now, more than ever.

"B-e-t-t-e-r," he said, a choke in his heart. He could not recall ever feeling this emotional. "What day this?"

"Tuesday. You had a long day yesterday. They g-a-v-e you a-n-t-i-b-i-o-t-i-c-s to get your fever down, and then took you to surgery late afternoon. Do you remember?"

"A little. What time now?"

"8:15 a.m."

A bubbly young woman wearing a lime green smock with tiny stethoscopes all over it entered the room. "Well, good morning! My name is Tamika, and I'll be taking care of you today."

Joe turned to Delia to catch the nurse's name. The previous day, he seemed to recall a Nurse G in the morning and then a different one for the night shift. The two surgeons assigned to his case, he remembered now, were Doctor B (for Brady) and Doctor Y (for Yu).

"How are you doing today, Mr. Joe?" Nurse Tamika asked before taking a look at his leg, and then touched the edge of his toes. "Color's good."

"Thirsty." Joe reached for the jug of water, but the tray was pushed aside.

"I can help you with that," she said. She raised his bed so that he could sit up, and then poured him half a cup.

Joe chugged it down, motioned for more. She poured

another cupful, when a second nurse brought in a tray of food.

"You must be hungry," Delia signed. "You haven't eaten in three days." The IV-drip must have kept him going because he didn't feel all that hungry.

"The doctor will be in shortly," Nurse Tamika told them. "See if he can eat something," she told Delia. "I'll be back to check on him later."

Delia positioned the tray of food near Joe's chest. He stared at the lumpy oatmeal, the cup of diced peaches coated in syrup, the slices of limp toast, and the carton of orange juice. Without a word, he reached for the juice, opened the carton and took a sip, before making a face, and then quivered.

"No good?"

He shook his head, pointed to his throat. "Sore."

"Try the oatmeal, something warm."

Joe took a spoonful. It was bland, no flavor at all. He tried another taste, and then pushed the tray away.

"You don't want a-n-y?"

He shook his head again.

"Did you get a good night's sleep?"

Joe shrugged. He was not about to tell her of the nightmares, the parts that he remembered, anyway. Though he made it out of the swamp, finally, he returned to it when he slept. "Yeah, I sleep okay."

"I called your mom again. She's worried about you. I told her I'd call her later after we speak with the doctor. M-icheline called last night, then D-ominic. A-lanzo left a message. I'll call him back later tonight. The phone has been ringing non-stop."

Joe nodded and then squinted. "What doctor say after my surgery? You talk to him?"

"Doctor Y said it took them more than four-hours to p-i-e-c-e portions of your leg back together again. You lost s-o-m-e blood, and required a p-i-n-t for them to complete the surgery. He said you w-o-u-l-d sleep for the night, that I should go home and get some rest."

"What time you leave?"

"Nine o'clock. I went home at six to feed the dogs and let them out, and then came back thirty-minutes later until they b-r-o-u-g-h-t you out of surgery."

Joe nodded. "What about you . . . you sleep last night?"

"Better than the last two." She gave a half-hearted grin.

"Sorry." Joe saw the dark circles beneath her eyes, could see she still looked tired. He could only imagine what *he* must look like.

Doctor Yu entered the room. "Good Morning," he said, acknowledging them both. "How are you feeling today, Joe?"

"Better."

"I see you didn't eat much."

Joe motioned he wasn't hungry.

"That's normal after being under general anesthesia, and in your case, we also did a peripheral nerve block for the leg."

Joe kept his eyes mostly on Delia, who was signing what was being said, and then he waited for more. He wanted to know if the surgery was successful, if he would eventually walk normal and return to his usual life. He knew it was probably too soon to ask these kinds of questions, and still, he wanted to know what he was up against.

"Let me start off by saying, you are one very lucky man." The doctor's eyes were mostly on Joe, but also on Delia, to make sure he was not speaking too fast. "The surgery itself was a very delicate procedure. For now . . . you're out of the woods," he said and then smirked. "Sorry, no pun intended. What I mean is that we were able to repair some of the damage, and save your leg."

Joe let out a breath, gave a brief nod, waited for him to go on.

"However . . . you have a long road ahead of you. This is not a simple case of resetting a broken bone. There was extensive damage. You will require several more surgeries in the next twelve months or so."

When Delia finished signing, Joe flinched. There was a lull in the room. A few moments passed before Joe signed back.

"He wants to know if his leg will be fine again," Delia said. "Will he be able to walk and run, and how long before he can return to work?"

Dr. Yu sighed heavily before taking a seat on the stool. He rolled himself over, clasped his hands before him, resting them on his lap before speaking. Joe braced himself for the news he suspected was not good.

"I understand you have a lot of questions. The injury you sustained is quite serious, and your night alone in the woods must have been terrifying for you. I can't stress upon this enough, Joe," he shook his head, "but you truly are one very lucky man. I'm sure you probably don't feel that way right now, but you very easily could have died, and for several different reasons. It's almost a wonder that you didn't." Dr. Yu glanced to Delia and then back to Joe again. "At the moment, I am somewhat optimistic that you will be able to resume some, not all, of your normal activities, in time and within reason. You'll have to be patient, though."

When Delia caught up with him, Dr. Yu continued. "Please understand. I cannot give you a clear, cut-and-dry answer. A lot of it depends on you and how well your leg heals. This kind of injury is more rare than common, so the healing process can be unpredictable."

After the translation was done, Joe signed to Delia, who

repeated out loud: "What do you mean, depends on me?"

"For now, you're stabilized. If we don't encounter any more problems, you might be able to go home tomorrow afternoon, but I'd like to keep you for another night at least, for observation." Dr. Yu paused, allowing Delia time to get the message across, and then went on. "This here is just a temporary cast. You'll need to come back in ten days for one made out of fiberglass, for six to eight weeks. We're keeping you on antibiotics—"

"Thank you," Joe was quick to show gratitude.

"Not so fast . . . there's more, I'm afraid. You'll have meds for the pain to keep you comfortable, but they will make you loopy, so you don't want to take more than you have to. It's very important that if there is any sign of fever or infection, any sign at all, you call me immediately."

Joe nodded. So far, he got it. It made sense.

"What kind of work do you do, Joe?"

Delia signed the question and gave the anticipated reply. "Construction mostly."

Dr. Yu shook his head slowly, shoved his hands in his pockets. "Consider yourself on vacation for a while. At the very minimum, I would say for a year, probably more."

Delia kept a neutral face, but Joe knew in that instant the devastating change their lives would take.

"Let's not worry about the what-ifs, and just take it one step at a time. Okay? At the moment, things are looking up—a thousand percent better than when we first laid eyes on you. But, please know, you will need to be very, very careful with this leg from now on."

Joe knew how these things worked. There were no money-back guarantees. They could not predict the final outcome nor would they make any promises they could not back up. Some of it was a crap-shoot. Whatever the end result, he would have to live with it.

Dr. Yu stood, rolled the stool back away from the bed. "I'll leave you two alone now. If there's anything you need, just buzz the nurse and let her know."

"Thank you, Doctor," Delia said. The two of them watched him leave the room.

They were alone now. Joe leaned back against his pillow, eyes closed. He felt numb. It was a lot to take in all at once. His mind was muddled with fear for their future. Being out of work for a year, *at a minimum*, with no health insurance, and having to depend on Delia for all of it with several more surgeries to endure. He knew the costs would accumulate fast. Just a single night in the hospital, a friend once told him, cost him twenty-five thousand for a routine appendix removal. Fortunately for him, it was the insurance company that paid, but he and Delia had none, and his surgeries, for sure, would not fall in the category of *routine*.

Would he even be able to work in construction again? Why had this happened to him? Why?

Delia touched his arm. Joe opened his eyes, stared at the blank wall across from him to avoid her gaze, a lump weighted down in his throat. There was so much to be grateful for, and the outcome could have been much worse. Being cold and alone was a thing of the past, and as far as he knew, he was going to be alright. And yet, he was overwhelmed by the doctor's words: *Consider yourself on vacation for a year, probably more.*

Delia placed her hand over his. "Do you want to talk about it?"

Talk about it? He'd already given her the short version. How far of a drop he'd fallen, the approximate time and condition of the wooded area, his repeated bouts of uncon-sciousness, dealing with the cold and the pain. He told her pretty much everything he wanted to, everything but what he regretted most. Delia would have more questions, but he didn't know where to start or how much he should tell her. He studied his fingers a bit, his mind never far from the actual incident. It was all too recent. He hoped that in time it would be a little easier to reflect back on. He looked up finally.

"My c-e-l-l phone s-t-i-l-l in woods. Wet. D-a-m-a-g-e-d. I could not call you. I didn't know . . ." He fought to hold it together, remembered how desperate he felt when the battery slipped from his fingers, lost in the muck, and he'd thrown and smashed the phone against the tree. "I didn't know if I ever see you again. I wish . . ." He pinched the area between his brows, and waited, trying to keep it together. He blinked hard and went on. "I should have tell you I go h-u-n-t-i-n-g. I should have left you note. Something. I thought maybe I might not make it. I thought I go crazy. I didn't want to die out there. It was hard to keep going. I black-out over and over. I didn't want to quit, but . . . I have no water, and pain . . . pain was k-i-l-l-i-n-g me. I pray. I keep g-o-i-n-g . . . I didn't give up. Didn't want to die out there." Joe was filled with re-lief now—that Delia was with him, that the pain had stopped due to the meds, that he was going to be okay. He could not contain his emotions, of everything he might have lost. Tears welled up in his eyes, no longer could he hold them back, his body trembled.

Delia was beside him in an instant, the nightmare finally over. He was safe now, where he needed to be. The two of them clung to one another and wept.

EPILOGUE

When Joe returned home, he adjusted the bag that was strapped to his waist. It held a clear tube that went straight to an area near the temporary cast to inject meds whenever he felt pain. He was told to use it sparingly if he still wanted to function, but that his not being in pain was crucial to his healing.

Delia helped him over to the sofa chair in the living room, where he could rest his leg on the ottoman and keep it elevated, as he waited for her to bring in his three loyal companions. A couple of days had passed, for the shock to wear off, or at least soften the blow to what the future would hold. As bleak as it seemed, Joe was grateful for so many things that he was determined, somehow, to stay positive. Delia's mom was there to help, and Delia herself insisted it was time to sell the Tipsy Teapot to allow herself more time to be available for work as a translator. The hours would be lighter, the pay much better, so it all made sense to Joe.

"Okay," Delia said, "here they come. Be careful with that leg." She opened the door to the sunroom to let them in. A few moments later, Prince, Jester, and Dingo came prancing in. The three of them and Joe were all over each other, like long lost friends, excited about the reunion. With thoughts that only Joe could feel, and not speak, he leaned over from his chair, gave them each a hug and a rub on the head. They danced about, licked his face, and seemed to sense and understand he suffered an injury. They each took a look and a sniff at the odd-looking contraption, the nuts and bolts that held the long rod in place, careful not to jar it in any way. Eventually, after the three of them settled down, Prince laid his head on Joe's lap, with the other two lounged out on the floor. He could not think of a better homecoming.

In the weeks and months that followed, Joe had many visitors, mostly from family near and far, but also some friends too. He shared with them the basics of what happened, answered their questions and inquiring minds. The local newspaper did a write-up, *Hunting Trip Turns Ugly*, the caption read, providing as many of the details that Joe was willing to share.

For months, he suffered occasional nightmares that eventually dissipated. But more than ever before, Joe had much time on his hands to reflect on it all, not just on the accident or the horror that came with it, but on the people in his life. Those that mattered, as well as things he may never be able to understand. There was a part of him that got it. We are who we are based on where we come from. It is not about shifting the blame on to our parents or even theirs—but about acceptance, flaws and all, with an understanding that it is not our job or responsibility to fix others, but rather to gain insight in the matter. We are often quick and discerning, experts even, at deciphering others' faults, precisely when it comes to family. We can point out every one of their shortcomings, angered by their ignorance of what we need most—to feel appreciated, to be understood, are of no lesser value than to be shown love.

It was not until September 2015, nearly three years later, when his father was on his deathbed, and all his siblings came out for one final visit that Joe came to see things a little clearer.

It was the first time in over thirty years that the entire family, all ten of them, came together. With everyone scattered among four different states across the country, there was no special occasion important enough, until now, that they all made it back home. His mother was always happy to see any of her children, though it made her nervous at times too. She worried something bad would get stirred up with their father. He was a complicated man, had not been easy to live with, as a father or as a husband, and no one knew that better than his mother. And yet she never spoke a harsh word about him, not once, that Joe could remember.

On the day that they all took turns, no more than two or three at a time entered the hospice room where his father lay, they each seemed to reach deep from within for something, anything, to say. There was a scrapbook of photos that Dominic made when they'd gone hunting together, some happier moments and memories to lighten the mood in the room. A few cards were set out that family members sent.

Joe wondered what one might say at a time like this. Aside from all their grievances and disappointments, what might his father want him to say? It was too late for *get-well-soon* and too early for condolences. At a loss for words, he watched his father's shallow breathing, noticed his pale skin and glazed eyes. No longer was he the robust man so sure of himself. It was then that Joe reflected on something he'd read, from *Gilead*, a novel Delia kept her nose in. For whatever reason, he decided to read a single paragraph, a short reading that now brought him clarity. *A man can know and love his father and a father his son, and there might still be nothing more between them but loyalty and mutual incomprehension.* Whether his father held any regrets, he would never know. If he were given a chance to do it all over again, would he do things differently or remain stuck in his stubborn ways?

Stubbornness was a trait his father passed down to his children. Some more than others. For Joe to reach even deeper for something more to say, something kinder and more valuable that his father taught them, would be that hard work and determination created a foundation, a set of values to become a responsible individual—to stand tall on their own two feet with their head held high, to earn whatever it was that they wanted, and not look for a handout. Those who felt entitled to a free ride were weakened by it.

In the spring of that same year, just six months before the death of his father, Joe was given the honor of walking Sarah down the aisle at her wedding. She'd been living on her own for quite some time, having studied and graduated from UNC in Wilmington, with a degree in marketing. When Delia first told him that Sarah wanted him to give her away, he was very much against the idea.

"She has a father," Joe said. "Not my right."

"Yes, but you have been there for her all these years, the one she looks up to and has g-r-o-w-n closer to."

Still, Joe felt awkward, uncomfortable with the idea. He did not want to antagonize the man, did not want any trouble, or to steal the limelight of what any father would expect to be his God-given right.

"Do you know what S-arah told me a few years ago," Delia said, "after she b-r-o-k-e up with that one d-u-d-e . . . the one with the H-a-r-l-e-y?"

"What?"

"I told her to think about the kind of man she wanted to marry, to write down the traits that were important to her. So that when she met a guy, after one or two dates, she could refer to her list and see if she wanted to invest any more time with him. Do you know what she told me?"

"What?"

"She said, 'I want to marry a man like J-o-e.'"

"Me?" Joe could not fathom what he'd done that was so special to warrant such a compliment. He was just an average guy with a high-school diploma who didn't even make much money. Why him?

"He's a nice g-u-y," Sarah said. "He has a good heart, and he's funny too—he makes me laugh. He never puts on a-i-r-s or b-e-l-i-t-t-l-e-s others. He's good at building t-h-i-n-g-s. He's h-a-n-d-y with house repairs, and he's smart—he taught his dogs to understand sign language."

Joe was speechless. He didn't know that Sarah felt those things about him, things he might not have even realized about himself. It felt good to hear them. Real good. But did that give him the right to step into another man's shoes, one who was still living, who may even be at the wedding?

When the time drew nearer, after much deliberation, and having Sarah tell him herself how much it would mean to her to have him walk her down the aisle, the man who was more of a father figure to her than her biological one, whom she loved since as far back as she could remember when he acted out the story of *Big Bird Says* . . . , Joe finally agreed.

On that warm, sunny day, Joe would never forget it. Sarah was decked out in her pearly white satin gown, a glow of happiness radiated through her as she walked beside him, arm-in-arm. He never would have imagined himself, ever, that he would experience this moment. How could he? The emotions swelled inside of him, feelings of pure joy he could not begin to explain. The slight ache in his leg was barely there. He survived four additional surgeries and was often reminded how fragile the leg remained. The injury in his workshop the previous winter was his wake-up call. It was something he would have to be mindful of for the rest of his life, the ongoing threat of losing his leg. It was a tough pill to swallow. Though a necessary one, he would be foolish not to take seriously. Life, as he knew it before, would never be the same. His days of climbing ladders, installing sheetrock, doing roof repair, or even keeping watch from a deer-stand, were all too risky and a thing of the past. Still hopeful of nabbing a buck or whitetail, he now hunts with his two feet firmly on the ground.

Joe reached the place where he was to release Sarah to her soon-to-be husband. As he turned to her, there was an undeniable sparkle in her eye, a look filled with such optimism and admiration. It made him realize that the role he played in her life was an incredibly worthwhile one, not just for her, but also for him, and that this was what life was all about. These precious moments that validate all the hard work, sweat, and tears of what life can sometimes offer. It isn't so much where we come from or how we were raised that dictates our future. Those things only play a small part. It is how we choose to view and believe in ourselves, to flip the script, right a wrong, and not repeat the same old patterns and excuses. It is also about having the ability to recognize the virtues that were passed down to us. For the one that his father instilled in them all—*hard work and determination*—may very well be what saved his life in those woods.

RESOURCES

Talking With Your Hands Listening With Your Eyes,
Gabriel Grayson

http://www.mksd.org/programs.htm

https://en.wikipedia.org/wiki/Rocky

https://en.wikipedia.org/wiki/Waardenburg_syndrome

https://www.imdb.com/title/tt0079817/quotes

https://www.imdb.com/title/tt0084602/characters/
nm0580565

ABOUT THE AUTHOR

Michèle Israel is the author of *Out of Darkness* and *Lessons of the Heart*. She studied with the Institute of Children's Literature, in West Redding, Connecticut. Having grown up in suburban New Jersey, the eldest of eight children, she worked her first job in her parents' beauty salon at the age of fourteen. After a 32-year career working for the State of Tennessee, where she currently resides, she now has the free-dom to focus more time on her writing, and continues her part-time work for the YMCA.

To learn more about the author, go to:
www.micheleisrael.net/

If you enjoyed this book, please consider posting a review on Amazon. Even if it's only a few sentences, it would be a huge help. Thank you.

CPSIA information can be obtained
at www.ICGtesting.com
Printed in the USA
LVHW110808020921
696500LV00002B/5

9 781977 206725